If you fly, read this book.
When you're done I guarantee you'll want to call (202) 224-3121
and demand that your Senator or Representative
support a reformed FAA and better airline
passenger health and safety protection.

CONGRESSMAN PETER A. DEFAZIO
Member of the U.S House of Representatives
Public Works and Transportation Committee
Subcommittee on Aviation

TAB Books
Division of McGraw-Hill, Inc.
Blue Ridge Summit, PA 17294-0850

Ralph Nader
Wesley J. Smith

COLLISION COURSE

The Truth about Airline Safety

FIRST EDITION
FIRST PRINTING

Library of Congress Cataloging-in-Publication Data

Nader, Ralph.
    Collision course : the truth about airline safety / Ralph Nader,
Wesley J. Smith.
        p.   cm.
    Includes index.
    ISBN 0-8306-4271-4 (h)
    1. Aeronautics, Commercial—United States—Safety measures.
I. Smith, Wesley J. II. Title.
TL553.5.N25 1993
363.12'4'0973—dc20   93-8266
                                                                   CIP

Acquisitions Editor: Jeff Worsinger
Book Editor: Norval G. Kennedy
Executive Editor: Steve Bolt
Production team: Katherine G. Brown, Director
                Wanda S. Ditch, Layout
                Ollie Harmon, Typesetting
                Sandy Hanson, Typesetting
                Susan E. Hansford, Typesetting
                Linda L. King, Proofreading
                Joann Woy, Indexer
                N. Nadine McFarland, Quality Control
Design team: Jaclyn J. Boone, Designer
            Brian Allison, Associate Designer
Front cover photograph: Craig Aurness/Westlight   TAB2
Cover design: Lori E. Schlosser   4305

For Nathra Nader
RN

For Arthur Lawrence Cribbs Jr., my friend—my brother
WJS

Contents

Acknowledgments

A book of this kind could not be possible without the cooperation of the many organizations and individuals that are responsible for the safety of aviation. They include:

The Federal Aviation Administration (despite the fact that it knew it would be criticized), the National Transportation Safety Board, the Department of Transportation, the Flight Safety Foundation, the Air Line Pilots Association, the Association of Flight Attendants, the Professional Association of Flight Attendants, the Aviation Subcommittee of the United States House of Representatives, the General Accounting Office, the Boeing Commercial Airplane Group, the United States Air Force, the International Society of Air Safety Investigators, the Transportation Safety Board of Canada, the Air Transport Association, the Regional Airlines Association, and the Aircraft Owners and Pilots Association.

Additionally, the National Association of Air Traffic Controllers, the Professional Airways Systems Specialists, the Aviation Consumer Action Project, Public Citizen, Airline Industry Resources, *Air Line Pilot Magazine*, the Aviation Safety Institute, University of Southern California Institute for Safety, the Oakland Airport, the San Francisco International Airport, the Oakland ARTCC, The University of San Diego, Center for the Study of Public Law, Associated Press, the National Aeronautics and Space Administration, Airport Safety Services International, the Air Traffic Control Association, Inc., The International Association of Machinists and Aerospace Workers, Fuji Safety, Inc. (U.S.A.).

We also thank the following individuals for their invaluable assistance: Robert Buckhorn, James Crook, Ira Rimson, Frank G. McGuire, Cornish Hitchcock, John H. Enders, Bill Taylor, Walter S. Coleman, William Faville Jr., Maura McGrath, Paul Hudson, William Reynard, Professor Clinton Oster, Louis A. Turpen, Captain William G. Frisbee, John O'Brien, Donald W. Madole, Justice Virgil P. Moshansky, U.S. Representative Peter A. DeFazio and staff, William Jackman, C.O. Miller, Julia Elhauge, Darlene Freeman, Captain B.V. Hewes, Kenneth Hacker, Linda Beckett, Chuck Usrey, Takao Kawakita, Johanna R. Maas, Tom O'Mara,

Paul S. Hudson, James K. Wolfe, Rosmary Wolfe, Captain Duane E. Woerth, Barry M. Sweedler, David Traynham, Marlene Thorpe, Drew Steketee, and Ted Lopatkiewicz.

Additionally, Edward J. DeVille Jr., Dave Duff, Christopher J. Witkowski, Lowell Dodge, Donald James, Hank Price, John Richard, Joseph Del Balzo, Jeff Worsinger, Richard Stafford, Elly Brekke, Chris Overmore, Norman Harris, Anthony J. Broderick, Theodore P. Harris, U.S. Senator William V. Roth and staff, Paul Stephen, Paul Dempsey, Hugh Wagner, Jim Portale, U.S. Representative James L. Oberstar and staff, U.S. Senator Christopher S. Bond and staff, David H. Koch, Caroline D. Gabel, Fred Farrar, Captain David J. Haase, John King, Major Todd Freuhling, Lauaretta A. Gin, Richard H. Wood, Daniel C. Cathcart, Mathew M. McCormick, Dave Dietz, the late John B. Galipault, Emanual Rappaport, John Mazor, Paul D. Russell, Randolph C. Harrison, Judith Terrill-Breuer, Don James, Drucilla Anderson, Elle Brekke, Robert Forsythe, John Albert, Esperison Martinez Jr., Lee S. Kreindler, and Debra J. Saunders.

We also want to express our sincere appreciation for the assistance and cooperation of the scores of individual airline pilots, flight attendants, maintenance workers, airport executives, government regulators and officials, consultants, and union officials who greatly assisted with this work, but who wish to remain anonymous.

Introduction
The challenge

"We have to halve the accident rate by the year 2000 just to stay where we are. Otherwise, we could face a major commercial jetliner accident somewhere in the world every couple of weeks."

Paul D. Russell, chief of product safety
Boeing Commercial Airplane Group, April 26, 1993

What's it like to be in a plane crash? Julia Elhauge knows.

July 30, 1992
John F. Kennedy International Airport

Julia is one of 292 passengers aboard TWA Flight 843. She's seated in the 17th row in a right-aisle seat aboard the L-1011, scheduled to fly from New York to San Francisco. She is returning to the Bay Area after a year of travelling in Europe with her husband while he researched a book project. She has flown separately to the United States so that she can attend the christening of her godchild. Now, she is looking forward to going home.

Later, Julia recalls the flight. "I was sitting next to a woman in the window seat who was telling me that she was terrified to fly. The woman had taken medicine prescribed by her doctor to calm her. My seatmate smiled and told me she felt fine. She looked as if she was feeling euphoric.

"We began the takeoff. I immediately felt that something was wrong. The plane felt sluggish, like it was going too slow. I wasn't alarmed, but I was aware. As the plane left the ground it felt like it was struggling to get in the air. We got as high as 30 to 100 feet. I expected the plane to soar. Instead, it suddenly slammed back to the ground.

"Gee, I thought. We're having an aborted takeoff. I turned to the woman to comfort her and said, 'Don't worry, flying is safer than driving.' I must have challenged Murphy's Law because I immediately heard a woman behind me exclaim in shock and surprise, 'Fire!'

"I turned to look over my left shoulder. The entire cabin was lighted in an eerie orange glow from the reflection of the fire that I was later to learn had started in the right engine. 'I can't believe this,' I thought, as adrenaline surged through my body, 'I am going to be in a plane crash!'

"I looked around at the people in the cabin and the sudden awful thought hit me; half of the people I am looking at will be dead less than two minutes from now. Then I thought, how can I be one of the 50 percent who are going to survive this thing?

"I was terrified. My arms were bare and I worried about them burning. I was in horror that my hair would catch fire. If only I could get to my leather jacket, I could give myself extra minutes. I was also afraid that if fire broke out in the cabin, people were going to be trampled in the panic. I didn't want to die in agony.

"The plane continued its fast, powerful, forward momentum toward the end of the runway. The passengers were deadly quiet. No one screamed. It was as if we were all holding our collective breath.

"Nor was there a word from the flight attendant or flight crew. A lot of time passed during the crash yet no one got on the intercom system to instruct us to assume the crash position, or to keep our seat belts buckled. I knew I wanted to get out of the plane fast when it finally stopped, so I unbuckled my seat belt with the intent to move up to the emergency exit before panic ensued and I was trampled. Then, I changed my mind when I realized that if the plane stopped suddenly while I was out of my seat, I could tumble down the aisle and break my neck. I tried but could not get the buckle latched back in place. All I could think of to do was to lean forward and assume the crash position as the seat-pocket emergency instruction card had described.

"We stopped with a sudden, very powerful jolt. My head smashed into the seat in front of me. I was shaken but remained conscious. I was running on pure adrenaline. I leaped out of my seat and tried to get down the aisle toward the emergency exit that a flight attendant had opened. Unbelievably, some older women were blocking the aisle as they tried to retrieve their carry-on luggage! I had to cut to the left aisle to get around them. No one had gotten on the intercom instructing passengers to leave everything and evacuate the plane. If the plane had not had two aisles, I am convinced these women would have caused fatalities.

"I got to the exit. People would pause at the exit and the flight attendant was yelling in people's ears, 'Move it! Move it! Move it!' to keep the people going. Thank God, the exit doors were huge. People were exiting two and three abreast and jumping onto the emergency exit-slide.

"On the ground, I ran behind a small building and watched as the plane was consumed by flames. I was alive. My plane had crashed but I was alive!"

Happily, no one was killed aboard Flight 843. For her part, Julia suffered a concussion, scrapes and bruises on her face, arms, and legs and soon experienced pain all over her body. In the months since, Julia, a writer, reports that she has been unable to write at her computer, has suffered terrible headaches, neck pain and other distress associated with her injuries. She experiences horrifying flashbacks and dizziness and can no longer drink cola or intake any caffeine without fainting. But, she was fortunate. She lived.

Julia says, "I was never afraid to fly. I used to rely on the naive belief that planes do not fall out of the sky. I was wrong. I used to believe that if there ever was an emergency, the system would work right if something went awry. It didn't. I used to believe that I could go merrily through my life believing that if something happened, there was nothing I could do about it. Again, I was mistaken.

"Now, I have a different attitude. I know that people can lobby for safety. I know that it is up to people to make a difference. I know I will, from now on."

Some things are worse than being in a plane crash.

July 19, 1989
Denver

For the O'Mara family, it is the worst of times as the mother and grandmother of 24-year-old Army lawyer Heather Rose O'Mara embrace the younger woman as she prepares to board United Airlines Flight 232, flying from Denver to Chicago. Heather's first-cousin had been killed in a mountain climbing accident. Now, the family is converging from around the country to Chicago to grieve and offer mutual support.

The three women are flying to Chicago on separate flights. Heather is flying into O'Hare International Airport where she is to be met at the gate by her cousins. The older women are taking a different flight into Midway Airport to accommodate Heather's grandfather who does not like to drive to O'Hare.

Heather has been told that this trip is unnecessary. But she recognizes her family's subterfuge. Her family needs her. This she knows. She is on a mission of love. "Dad needs to see me alive," Heather tells her mother. And then, she is gone.

Later, at O'Hare International Airport, Heather's cousin Jill Zengler is waiting for Heather to arrive. But something is amiss. The people from United are asking anyone awaiting Flight 232 to step into a separate lounge at the terminal.

"What's wrong?" she asks. "Did the plane crash?"

The attendant's face turns chalk-white.

Tom O'Mara, Heather's father, is at his nephew's wake speaking with a woman he has not seen in 20 years. She apologizes for her husband's absence. "He works for United Airlines. There's been a crash . . . some flight from Denver to Chicago."

"My daughter is on a flight from Denver to Chicago," Tom says, his heart frozen in his chest. The woman lowers her eyes. "I'm sorry," is all she can say.

For hours the family desperately seeks information on their daughter. The plane has crashed in a place called Sioux City, Iowa, that much they know. The plane has broken apart during an emergency landing and burned. There are survivors. But, many are also dead.

"It was the most frustrating, gut-wrenching time of my life," Tom O'Mara says. "As her father, I was supposed to protect Heather from danger. But I could do nothing. I could not mourn for my sister's son. I could only think about the fate of my daughter."

Heather's family boards a special United Airlines flight for Sioux City. On board, it is very quiet. Tom O'Mara hugs a pillow and caresses it as he did to Heather when she was a small child falling asleep in her Daddy's arms. He looks out the window at the clouds and thinks of the many flights he and his daughter have taken together and how they always marveled at the clouds.

At the airport, the imagined horror of Flight 232 becomes all too real. Three large chunks of charred, twisted metal lay about. Black lines are gouged into the runway pavement, evidence of metal scraping concrete as the huge DC-10 cartwheeled out of control. Other pieces of the wreckage lie in a nearby corn field.

Then the worst: Heather has been killed.

Two days later, her body is released to her parents. The coffin remains closed. Heather suffered 17 separate skull fractures when her seat was ejected from the plane. The O'Mara's never see the body of their beloved daughter. It is better that way.

An aftermath that never ends. "The void our daughter's death has caused in our lives cannot be articulated," Tom says. "And the questions: We are plagued by the questions. Why Heather? Why us? Was the accident preventable? Will justice be done? Will life ever be the same? As sweet? As hopeful?"

Aviation safety: It is about lives saved and lives lost. It is about the Julia's, the Heather's and the Tom's, about you, your neighbor, your spouse, and your siblings. It is a matter of vital concern to everyone who will ever board a plane or wave good-bye to a loved one at an airport gate.

But there is more to the topic of aviation safety than the humanitarian issue. Aviation safety is also a matter of economics. The viability of the entire $75 billion-plus commercial aviation industry depends upon there being an almost zero accident rate. If passengers ever believe that their lives are endangered by getting on an airliner, the industry itself would be what crashed and burned.

So, is flying safe? That question is not easy to answer. Aviation safety is a complex and dynamic subject. The safety levels built into the system are always changing, always in flux. Change comes by degrees. Safety levels are not degraded in a day, but over years. And it often takes years to correct deficiencies.

Still, the question must be answered. After much research, study, contemplation and analysis, the best answer we can give is that in many areas, it is not safe enough. More disturbingly, the level of risk appears to be growing.

Government regulators, the airlines, and other members of the aviation establishment do not want to face this truth. Knowing that the passenger's perceptions of airline safety and industry economics are inextricably linked, they are ever about the business of assuring the public that all is well. "The skies are safe," they say. "Regulation is adequate," they insist. "There's nothing to fear," they soothe. "Trust us. It's all under control."

As proof, they will pull out the accident statistics of the past to demonstrate that flying is safe and will ever be so. They will proudly proclaim that between 1980 and 1989, according to the National Transportation Safety Board *1990 Annual Report to Congress*, there were 44 fatal accidents involving large commercial jet aircraft, with a total of 1,554 passenger deaths. During this same time period, there were 64,353,112 departures. That amounts to far less than one fatal aircraft accident per 1,000,000 departures.

Those statistics sound impressive. But are they relevant? John H. Enders, president of the Flight Safety Foundation says, that "the accident rate is history. It is a record of what happened, not the current direction or trend." Because no passengers were killed on large commercial jetliners in 1980, does that mean commercial flight was safer than in 1985 when 525 passengers lost their lives? Or was the difference between 1980 and 1985 simply a matter of luck? Then, in 1986, was there a sudden and tremendous increase in safety because a mere eight jetliner passengers were killed? Of course not. In all likelihood, the safety levels were roughly equivalent in 1985 and 1986.

Fatality statistics simply are not a reliable measure of safety. For example, no one was killed in the TWA accident of July 30, 1992, at Kennedy Airport. The 292 passengers who escaped with their lives are not part of the mortality statistics. Yet, had the plane crashed after getting only a little higher into the air, there might have been no survivors.

Some would argue that aviation statistics are good prophesiers of coming trends. If that is true, then the aviation statistics of the last five years have been going in the wrong direction. According to Gerard M. Bruggink, aviation safety consultant, in an article published in *Flight Safety Digest* (January, 1991, Flight Safety Foundation), the "best-ever performance of the industry occurred" during the years 1980–1984. Bruggink said "the 1985–1989 period shows an abrupt reversal of that trend."

Indeed, Bruggink, the former deputy director of the Bureau of Accident Investigation for the National Transportation Safety Board, cites the following statistics to prove his point:

Year	Fatal accidents	Aircraft occupant deaths	Hours flown between fatal accidents
1977–74	19	1058	1,500,000
1975–79	11	1030	2,700,000
1980–84	5	222	6,600,000
1985–89	15	1216	3,100,000

Using these statistics, the last five years of the 1980s not only went in the wrong direction, but produced more deaths than any other five-year period in the previous 20 years.

We are convinced that statistics do not tell half of the tale. What is needed to answer the query, "Is flying safe?," is an analysis of the current issues and trends affecting aviation safety as seen by those who work in the field, from pilots, to regulators, to aircraft mechanics, to air traffic controllers, to those involved in congressional oversight, to consumer groups who monitor the industry. How do they evaluate the safety of the system? What are their concerns? Where is the complacency? What is being done to maintain and improve safety? What problems are not being adequately addressed? How can we do a better job? These are only some of the questions this book attempts to answer.

"The whole air safety system, without equivocation, is being degraded."

              Laurence A. Sump, with
              Professional Airway System Specialists (PASS),
              an aviation-related union

"The system is saturated to the point of overcapacity, which threatens safety. We have to get a handle on it."

     Captain William G. Frisbie,
     former Air Force One pilot and former chief pilot
     for Pan American, now a consultant to the industry

Strong words made all the more powerful coming from commentators who work in the heart of the aviation safety system. Nor are these isolated sentiments. In researching this book and in speaking both on and off-the-record with scores of people who work in virtually all areas of aviation, we frequently heard the same worrisome lament: The system is growing less safe. Corners are being cut. Government regulators either don't really know what is going on, or don't want to act on what they do know.

Despite the official denials of the Federal Aviation Administration (FAA) and the airline industry, these concerns seem to be supported by the facts. Aviation safety is threatened on many fronts at the same time. Individually, each presents a significant challenge. Collectively, they pose a clear and present danger to existing safety levels. These issues include:

- The economic near collapse of the industry after the airlines were deregulated.
- Pressure from the airline industry to increase capacity, which has caused the FAA to approve compromises in safety procedures and to contemplate further changes.
- The aging of our domestic aircraft fleet.
- The obsolescence of the current air traffic control equipment and the failure of the FAA to modernize it.
- The growth of commuter airlines that fly smaller planes with less safety equipment.
- The need to substantially upgrade the crash survivability of most commercial transport jets.
- Problems with human factors such as management and pilot performance that adversely affect safety.
- The threat of sabotage and criminal attacks against airplanes and the feeble security measures taken to prevent it.

- The need to improve ground control technology to prevent accidents from happening while planes are on the ground.
- The underfunding of the FAA that has overwhelmed the already too-passive agency and rendered it unable to fully perform its legal mandate.

Singularly and collectively these and other matters of concern present a formidable challenge—merely to maintain current levels of safety. Of even greater concern, this poses a significant threat to the system's ability to make the necessary improvements required in the coming years to accommodate the anticipated increase in the number of people who are expected to fly. If the system cannot safely be made more efficient, the very economic foundation of the entire commercial aviation industry could be threatened with collapse.

Upon hearing the topic of this book, one woman told us that she was afraid of the information it would contain, adding, "I am a frequent flyer. I don't want to know." Such head-in-the-sand fatalism is harmful to aviation safety. As Barry Sweedler, director of the office of safety recommendations for the National Transportation Safety Board told us, "It is the public that drives the whole (safety) machine." He is right. In the final analysis, flying will only be as safe as people who fly demand.

That means consumers are going to have to exert their power as citizens and customers to reverse the downward trend in safety levels. The flying public is going to have to get involved. They are going to have to let their elected officials know that they care about the issue. They are going to have to insist that safety considerations be upmost in the mind of federal regulators. Toward that end, we will propose systemic reform that we hope will lead to greater consumer involvement and safer skies. We will also advocate the creation of a broad-based consumer organization dedicated solely to advocating for airline safety.

Nay sayers will tell you to leave safety to the experts. They will argue that the subject is too complicated for consumers to understand. Pay no heed. By joining an airline passenger advocacy group, each and every one of you and each of your friends will be able to force regulators to do a better job. You will be able to compel the airlines to make their planes more crashworthy. You will be able to pressure the industry to compete for your consumer dollars based upon its safety efforts, as well as other considerations, such as price and convenience.

One last point: This book concentrates on aviation issues that directly affect safety in the United States. There is a reason for this emphasis. For the most part, the United States is the world leader in aviation safety regulation. Many nations take their safety cues from this country. If the United States seriously upgrades safety levels, it will create a rising tide that should raise all boats.

"Aviation has to meet our society's higher safety standard for aviation. Arguing against that standard is like arguing against gravity or against the sun rising in the East. These things are simply given. If aviation is to thrive and grow in our society it has to meet our society's standards, whatever those standards might be."

Congressman Norman Y. Mineta, May 2, 1984

Part I

The system

"Most airlines once did much more than the FAA required in such matters as training, programs, maintenance and replacement of aircraft, but firms today tend to satisfy minimum safety requirements."

**Leon N. Moses and Ian Savage, in their article,
"Air Safety in the Age of Deregulation,
Issues in Science and Technology," 1988**

"During the 1980s, we were blindsided by economic theory to the detriment of safety."

A disgruntled Department of Transportation official, 1992

The $75 billion dollar-plus commercial aviation industry is necessary to the welfare of the United States. It provides swift transportation of people and goods, employs over one million people (not including people who work for manufacturers and support services), and is essential to national security as evidenced by the use of civil transport aircraft to transport troops in times of military action. The aviation system is so important that it is considered basic infrastructure.

For aviation to prosper it must be safe. Safety depends on many factors, such as the quality of aircraft design, the training of pilots, and excellent maintenance. But the genesis of the safety system, from which all else follows, is the vigor and enthusiasm with which the government issues and enforces effective safety standards.

The FAA is the government agency primarily in charge of aviation safety regulation. Through rule making, the FAA establishes the minimum safety levels under which the airlines can legally operate. It is vital then, for the FAA to write and enforce regulations that are sufficiently substantive to fully protect the flying public. Unfortunately, that is a task that is often difficult to convince the FAA to perform. Why? Because when it comes to safety, money talks. As will be detailed throughout this book, the regulatory system's function of fostering safety often takes second place to protecting the airline's short-term bottom line.

This is indeed ironic. During the 1980s, while the FAA often foot dragged and otherwise stepped lightly in pushing safety, its parent governmental branch, the Department of Transportation, allowed airlines to fall deeply into debt, be victimized by leveraged-option-buyouts and to be otherwise financially mismanaged. This has resulted in a surrealistic tableau of a government that accepted financial excuses as a reason to constrain safety rules while at the same time, it was smiling upon corporate raiders and irresponsible airline executives who were burdening the industry with enormous debt. This dichotomy speaks volumes about the government's priorities.

The following chapters explain how the aviation safety system operates both in theory and in the practical world. Part I describes how safety is measured, the workings of the regulatory process and the reasons it can take years to create and implement new safety rules. Economic deregulation of the airlines is described, as well as its adverse impact on safety.

Let's start with a little history to put the current system into context.

1

The past leads to the present

"The first air traffic controller got his job as a result of a coin toss. To determine who would be the first to pilot the Wright Flyer at Kitty Hawk, North Carolina, Orville and Wilbur flipped a coin. Wilbur won but used up his turn in an unsuccessful attempt at first flight. And so, Wilbur Wright had to be content in the role of an incipient air traffic controller, running along side his brother on the sand dunes, shouting instructions and word of encouragement to Orville, as the plane lifted in the air."

> **Joseph M. Del Balzo, then
> executive director for FAA systems operations,
> from a lecture, "Air Traffic Control: The Sky's the Limit,"
> February 6, 1992**

Return with us to those glorious days of yesteryear, when young daredevil pilots barnstormed around the country putting on air shows and offering people airplane rides. On the surface, it would appear that these early aviator-pioneers in their flimsy bi-planes were entertainers. But what they were really about, whether they knew it or not, was the important business of creating a new era in the history of transportation.

The early days of government regulation

"Passed at the behest of the aviation industry, which believed the airplane could not reach its full commercial potential without Federal safety regulation, the (Air Commerce) Act charged the Secretary of Commerce with fostering air commerce, certification of aircraft, establishing airways, and operating and maintaining aids to navigation."

From the Department of Transportation tract,
History of the Federal Aviation Administration

Civil aviation was given its first powerful boost with the government's efforts to speed up delivery of the mail. Mail delivery always has been an important component promoting commerce and the growth of the country. For example, government contracts with the Pony Express and later, the railroads, helped our forebears open the West. In the early 1920s, this tradition was continued with the creation of the United States Air Mail Service. The impact on flying would be profound.

In establishing airmail service, the Post Office Department created the first federal regulations designed to promote aviation safety. These rules mandated minimum experience and proficiency testing for mail-carrying pilots and established aircraft inspection and preventative maintenance programs. The value of safety rules soon became evident in the flying record of Post Office pilots. While other commercial flyers experienced one fatality every 13,500 miles, the Air Mail Service had one fatality every 463,000 miles.

The government wanted to do more. It wanted to stimulate the growth of private sector aviation as a commercial enterprise. Toward that end, in 1925, the government enacted the Air Mail Act. This legislation authorized the Post Office Department to contract with private companies to carry the mail by air, creating a business opportunity of enormous potential. Businesses were created to take the government up on its offer. Several of these companies also began offering limited passenger service. Many of these early air transport carriers evolved into major airlines of the modern era.

In 1926, the Air Commerce Act became law, which brought safety regulation of aviation under the authority of the U.S.

Department of Commerce. The law was designed primarily to promote the growth of the fledgling aviation industry by providing federal participation in promoting safety and assisting growth.

The government's misguided approach—combining industry promotion and safety enforcement into the work of the same governmental body—began here, a policy that continues within the FAA today. As flying increased in popularity and the number of planes increased, chaos threatened. With no centralized authority in existence to regulate flow, midair collisions became an increasing threat to safety. It was soon clear to everyone involved in aviation that an organized and systematic set of procedures would have to be created to prevent accidents. This process became known as *air traffic control* (ATC).

The U.S. government took formal responsibility for ATC in 1935. Created before the development of radar, this first nationwide ATC system used a rudimentary method that utilized Teletype machines, wall-sized blackboards, and large table maps where markers, representing planes, were moved across the board based upon the controllers' best estimates of the location of the aircraft. Available technology did not allow pilots and controllers to communicate directly with each other, so a cumbersome communications triangle was created whereby information between pilot and controller and controller and pilot was routed through the airline dispatcher in charge of the flight.

Government economic regulation of the industry commenced in 1938 with the Civil Aeronautics Act. Safety and economic regulation over aviation was taken out of the Department of Commerce and placed into a newly created independent executive agency called the *Civil Aeronautics Authority*. Among the economic responsibilities of the authority were the establishment of airmail rates and the issuance of route certificates. The growing importance of aviation to the economic life of the nation was clearly symbolized by the fact that the administrator of the CAA answered directly to the president of the United States.

In 1940, more tinkering with the regulatory process occurred. Some of the Civil Aeronautics Authority's responsibility was split into a separate regulatory agency called the *Civil Aeronautics Board* (CAB). CAB was given jurisdiction over safety and economic regulation while the Civil Aeronautics Authority maintained jurisdiction over air traffic control, aircraft certification of airworthiness, safety enforcement, and airway development.

The modern era

"Transportation has truly emerged as a significant part of our national life. As a basic force in our society, its progress must be accelerated so that the quality of our life can be improved."

**President Lyndon Baines Johnson,
upon signing the law creating the
Department of Transportation, October 15, 1966**

Technical advances in aviation that resulted from World War II were enormous. The might and power of aircraft as weapons of war caught people's imagination. The future of flight seemed unlimited.

In commercial aviation, nonscheduled operators, sometimes called *air taxi operators*, began to operate in growing numbers. The government exempted these small commercial carriers from many of the safety regulations that were being required of the larger airlines. That set a precedent for today's system of unequal safety regulations in which air taxis, charter services that fly small aircraft, and *regional airlines* (also known as *commuter airlines*), often operate under less stringent safety requirements than the large air transport commercial carriers. This is one reason why such air carriers generally have a worse safety record than the large airlines.

Midair collisions became a growing concern in the late forties and into the fifties. By this time, pressurized passenger aircraft were flying coast to coast and the race was on among aircraft manufacturers to build bigger and faster air transport planes as the airlines vied to increase their market share. The growth in commercial aviation and improved aeronautical technology began to outpace the regulators' ability to keep up, threatening safety—a condition that is mirrored in the nineties aviation environment.

The government failed to respond effectively to the deteriorating safety margins. New ATC technology was desperately needed to maintain separation between the growing number of aircraft flying in the same areas of sky. Radar had been developed and was available to perform the task, but Congress refused to allocate sufficient funds to modernize the system. Worse, many government safety functions and airway development activities were actually reduced. As a direct result, the safety margin was endangered.

As has happened repeatedly over the years, it took tragedy and death to break the government's complacency. The first catastrophe happened over the Grand Canyon in 1956 when two large passenger planes collided in midair, killing 128 people. Soon, other midair tragedies took additional lives. Political pressure that was applied by an alarmed public and a concerned aviation industry, put heat on government officials and elected representatives. Too much blood was being spilled. The people's faith in flying was threatened. The safety-gridlock in government began to break. The spirit of reform was finally in the air.

In 1958, the *Federal Aviation Agency* (FAA) was created to improve government safety regulation. (The CAB retained jurisdiction over economic regulation of the industry and remained charged with accident investigation.) The renewed commitment to safety that the creation of the agency represented was a positive development. But a rare opportunity for truly meaningful reform was missed. Rather than restrict the jurisdiction of the FAA to issues of safety, politicians once again placed upon the backs of regulators the legal charge to promote air commerce.

With the creation of the FAA and with Congress recognizing that a jet age was dawning in commercial flight, sufficient funds were finally allocated to upgrade the ATC system. Eighty-two long-range radars were purchased, giving air traffic controllers the "eyes" to see airspace above the whole country. Controllers now had the ability to separate slower flying aircraft using *visual flight rules* (VFR) from faster planes flying on *instrument flight rules* (IFR). The threat of midair collisions now reduced, flying became a safer mode of transportation.

As transport jets came increasingly into commercial use, the ATC equipment needed further modernization. In the 1960s, newly designed air traffic control equipment came online that used the signal from aircraft transponders to precisely identify an aircraft. ATC computers translate information from the transponder to display on the radarscope the aircraft identification, course heading, and altitude of aircraft that have a transponder. Radar equipment installed in the 1960s was a tremendous step forward. Without it, the eventual burst of growth in commercial aviation could not have been accommodated safely.

The next big change in the regulation of aviation came in 1966 with the creation of the *Department of Transportation* (DOT). The Federal Aviation Agency was renamed the Federal Aviation Administration. But more than the name was changed. The FAA became a part of the new DOT. At the same time, an important reform occurred—removing accident investigation from CAB and placing the responsibility with the newly created and independent *National Transportation Safety Board* (NTSB).

In 1970, the *Airport and Airway Trust Fund* (also known as the *Aviation Trust Fund*), was created, financed in part by user fees imposed upon every airline ticket. The purpose of the fund was to help pay for improvements in ATC, navigation systems, and airports. Today, the fund pays for approximately 75 percent of the budget costs of the FAA; however, there is a $6.3 billion uncommitted surplus in the trust fund projected for fiscal year 1993, meaning more money is available for safety related expenditures than the government is willing to spend. This too, adversely impacts the margin of safety.

The last big change in the regulation of our airways came with passage of the Airline Deregulation Act of 1978. With deregulation, CAB was phased out of existence and the government ceased setting prices and mandating carrier routes. Market forces were unleashed stimulating tremendous growth in the industry, particularly in the area of commuter airlines. Unfortunately, deregulation—as managed by the laissez faire ideology of the Reagan/ Bush years—also subverted the economic foundation of commercial aviation; at the same time, a raging controversy has arisen over the effect that economic deregulation has had on safety.

But, we are getting ahead or ourselves. Let's turn now from history to a discussion of the different government entities and private organizations that have the greatest impact on aviation safety.

2

The aviation safety community

The role of government

"All regulation of aviation has to stem from statutory authority."
Anthony J. Broderick,
associate administrator for regulations and certifications,
Federal Aviation Administration

The power of the government to regulate aviation has its source in the U.S. Constitution. One of the specific purposes for which the federal government was created is to promote the general welfare. The federal government is also given explicit authority in the Constitution to regulate interstate commerce. A healthy and safe aviation industry is vital to both of these important goals.

In the United States, laws are written by the legislative branch and executed and enforced by the executive. That is basic civics. But this fundamental principle of governance only provides a bare bones outline of how the government operates. The real power can be found in the details.

The details are created by the executive branch when an executive agency, such as the FAA, promulgates rules. The distinction between a *law* and a *rule* is profound. Congress enacts general laws that empower the government to act in a given area, such as the regulation of aviation safety. The specific rules then are written by the executive branch to implement the law; the executive branch also enforces the rules and law. If the executive branch wants lax execution and enforcement, that will happen. On the other hand, if the executive branch wants to move with vigor and persistence, the law is more likely to have impact.

Another point: The federal government has grown so bloated that it is almost beyond management. That means that the president and the cabinet officers, who are nominally in charge of rule-making, must rely upon the vast bureaucracy to implement their desires and execute the law; thus, agencies such as the FAA have tremendous potential power.

Aviation safety and the role of Congress

Congress exerts a great deal of power over aviation safety in addition to passing laws.

The power of the purse The FAA is limited in what it can accomplish by the funds that it is provided. The FAA is dependent upon the amount of money appropriated by Congress. One of the reasons that the FAA has performed inadequately is the fact that it has not been given the financial resources to fully perform all of its many responsibilities.

Committee recommendations Congressional committees also exercise power over aviation regulation. For example, one of the most powerful committees is the House Committee on Public Works and Transportation, which has a Subcommittee on Aviation (hereafter called the *Aviation Subcommittee*). If a bill is introduced in the field of aviation, the Aviation Subcommittee holds hearings and takes expert testimony from interested parties. Often, those testifying are *special interests* who have a financial stake in the proposed legislation.

Committee oversight The appropriate legislative committees and subcommittees also exert general oversight over aviation safety regulation. In this capacity, they may hold hearings and require FAA officials to report on the status of rulemaking and enforcement actions. They may also take testimony from interested parties in the industry such as officials of the professional unions and commercial trade associations.

Staff work Legislators are not involved in their committee assignments on a full-time basis. Instead, they rely upon people called the *professional staff* to investigate the issues and understand the details. These staffers work full-time, researching, analyzing, and applying their expertise to the issues, subsequently advising committee members.

General accounting office

The scope of government operations is so vast that it is impossible for the Congress alone to keep fully informed on the operations of the government. This is one of the reasons for the *General Accounting Office* (GAO). The GAO is an independent and nonpartisan investigative agency that acts as the eyes and ears of the government. When requested to investigate an area of government performance, the experts within the GAO will conduct in-depth investigations and publish written reports detailing their findings and offering recommendations.

Scores of such reports have been issued on topics relevant to aviation safety. Most of these reports paint a disturbing and troubling picture of FAA mismanagement, regulatory failures, poor administration, and occasional ineptitude.

The executive branch and safety regulation

As described earlier, the executive branch possesses most of the real power over the levels of safety that will be established by government regulation. This power resides in the following offices:

The Department of Transportation (DOT)

The DOT is an umbrella Cabinet department that exerts oversight of the varied transportation agencies of the government: Federal Railroad Administration, Maritime Administration, Federal Highway Administration, U.S. Coast Guard, and, of course, the Federal Aviation Administration.

Most of the work regulating aviation safety is performed by the FAA; however, DOT does have direct responsibility over the financial fitness of airlines, that is, assuring that airlines have the monetary resources to comply with minimum safety regulations promulgated by the FAA and to conduct business in an appropriate and safe manner. Unfortunately, recall that the DOT was lax in enforcing financial fitness standards in the 1980s, which played a large part in the foundering of the commercial aviation industry during the era of deregulation.

The Federal Aviation Administration (FAA)

"The FAA administers the world's busiest civil aviation system .... They are responsible for the safety of half a billion airline passengers a year .... In the same period, other FAA specialists perform 30,000 security inspections and assessments, host more than 5,000 safety seminars and conduct 300,000 safety inspections of airlines and aviation activities."

From the public relations publication ***This is the FAA***

The FAA is primarily responsible for ensuring the safety of aviation. This is a daunting task, requiring a huge organization, employing approximately 53,000 people and operating on a $9.4 billion budget in fiscal year 1993. To underscore the importance of the work of the FAA, the director is appointed by the president, subject to ratification or rejection by the Congress.

Responsibilities of the FAA are enormous:

- Operating the air traffic control system.
- Promulgating safety regulations, ranging from establishing maximum pilot duty-hours to mandating minimum aircraft maintenance standards.
- Enforcing safety regulations when the regs become effective.
- Conducting safety inspections.
- Establishing minimum standards for the design, materials, workmanship, construction, and performance of aircraft, aircraft engines, and related equipment.
- Certification (licensing) of pilots, airports, aircraft, airlines, mechanics, and flight schools.
- Establishing minimum standards for aviation security.
- Establishing airport noise abatement standards.
- Administering the Airport Improvement Program, which helps fund local airport construction and safety improvements.
- Conducting research and development of new aviation technologies.

- Enforcing safety standards overseas where U.S. air carriers operate.
- Working with the International Civil Aviation Organization (ICAO) to establish and maintain worldwide aviation safety standards.

That's a lot of responsibility and the success or failure of the FAA in performing its responsibilities has a direct impact upon safety levels.

The Office of Management and Budget (OMB)

"Proposed safety regulations must go to the OMB for final approval."

Joseph M. Del Bazo,
FAA director of systems operation

The Office of Management and Budget works on behalf of the president to develop economic policy and to help manage the economy. What does an office that focuses on economic affairs have to do with aviation safety? Unfortunately, too much. If the OMB determines that the cost of a proposed safety regulation to the industry or the public exceeds what OMB perceives to be proposed rule's benefit, OMB will veto the proposed regulation, even if the FAA wants implementation. The effect of OMB oversight upon the safety regulatory process too often has been to place more importance on the level of profits rather than the safety of people.

National Aeronautics and Space Administration (NASA)

"Very few people recognize that the first A in NASA, is, aeronautics."

William Reynard, with the office of the
Aviation Safety Reporting System at the
NASA Ames Research Center

NASA is an important research arm of the government in the areas of aviation safety and emerging technologies. NASA is involved with many projects of interest to the flying public.

The Aviation Safety Reporting System (ASRS) ASRS is an important safety project. Under the shield of anonymity, pilots, controllers, and others who work in aviation are able to candidly—without fear of punishment or reprisal—report safety violations to NASA. NASA maintains these reports in a computer data base. According to NASA, more than 180,000 confidential reports were on file as of 1991. ASRS information is vital because the data can reveal emerging safety threats before they cause accidents and loss of life.

Human factors research NASA has several programs to research and improve human performance in aviation. NASA played a vital role in creating a new flight crew training program called *cockpit resource management* (CRM) (also *crew resource management),* which teaches pilot, copilot, and flight engineer to work together as a team. This is important because cockpit miscommunication and poor work attitudes have led to accidents and death. NASA also utilizes *line oriented flight training* (LOFT), which uses flight simulators to allow flight crews to experience flight emergency situations, for instance encountering wind shear during a landing approach, and receive hands-on training to cope with them. NASA also researches the effect of fatigue on crew performance, with efforts aimed at understanding and preventing flight crew fatigue that could endanger safety.

Weather research NASA studies wind shears and other weather phenomenon that can cause a large transport jet to suddenly crash. Also, the problem of deicing has engaged the researchers at NASA who research the effects of ice buildup on aircraft components and the efficiency of lifting surfaces that are covered with ice.

The National Transportation Safety Board (NTSB)

"The sole purpose of the National Transportation Safety Board is to improve transportation safety."

**Barry Sweedler,
director of the NTSB
office of safety recommendations**

It is a surrealistic experience to walk into the reception area of the NTSB headquarters in Washington and see the huge color photographs of air, train, and other transportation disasters hanging on the walls. But accidents are what its work is all about—not in a ghoulish or voyeuristic sense, but for the specific purpose of promoting safety.

The NTSB investigates major accidents, whether aviation, highway, railroad, marine, or pipeline, in order to determine the "probable" and "contributing" causes of the mishap. The purpose of the investigations is not to affix "legal blame." Indeed, the analysis and the conclusions regarding the causes of an accident contained in an NTSB investigation report are not admissible in court. (Other matters in the investigation report might be admissable.) Rather, the NTSB investigations are intended as learning experiences so that the tragedy of yesterday can be used to prevent accidents today and tomorrow.

After each accident investigation, the NTSB issues a report, giving the board's expert opinion on the reasons the accident took place. From these accident investigations (and from the independent safety studies the NTSB conducts), safety recommendations are issued by the NTSB advising the appropriate agencies on regulatory actions that the agency could take to improve transportation safety. In aviation, the recommendations will generally be addressed to the FAA and/or Congress, as well as organizations in the private sector, such as the airlines or manufacturers.

The NTSB is completely independent of any other department or agency in government and is less subject to political pressure, worries about industry profits or the political desires of the secretary of transportation and the president.

On the other hand, the NTSB has no power. The board cannot regulate; its work is advisory and its primary tool is persuasion. Members of the NTSB testify before Congress, they interact with the FAA and they inform the media about their recommendations. For example, the NTSB created the "Most Wanted List" of safety recommendations in order to get press attention and pressure regulators to adopt their proposals. Since then, two aviation safety recommendations on the list have been adopted by the FAA, recommendations that had been ignored by the FAA for years.

(The NTSB is prohibited from addressing areas of airport and airline security. If the board were not restricted, the distressing truth about the quality and level of aviation security might be better known.)

The International Civil Aviation Organization (ICAO)

ICAO is an agency of the United Nations made up of members who have joined together for the purpose of reaching international accord on issues of importance to world aviation. One of ICAO's principle purposes is to establish international safety standards to govern the rules to be established by its members and their respective air carriers. This is less noteworthy than it might first appear because ICAO has no enforcement capabilities and must rely upon the good faith compliance of each member. Moreover, members have the power to declare that they differ from established ICAO standards. Also, the bureaucracy within the organization reduces its effectiveness.

The private sector

It is an unfortunate fact that government oversight and enforcement is so underfunded and understaffed that regulators and inspectors must rely upon the integrity and good faith of those they regulate to obey the rules. Also, as safety professional C.O. Miller says, you can't have a rule for everything. The private sector must be committed to safety in the way that they conduct their businesses. Unfortunately, if a company is determined to cut corners, there is every likelihood that it will succeed, at least for a while. Many different industries impact the safety of flying.

Equipment manufacturers

"About 30 percent of air safety incidents have material malfunction as a causal factor—usually the first event."

Colin Torkington and Alan Emmerson, with the Civil Aviation Authority of Australia at the 22nd International Seminar of the International Society of Air Safety Investigators

By definition, aviation safety has to begin with quality equipment. A plane that is poorly designed is likely to develop serious flight problems that might result in an accident. For example, when a faulty engine component in a DC-10 failed and the engine disintegrated (United Flight 232), parts from the engine severed redundant aircraft control system (the hydraulic systems) components that had been unwisely bundled in one area. Failure of the redundant systems caused the pilots to lose normal control of the aircraft, which subsequently crashed during an emergency landing, taking the lives of 111 people, including that of Heather Rose O'Mara. Engines that are not properly manufactured, that are repaired with defective parts, or are maintained negligently can fail, leading to tragedy, as was also the case with the United Airlines plane. Aircraft interiors that are insufficiently crashworthy have caused needless death and injury to those who would have otherwise survived a crash. New technology, designed to increase safety, can instead endanger the public when it fails to perform as designed.

Boeing Aircraft, McDonnell Douglas, Airbus, Beech Aircraft, Fokker, General Electric and the many other manufacturers of airplanes, engines, and parts, have a tremendous responsibility to the public. First, the companies must manufacture safe aircraft and replacement parts. Then, adequately educate customers on the proper use of the product. Finally, the companies must continually inform airlines and regulators when defects or equipment failures are discovered. Such information is passed along to the aviation community in the form of official *service bulletins* published and distributed by the company, in educational seminars, and in manuals that govern the operation of the equipment.

Air carriers

"You cannot prevent accidents if you believe that safety depends only on pilots and engineers. You must admit that each person of the company is doing it together."

Japan Airline executive in
JAL training video *What is Safety to You?*

Commercial air carriers involve themselves in public safety issues as well as performing the day-to-day tasks of operating the business of public transport. Air carriers have powerful lobbying capabilities. They are effective advocates of their own business interests in the political and regulatory systems of the government and have a large voice in the manner and extent to which they, themselves, are regulated.

The airlines are also given the right by the FAA to decide the manner in which the safety regulations will be obeyed; thus, the airlines not only have major input into the nature and extent of the safety rules, but are then frequently permitted to create their own plan for compliance, subject to FAA approval. In a very real sense, so long as the public remains passive, the level of aviation safety will be only as high as the industry chooses.

Insurance companies

"We, the aviation insurers, on a worldwide basis, collected between $300–$400 million in premiums for air carriers only. However, the losses (read in claims or reserves set aside for those claims), will extend beyond $1 billion."

Edward R. Williams,
vice president and director of flight operations,
Associated Aviation Underwriters, to the
43rd annual International Air Safety Seminar of the
Flight Safety Foundation

Insurance companies should be in the business of risk reduction, that is they should promote safety to protect their own bottom line. Good aviation insurance companies do that. Good insurance companies are in continual contact with the air carriers they insure to make sure that safety programs are created and implemented, then consequently offer lower premiums to companies that pass safety muster. Good insurance companies help educate air carrier employees in issues of safety, help with research, and use the threat of higher premiums or policy cancellation to keep safety at the forefront of airline management's thinking. In short, good insurance companies concurrently promote safety and pay the consequences when safety falters. Unfortunately, all insurers aren't good.

The civil justice system

"The tort system ... creates an economic motive to comply with elementary norms of care and safety because of the potential liability which exists if the actor transgresses standards of acceptable behavior."

Charles P. Kindregan and Edward M. Swartz, in their article
"The Assault on the Captive Consumer:
Emasculating the Common Law of Torts
in the Name of Reform ," published in the
***St. Mary's Law Journal*, Volume 18, Number 3, 1987**

Translation: The threat of a lawsuit creates a powerful financial incentive toward safety.

This truth is an important element in the aviation safety system. Airlines, like all commercial enterprises, are in the business of making a profit. The potential to earn a profit is materially affected by the potential cost of an accident. A major expense in any accident is the money that must be paid to the passenger-victims and/or their families. The more that airlines know they will pay victims if disaster strikes, the more likely that airlines conduct their business in a safe and responsible manner. Even when the bulk of the losses are insured, the information garnered in a lawsuit about an airline's private business practices is an inducement to safety. In addition to promoting safety by financially deterring unsafe practices, the civil justice system shines a public light on safety lapses—deficiencies that have often been overlooked by government regulators or missed by government inspectors or investigators.

Industry lobbyists, unions, and citizen activists

"The pilots' and flight attendants' unions are the most effective fighters for consumers in the regulatory process, whereas trade associations have tremendous power within the FAA."

Congressman Peter DeFazio,
member of the House Aviation Subcommittee, 1992

Many organizations and associations work tirelessly to affect the level of aviation safety by pushing Congress to pass laws they want or reject pending legislation they oppose and by urging rule-makers in the FAA and other agencies to implement the law in a way that is beneficial to their point-of-view. Many of these groups have full-time staff to attend to these matters and often have a forceful voice in the halls of government.

The following is a list of some of the most important groups and organizations.

• *Air Transport Association* (ATA) is the trade organization for the major airlines. It is a powerful voice within Congress and the FAA.

- *Regional Airline Association* (RAA) represents the interests of commuter and regional airlines.
- *Aircraft Owners and Pilots Association* (AOPA) is the loudest voice for the interests of general aviation (private aviators).
- *Air Line Pilots Association* (ALPA) is the biggest union of airline pilots and a very powerful voice advocating for increased safety levels.
- *Association of Professional Flight Attendants* (APFA) and the *Association of Flight Attendants* (AFA) are the largest unions that represent flight attendants. They too have vigorous safety programs.
- *National Air Traffic Control Association* (NATCA) is the air traffic controllers' union and is an indirect successor to PATCO. (Recall that PATCO called for the ATC strike in the early eighties; the strikers were fired by President Reagan and PATCO subsequently ceased to legally exist.) NATCA speaks loudly on issues involving air traffic control.
- *Professional Airway Systems Specialists* (PASS) is the union that represents FAA inspectors and the technicians who maintain and repair air traffic control equipment.
- *Flight Safety Foundation* (FSF) is funded by the many and varied interests of the aviation industry. The foundation's sole function is the promotion of safety.
- *Aviation Safety Institute* (ASI) is a nonprofit organization out of Worthington, Ohio, that studies safety issues and publishes reports and recommendations to improve the system.
- *Aviation Consumer Action Project* (ACAP) is an activist consumer group founded by Ralph Nader in the early seventies that has advocated on behalf of airline passengers in the areas of aviation safety and economic fairness.
- *Surviving family groups* have organized after aviation tragedies to promote airline safety. The most famous of these are the groups made up of surviving family members of those killed in the infamous Pan Am 103 bombing over Lockerbee, Scotland, and in the aftermath of the Sioux City tragedy. Many of these groups are endeavoring to form a united front group to advocate for airline safety.

- *Safety professionals and consultants* also work with government and industry to prevent accidents. These individuals, who do not usually align themselves with any particular segment of the system, frequently work behind the scenes to improve safety.

These groups and individuals and others like them are advocates for their individual perspectives on aviation safety. Sometimes their voices conflict, at other times they are in harmony. Their varying points of view are presented in the discussion of the many safety issues that are addressed throughout the book.

Now that you know the forces that influence the safety system, let's take a brief look at how aviation safety is measured.

3

Taking safety's measure

"Two jet liners converging almost head-on missed colliding over North Carolina on Sunday by less than a mile and a half .... It was one of the most disturbing close calls in recent memory ...."

News story in *The New York Times*, July 4, 1991

The statistical record

The incident reported by *The New York Times* of the near miss over North Carolina, is now part of the statistical record of the Department of Transportation, the FAA, and the NTSB. These statistics are kept by the government for many purposes, primary among them, to analyze the safety of the aviation system and to attempt to discover emerging problems that can be determined from the statistical record. The government tracks safety data for several key areas.

Accidents An accident is an event that occurs when a person on board an aircraft in flight, or who has boarded with the intention of flight, suffers a serious injury or is killed, or an occurrence in which an aircraft is *substantially damaged* (called a *hull loss*), which is a categorization that is typically referenced in accident reports. An accident can occur in the air or on the ground.

Incidents An incident is a near-accident that adversely affects the safety of an aircraft or the people on board an aircraft. Aviation safety records would be incomplete if the records only tracked the number of planes that crash or the number of people injured or killed. Accordingly, the government also attempts to keep a count of the number of incidents.

Near midair collisions (NMAC) An NMAC occurs when aircraft come close to colliding in midair. A *critical* NMAC is defined by the DOT as a near collision that was avoided "due to chance" rather than avoidance by the pilot; a separation of fewer than 100 feet would be considered critical. A *potential* NMAC occurs when the incident probably would have resulted in a collision if no action had been taken by either pilot; a potential NMAC usually requires fewer than 500 feet separation. A *no-hazard* NMAC occurs when, by the nature of the circumstances, an accident probably would not have happened regardless of any evasive action taken.

Other safety measures Other statistics are also kept by government in an attempt to measure the safety record. An *operational error* occurs when an air traffic controller violates FAA-mandated separation standards between two or more aircraft, or separation between aircraft and other objects. This might not significantly threaten air safety. The same can be said of the *pilot deviation*, which occurs when the action of a pilot results in the violation of an FAA regulation.

The government also differentiates among the different kinds of planes flown and the different purposes for which they are flown.

FAR Part 121 carriers FAR 121 carriers (also known as Part 121) are governed by Section 121 of the Federal Aviation Regulations. FAR 121 applies to aircraft that carry more than 60 seats, including all regularly scheduled airlines that operate transport jets.

FAR Part 135 carriers Operators of smaller aircraft that carry 60 or fewer passengers are governed by less-stringent rules: Part 135. FAR 135 carriers are subject to less-stringent safety standards in many aspects of aviation safety, such as maximum pilot duty hours, and minimum levels of required safety equipment.

General Aviation (GA) GA pilots fly small private aircraft. The safety requirements for GA aircraft are governed by FAR Part 91 General Operating and Flight Rules and are less stringent than Part 135 requirements.

All Federal Aviation Regulations are part of the broader U.S. government Code of Federal Regulations (CFRs). CFR referencing is identical to FAR parts and paragraphs; CFR 135.119 is FAR 135.119, which is a prohibition against carriage of weapons.

Statistics

This table reflects the accident and fatality statistics from 1980–1990 for all Part 121 commercial carriers, scheduled, and unscheduled service. (Source: 1990 NTSB)

	Accidents		*Fatalities*	
Year	Total	Fatal	Total	Aboard
1980	19	1	1	0
1981	26	4	4	2
1982	20	5	235	233
1983	24	4	15	14
1984	17	1	4	4
1985	22	7	526	525
1986	24	3	8	7
1987	36	5	232	229
1988	29	3	285	274
1989	30	11	278	276
1990	26	6	39	12
1991	27	4	50	49
1992	19	4	33	31

The government also keeps track of Part 135 accidents. This table reflects the accidents and fatalities of Part 135 carriers, including scheduled carriers and nonscheduled carriers. (The nonscheduled carriers are *air taxi operators* that would typically—but not always—fly a smaller general aviation airplane that has been maintained according to regulations for the purpose for revenue flying.)

| | Accidents | | Fatalities | |
Year	Total	Fatal	Total	Aboard
1980	209	54	142	138
1981	188	49	128	124
1982	158	36	86	86
1983	158	29	73	67
1984	168	30	100	98
1985	173	42	113	111
1986	177	37	69	65
1987	129	40	124	120
1988	115	29	79	75
1989	130	31	119	119
1990	118	28	44	44
1991	110	34	150	146
1992	97	31	87	87

Accidents and the mortality level of general aviation (private flying) as recorded by the government are in this table.

	Accidents	Deaths
1980	3590	1239
1981	3500	1282
1982	3233	1187
1983	3075	1064
1984	3011	1039
1985	2737	951
1986	2576	965
1987	2464	807
1988	2354	777
1989	2233	768
1990	2218	763
1991	2143	746
1992	1956	812

The FAA also keeps track of NMACs as reported by pilots. The following chart reflects NMAC statistics from 1980–1990. (DOT Annual Report of National Transportation Statistics, June 1992.)

Year	Critical	Potential	No hazard	Unclassified*
1980	118	319	122	9
1981	84	232	76	3
1982	56	191	64	0
1983	98	283	84	10
1984	127	317	115	30
1985	180	423	133	22
1986	162	473	198	7
1987	190	605	263	0
1988	110	442	158	0
1989	93	322	135	0
1990	73	244	107	0
1991	52	196	99	Unknown

*No determination could be made due to insufficient evidence or unusual circumstances.

These statistics and many other measurements that are compiled by the government are used by analysts seeking to learn lessons and draw conclusions about aviation safety. As a simple illustration, if an analyst sought to determine whether the toughness of safety regulations had an impact upon the safety of flying, that analyst might note that the accident statistics indicate that Part 135 carriers consistently had more accidents per year than Part 121 carriers and that general aviation had a worse safety record than commuter airlines and air taxis. It would then be noted that Part 121 carriers are governed by the strongest FARs and the Part 121 carriers are in the sector of the industry that suffered the fewest accidents and fatalities. General aviation, which is held to the least stringent safety requirements by the government, suffered the highest accident and fatality levels.

Commuter carriers and air taxis, subject to less-stringent safety rules than Part 121 carriers, but to a higher standard than general aviation aircraft and pilots, had a safety record in the middle; thus, the analyst might hypothesize that the statistics indicate that tougher safety regulations make for safer flying. The hypothesis would then be subjected to testing and analysis and intellectual challenges, perhaps relying upon different sets of statistics, in order to verify or disprove its truth. These studies, in turn, stimulate further responses and challenges. And so it goes ....

NASA's Aviation
Safety Reporting System

The government's statistics only provide a partial picture of the safety playing field at a given time. There is also an abundance of safety data that might never make it into statistics officially reported by the federal government.

One of these data sources comes from NASA's Aviation Safety Reporting System, the program that allows pilots, air traffic controllers, and others to report incidents involving the violation of safety rules in anonymity. These reports read like mini-dramas. Many reveal disturbing lapses in safe operating procedures. For example, a pilot reported an unauthorized landing to NASA, an occurrence that probably never made it into the FAA aviation safety statistics: (PIT in the report is a code for the airport in question. Word-contractions that were used in the original report have been altered to spell out the whole word.)

> I was the pilot of a flight into PIT. The weather was exceptionally good and the flight proceeded normally. Upon entering PIT airspace we were told to look for a medium large transport plane. We found the craft and were cleared for a visual approach to [Runway] 28-L. Since I was flying, I was concentrating on keeping [the other] aircraft in sight. Since it was dusk I was looking into the sun. The captain of the flight was new to this airplane. This was his second day of line flying and he wasn't yet settled into the "flow" of the checklists and handling the aircraft. We continued the approach and landed. Upon clearing the runway, we were not told to contact ground control [the controller who controls the aircraft as it taxis]. So I announced [the captain was now in control of the aircraft] that flight XXX was clear of the active [runway]. After a pause, we were told to contact ground control. This pause was the first hint that something was wrong. Ground told us to taxi to the ramp, and after we had, he replied that the tower must be getting forgetful. [The tower controller is in charge of landings and takeoffs.] Nothing else was said. After further thinking we realized that approach [the controller in charge of the approach to

the airport] never switched us to tower and that we had forgotten to remind them. I believe that I was trying to keep the [other] aircraft in sight and follow the visual approach so intently while looking into the sun that I failed to notice that we had never swapped frequencies. [The approach controller should have "handed" the flight off to the tower controller, who would have communicated with the aircraft on a different radio frequency.] We had been cleared for the approach but it stuck in our heads that we had been cleared to land ....

In other words, this plane landed without the air traffic controller advising the pilot that it was safe to do so. This was a serious safety lapse. Had there been another plane on the runway, real tragedy could have resulted.

William Reynard, ASRS director, states that more than 200,000 safety lapses have been reported to NASA since 1986, building up a significant data base as to what is happening in commercial aviation. He adds, "If you want to know what's going on out there, just ask us, and we can search our records and put together a package telling you what we see."

ASRS material also has value because it not only describes what happened, but why it happened. As such, it is a valuable accident prevention tool that, according to Reynard, is being underutilized. "Everybody hasn't yet taken advantage of the potential of our incident records. That's too bad. I am convinced that incidents are surrogates for accidents. Each incident we record is a 'mini-accident investigation report.' We get data you can't find anywhere else."

As an experiment, the authors requested ASRS material regarding safety lapses that were caused by pilot fatigue in Part 121 aircraft, the airlines. Within six weeks, we were sent 100 separate incident reports and were told that 843 more were available if we wanted them. Moreover, we were warned that the reports represent the "lower measure of the true number of such events which are occurring" because all reports were voluntarily given. The reports indicate that pilot fatigue is a potential threat to safety.

What does all this mean? The statistics published by the government are of interest, but as history lessons; their inherent value in preventing future accidents is limited. More can be accomplished by utilizing the NASA ASRS because an area of degrading safety might first appear in anonymous incident reports before resulting in an accident.

The reports are also helpful in learning why an incident did not metastasize into an accident. Reynard explains: "The reports are excellent at revealing the recovery factors that prevent an incident from becoming an accident. For example, there was one report where a captain failed to hold his jet short of a runway as instructed by the ground controller. The flight engineer brought it to the pilot's attention because of the training he had received in flight crew communications during cockpit recourse management training. The pilot immediately stopped the aircraft and a potential accident was avoided. Before the training, the flight engineer stated he probably would have kept his mouth shut and the pilot acknowledged that he might not have been willing to listen. That tells us the [CRM] training is an effective deterrent to accidents."

The FAA and other government agencies can learn about the current state of aviation safety by utilizing ASRS. Add a solid safety indicator program, which would project future safety issues in much the same way economic indicators predict future movements of the economy, and the FAA could go a long way toward making itself a proactive preventer of accidents rather than a Johnny-come-lately reactor to them.

Missing stats

The government is a prodigious statistic collector, but does not keep track of everything related to safety. For example, the government tracks on-time performance and the number of flight delays by airlines and makes them available to the public. That places pressure on the airlines to maintain their schedules. But at the same time, the FAA refuses to divulge any knowledge that it might have concerning the differing safety levels that exist among the competing airlines. The result of this policy, if not it's design, is to leave the false impression with the flying public that all airlines are equally safe, that no one airline has a higher standard of safety than another.

This policy is at best misguided. Think about what would happen if the FAA provided the public with reports and statistics that would allow a passenger to compare safety efforts among the competing airlines before purchasing a ticket. The information would force the airlines to compete on issues of safety, not just price, comfort, and convenience. If the proponents of free markets are correct about the benefits of competition and free markets, would that not lead to safer flying?

Later, these and related issues will be discussed in more detail. But now, it's time to explore the dark recesses of that bureaucratic swamp known as Washington, D.C.

4

Bureaucratic quicksand

"It is true that throughout the history of aviation safety, regulators have been reactive to accidents. It is also true that subjecting newly proposed safety regulations to the cost/benefit analysis and OMB approval slows things up."

Clint Oster,
coauthor of *Why Airplanes Crash*

The rule making pace of the FAA can be compared to continental drift: science can prove that there is movement but the movement cannot be seen by the naked eye. While that might be a bit hyperbolic, it does reflect frequently heard criticism of the FAA from people in government, the professional unions and consumer advocates, who claim that the snail's pace at which the FAA usually performs its regulatory functions often adversely impacts safety.

In reviewing the record, these critics do have a point. The FAA often takes many years to create rules needed to upgrade safety, even when a problem and cure have been well identified.

Snail's-pace regulating has adverse consequences. When the FAA fails to act to improve safety in a timely manner, the lives of the flying public are put at risk unnecessarily. For example, many safety experts believe that the FAA's failure to adequately upgrade safety regulations that apply to commuter airlines (Part 135 carriers) is one reason why these carriers have a worse safety record than airlines that fly large transport jets (Part 121 carriers).

There are many reasons why the FAA suffers from "the slows" (to borrow an apt phrase from Abraham Lincoln). Part of the problem lies in the conflicting legal mandate of the FAA, which is directed to both promote aviation and to foster safety. This "dual mandate" might make regulators unduly sensitive to the expense side of the airline's safety ledger. In addition, regulatory gridlock exists partly because the FAA is provided with insufficient funds and resources, or perhaps FAA personnel do not pursue their tasks with sufficient vigor. But a large part of the problem can also be traced to the rules of the regulatory process itself.

Bureaucracy in inaction

"If there is not a driving force pushing a safety regulation, it can be killed in a bureaucrat's in-box."

A Washington, D.C., consultant
who advises several regulatory agencies on
issues of government regulation

The path that a new safety regulation takes from idea to completion is often long and tortuous. Here are some of the landmarks along the way.

The need is identified

The first step in creating new or improved safety rule is for the need to come to the attention of the FAA. The inspiration for change can come from many sources. After an accident investigation, the National Transportation Safety Board might submit a formal recommendation to the FAA calling for regulatory action to improve safety. A citizen, a private organization, or a public advocacy group may request that the FAA issue a new rule by filing a document known as the *Petition for Proposed Rulemaking*. Congress might pass a law that requires the FAA to engage in rulemaking. Or, the internal processes within the FAA itself might identify an area of need.

Once the proposed reform is formally identified, the ball moves to the FAA's court.

The FAA chews its cud

"The NTSB keeps a list of unacceptable responses by the FAA and other regulatory agencies to its safety recommendations. Open

*unacceptable responses are ones in which we have a
disagreement with the FAA and continue to try and persuade
them to take the action we have recommended. Closed (or)
unacceptable responses are those files where we have basically
thrown up our hands and have accepted that we will not be able
to persuade them to our point of view."*

**Barry Sweedler, director of the
NTSB office of safety recommendations**

The safety proposal is soon immersed in a bureaucratic labyrinth.
The people of the FAA will confer with each other. They will so-
licit the opinion of people in the DOT and other relevant government agencies. Research will be undertaken, issue papers written
and consultants commissioned to write reports. Let's call this
process, cud chewing. Why? Because the idea is swallowed
whole, bureaucratically regurgitated, swallowed again, masti-
cated, brought up for renewed consideration, swallowed, perhaps
chewed some more and then, maybe, digested.

The cost/benefit analysis

*"If the flying public knew that regulations protecting their safety
depended on a cost/benefit analysis, there would be a
revolution!"*

Congressman Peter A. DeFazio, D-Oregon

Many readers might remember the infamous Ford Pinto scandal;
for those who do not, here's what happened in a nutshell. In
1971, the Ford Motor Company introduced to the automobile market a small, sporty sedan called the Pinto. Unbeknownst to pur-
chasers of the car, the Pinto had a dangerous safety problem: It
was not able to safely withstand a rearend collision at moderate
speeds, making the car susceptible to explosion and fire when hit
from the rear.

In 1973, the federal government was considering passing a
regulation requiring automobiles to be manufactured so as to be
able to withstand rearend collisions of 30 mph or fewer without
having the fuel tank rupture. The Pinto, as then produced, could
not meet this proposed regulation. Ford decided to fight the regulation because they did not wish to refit or remodel the Pinto to
make it more crashworthy (a procedure the company knew how
to accomplish). The issue was money. Ford simply did not want

to spend the money to make the Pinto comply with the proposed rule and thus prevent deaths and serious injuries.

Ford asked the government to reconsider the proposal on the basis that the benefits in lives saved and injuries prevented in making their automobile safer was outweighed by the cost that would be incurred by the company if the proposed 30 mph standard was enacted. To support its thesis, Ford attached a mathematical formula. The formula worked as follows: Ford set the cost of a human life at $200,000, a burn injury at $67,000, and the value of an incinerated auto at $700. Ford then figured that in Pintos there would be 180 deaths, 180 burn injuries, and 2,100 burned vehicles per year. Using those figures, Ford set the benefit of the 30 mph standard at $49.5 million per year. Ford then stated that it would cost the company $11 per auto to meet the standard for a total cost to the company of $137.5 million. At the time, people were outraged that Ford would advocate such a stark cost/benefit analysis in determining whether auto safety should be improved by regulation. Yet today in the FAA—and other government agencies—that is the exact kind of analysis that is engaged in when determining whether a proposed safety regulation should be made law.

Meanwhile, people were being killed and maimed in Pintos that exploded into flames when rearended. This resulted in lawsuits. In one of these suits, the lawyers for the family of a man killed in a Pinto and a person disfigured in the car by burns, discovered the cost/benefit memo and other evidence indicating that Ford knew the Pinto was dangerous before it was marketed. The jury was furious. They awarded millions in compensatory damages and also found Ford liable for $125 million in punitive damages (punishment damages) for willfully disregarding the safety of the Pinto occupants. (The punitive damage award was later reduced by a court to $3.5 million.)

What does the conduct of Ford Motor Company have to do with aviation safety? Unfortunately, too much. The FAA is required by Executive Order No. 12,291, signed by Ronald Reagan, to conduct a similar cost/benefit analysis—as that proposed by Ford in 1973—before approving any new safety regulation. The Order specifically states in Section 2 (b):

> Regulatory action shall not be undertaken unless the
> potential benefits to society for the regulation
> outweigh the potential costs to society.

This might appear reasonable, but the way it works is a different story. In a somewhat simplified form, here is how the cost/benefit analysis operates at the FAA:

- First, a study is undertaken that attempts to predict how many lives will be saved if the proposed rule is adopted. The FAA usually looks into the history of aviation accidents and, using the historical record, projects the number of lives expected to be saved if the proposed rule is adopted.
- At the same time, another study, relying in large part on information supplied by the airlines, estimates the dollar cost of implementing the proposed rule. This is the *cost to society.*
- A dollar amount is arbitrarily picked to represent the value of one human life for the purposes of the cost/benefit analysis. As of the time of this writing, the FAA uses $1.5 million to represent the value of a human life. (Other government agencies use different figures.)
- Next, the number of projected lives saved is multiplied by the dollar value of each life. This amount constitutes the projected *benefit to society.*
- Finally, that figure is compared to the expected cost of implementing the rule.

Here's an illustration of how all of this works. Assume that a proposed rule is projected to save 10 lives at a cost of $30 million. The equation would work out as follows:

10 lives saved × $1.5 million value per life = $15 million.

If, as in this example, the anticipated cost, $30 million, is higher than the projected benefit, $15 million, the rule is said to have a negative cost/benefit effect. Under Executive Order No. 12,291 the rule cannot be implemented.

The manner in which the cost/benefit analysis has been used to stifle safety is a travesty. It is wrong to deny the flying public safer transport because of some arbitrary equation, especially one that is so imprecise. The bean counters in the FAA aren't psychics. They cannot know how many lives actually will be saved by a proposed rule. So, instead they ask, "How many lives have been lost because of this safety defect?"

Determining a future benefit by relying on history is inadequate to the task. First, you need dead bodies. If no one has died from an identified danger, there can be little benefit shown. In the real world of uncertain results, that simply does not make sense. Just because a tragedy has not yet been caused by a safety hazard, that does not mean lives will not be lost because of the hazard in the future. For example, to date, nobody has been killed by a bomb planted by terrorists on a domestic jet airliner; therefore, the FAA has refused to require the airlines to screen domestic check-in luggage with explosive screening devices, one of the increased security measures that the FAA mandated on international flights after the Pan Am 103 bombing. (*See* chapter 15.)

This is fallacious reasoning. The mere fact that we thankfully have not suffered the horror of a "domestic Pan Am 103," does not mean that we never will. Domestic sabotage is a foreseeable event. (If you have any doubts, witness the 1993 bombing of the World Trade Center in New York City.) It shouldn't take a high body count in the past to justify safety measures today that could keep people from becoming fatality statistics tomorrow, fatalities that then would be used in a cost/benefit analysis to justify new security measures on domestic flights.

There is another problem with using past fatalities as the basis for predicting the number of lives that could be saved by a regulation. The number of people killed in an accident does not accurately predict the danger to the flying public because some passengers often survive air crashes. For example, the 1989 crash at Sioux City began when the tail engine on a DC-10 exploded in-flight because of a defective part. The explosion severed the flight controls, disabling the aircraft. The pilots were able to crash-land the plane at the Sioux City airport. (Who can ever forget the dramatic footage of the burning jet cartwheeling down the runway?) The tragedy claimed 111 lives, but miraculously, 187 survived. Taking that into account, which figure should be used when projecting the number of lives that will be saved by rules that could prevent that accident from recurring—the number of people actually killed or the total number of people on the plane? The benefit to society could vary dramatically depending on the statistic chosen.

Despite these flaws, the cost/benefit analysis is the most important criterion used by regulators when determining the level of safety that the Federal Aviation Regulations will require. The effect of this (at least during the Reagan/Bush years) has been to stifle safety and prevent many useful and important safety rules from being implemented. Moreover, the rule also has been used as justification for watering down many of the safety rules that managed to get past the cost/benefit analysis bottleneck.

Executive Order 12,291 should be rescinded, or at least the FAA should be exempted from its requirements. That is not to say that the cost of safety should not be considered in the regulatory scheme of things. But cost of safety should be **a** consideration, not **the** consideration.

Notice of proposed rulemaking
"Politically, some comments are worth more than others."

**A Washington, D. C.,
consultant to the government
regarding regulatory issues**

Assuming that a proposal survives its initial consideration by the FAA, the agency will draft the proposed new rule and publish it in the *Federal Register* as a Notice of Proposed Rulemaking (NPRM). Here's how the NPRM works, according to Anthony J. Broderick, associate administrator for regulations and certifications:

> The public gets a period of time to comment on the proposed rule. We generally like about a four-month period. They tell us what they like and what they don't like about it. Then, we basically start the whole process over again, modifying the rule, reanalyzing its effect in various ways on society, then taking that package, getting it through the administrator's office, on over to the office of the Secretary of Transportation and then, to the OMB.

In other words, more cud chewing. With all of that going on, it's amazing that safety rules are ever enacted at all.

The "public" that Mr. Broderick mentioned that is given the opportunity to comment are not usually interested citizens performing their civic duty. In real life, the general public rarely hears about NPRMs. Few people subscribe to the *Federal Register* and the news media rarely covers the publication of an NPRM. The comments that the FAA does receive generally come from the aviation industry, through the Air Transport Association, the Regional Airlines Association, individual airlines, manufacturers, and manufacturers groups. The pilots and flight attendants unions also let their collective voices be heard as might consumer activist groups, such as the Aviation Consumer Action Project (ACAP).

According to one knowledgeable insider who asked to remain anonymous, the comments received by the FAA are not given equal weight:

> Regulators may ask themselves, where's the trouble
> out there? Who's going to sue? Who's going to run to
> the Hill? Who's going to leak to *The Washington Post?*
> The more perceived power the commentator has to
> affect the public debate, the greater will be their clout
> with regulators and legislators.

In other words, rulemaking, like legislating, is an insider's game. In such an atmosphere, it is not surprising that safety might take a back seat to bureaucratic maneuvering and the corporate bottom line.

The final rule is promulgated

"Numerous delays can occur in the latter stages of rulemaking. The record, often lengthy, must be assessed by the staff and summarized for decision making. Recommendations must be prepared. Different disciplines might become involved, and coordination with other agencies and OMB review will typically take place. Sometimes, internal policy disputes arise at the deliberative stage. All of these, as well as other factors, may delay the issuance of a rule."

From, "A Guide to Agency Rulemaking—2nd edition"

Just because an NPRM is published, that does not mean that the rule will be finalized. There is still a swamp of bureaucratic quicksand to maneuver past, quicksand that can trap or bury the most valuable safety regulation. Many a worthwhile aviation safety rule has fallen into this bureaucratic black hole and died a' borning.

A proposed rule that does emerge from the quicksand is published in the *Federal Register* as a final rule. Often, many years will have passed between the identification of the need to create a new safety regulation and its final implementation. And then, the content of the final rule might bear little resemblance to what was initially proposed. Moreover, the rule might be so watered-down that its effectiveness is questionable or the rule might be so vague that the FAA's enforcement ability might be in doubt.

A true story from the quicksand

Cornish F. Hitchcock, an attorney at the citizen activist organization, Public Citizen, tells of the time he walked the Byzantine maze of FAA rulemaking trying to upgrade the FAA regulation that sets the minimum contents of medical kits that airlines are required to have on-board their transport jets. The episode began when Hitchcock received a letter from a doctor who wrote: "I was on a plane recently, and a passenger on board had a heart attack. And they made the announcement, 'Is there a doctor on the plane?' I stood up and offered to help and I felt utterly helpless because there was no equipment that I could use to respond to this. There was a first-aid kit that had some band-aids and some splints but it was one of the most frustrating experiences I've had in my medical career. Can't you do something about this or can somebody do something to try to provide equipment so that qualified professionals can deal with this emergency?"

Hitchcock thought that was a fair question and decided to do a little digging, which started a nearly five-year odyssey:

> We looked at the current standard that the FAA had on its books, and we were surprised to learn that the (then) existing regulation incorporated a kit called the Johnson & Johnson In-flight Kit, which was established in 1924, and which you will see on display at the Smithsonian.
>
> That was the state of medical technology available on U.S. aircraft. It was an area where it seemed desirable to catch up. So, in conjunction with a medical student, we did a literature search. To my astonishment, there was quite a bit of literature by various medical groups listing the medical equipment that should be on board airliners, so that the patient could be treated very quickly and the suffering could be relieved until the plane reached its destination or made an emergency landing. We also did a survey and the literature showed a report in the American Medical Association Journal that nine out of ten doctors agreed

that there ought to be this sort of equipment on the plane.

With such solid support from the medical establishment, Hitchcock idealistically believed that it would be easy to convince the FAA to update the rules. He was wrong.

We filed the Petition for Rulemaking with the FAA in 1981. The FAA took the petition and sat on it for more than a year.

Then, in the spring of 1982, I got a call from a member of the Senate Aviation Subcommittee about a hearing they were going to hold. We convinced them to add the issue of in-flight medical emergencies to the agenda and told them of some doctors who might be good witnesses. They agreed and the hearing was announced and proceeded on that basis.

The day before the hearing, the FAA acted on our petition. They turned us down. They said, 'Sorry, we do not have the legal authority to issue a rule upgrading the quality of the kits.'

That did not make sense to us. On the one hand, there is a broad safety statute authorizing the FAA to regulate the safety of flight. And they had used that authority to require oxygen and band-aids and splints. But for the life of us, we could not read the statute to say, 'Band-aids, yes; stethoscopes, no; splints, yes; blood pressure cuffs, no.' But that was the position the agency took.

Frustrated by the FAA, Hitchcock moved the matter to another forum. Suit was filed in the D.C. Circuit Court of Appeals. In 1983, the court unanimously held that the FAA did, indeed, have the authority to consider the petition on the merits. Nearly two years had passed from the beginning of the effort and Mr. Hitchcock was still at square one.

Meanwhile, the Congress was getting into the act. Senator Barry Goldwater (R-Arizona), authored a bill in the Senate designed to compel the FAA to issue rules updating the medical kits and the Aviation Subcommittee was also interested in the issue. Cornish F. Hitchcock continues:

What happened at that point was a form of regulatory negotiation. In an effort to head off the legislation, the FAA agreed it would undertake rulemaking on a number of issues that were of concern to the subcommittee leadership. It so happened that improving the emergency medical kits was one such regulation.

The cost/benefit analysis showed that this rule would be effective if it saved one life a year. The Air Transport Association finally announced that it would not oppose such an effort; thus, by the summer of 1984, we were pretty much on track. The notice of proposed rulemaking went out the following spring, and the final regulation was adopted at the end of 1985. It did not go as far as we had hoped in terms of adopting some of the recommendations from outside medical groups, but it did include a number of important improvements to the existing kit. We moved forward from 1924 to 1985 with remarkable speed.

(The above material was taken from a presentation by Mr. Hitchcock that first appeared in print in *The Administrative Law Journal* of The American University, Volume 5, Number 1, Spring 1991. This abridged version has been republished with the consent of Mr. Hitchcock.)

If it took nearly five years for Mr. Hitchcock and his allies to convince the FAA to promulgate a relatively simple rule requiring that stethoscopes and other emergency medical equipment be placed on board airplanes, imagine the heroic struggle it takes to convince the FAA to engage in rulemaking over issues of more intense concern and greater expense.

5

Deregulation

"Air transportation, is de facto, our national mass transit system—yet it is virtually bankrupt."

Theodore P. Harris,
chairman of Airline Industry Resources, Inc., 1992

"It is frustrating that the most damaging thing that happened to the airlines in the 1980s was the leveraged-option-buyout."

Professional staff member in the
Department of Transportation

In 1978, the U.S. Congress passed and President Carter signed the Airline Deregulation Act, probably the most radical alteration in the relationship between government and the commercial aviation industry since the 1920s. The new law phased out the Civil Aeronautics Board (CAB) and ended most of the government's economic regulation of the airlines. Gone were the days when the CAB controlled the economics of air travel in order to ensure the economic viability of the industry. No longer would ticket prices be established by the government. Regulation of domestic air routes was a policy of the past. Now had come the time for bare-knuckled competition, in which the invisible hand of the free market would bring about greater business opportunity, lower air fares and a tougher, more efficient national air system.

After nearly a decade of this experiment in free market economics, the results are coming in. First, the good news: There have been some financial successes under deregulation. Regional airlines have been the big winners, growing at an exponential rate and making money in the bargain. Southwest Airlines has been able to create a profitable market niche by offering direct route air travel at a reasonable price throughout Texas, California, Arizona, and the Southwest. In some ways, consumers have benefited too. Prices are down on many routes, subject to restrictions, although they are much higher on others. Fare wars occasionally have reduced the cost of air travel by up to 50 percent for limited seats. Despite the current slump, commercial aviation is projected by industry and government observers to be a large growth industry during the 1990s and beyond.

Now the bad news and it is very bad indeed: Thanks to the combination of deregulation and the laissez faire approach to government of the Reagan/Bush years, the worst face of capitalism has carried the day. Overall, the commercial industry is nearing financial collapse, having lost approximately $10 billion dollars in the last three years. Mergers, leveraged-option-buyouts (LOBs), predatory pricing, and monopolistic practices all have resulted in an industry that is strongly trending toward oligolopy, with the "Big Three," United Airlines, American Airlines, and Delta dominating the industry.

Venerable carriers such as Pan American, Piedmont, and Eastern have gone out of business or merged. TWA, Continental Airlines, and other large and once financially healthy companies have been forced to seek the shelter of bankruptcy court in a last ditch effort to stay in business. (Continental subsequently emerged from bankruptcy court protection.) Other companies, such as USAir and Northwest Airlines have gone deeply into debt. For example, in its June 30, 1992, Report of Financial and Operating Statistics made to the Department of Transportation (known as a Form 41 Financial Disclosure), USAir reported that it had incurred $2,026,086,000 in long-term debt. Northwest's debt problem wasn't much better; the August 10, 1992, Form 41 Disclosure Statement revealed $2,494,601,000 in "total current liabilities" and $2,720,942,000 in "total noncurrent liabilities," of which $998,066,000 was for long-term debt. Thanks in large part to deregulation, the once thriving and world dominant American aviation industry is in deep financial distress and might need to be saved by investors from overseas. In fact, that trend has already begun. British Airways has been allowed to invest in USAir, KLM owns almost half of Northwest Airlines and Air Canada owns a large stake in Continental.

(Isn't it interesting that while every proposed safety regulation must pass a rigorous cost/benefit analysis, the government has permitted the airlines to incur massive debt requiring huge interest payments, without so much as a peep of protest? This speaks volumes about the priorities of the Department of Transportation during the Reagan/Bush years.)

The proponents of deregulation also assured the country that deregulation would not cost smaller communities access to commercial flight. And that has proved true—but only because the government subsidizes small carriers to induce them to service these communities.

The program is called the *subsidized essential air service* and it spends millions of dollars annually to provide air service to small communities. For example, according to DOT documents, the commuter carrier WestAir is paid $305,374 annually to provide service between Crescent City, California, and Sacramento and San Francisco. The carrier also receives $716,353 to fly between Merced and San Francisco. Another commuter carrier, Big Sky Airlines, is paid $2,322,144 per year to fly from various locales in Montana to the large airport at Billings. (Source: October 1992 EAS Report.) So, in the name of free markets, deregulation freed the carriers to pursue the profitable markets while sticking the taxpayer with part of the bill for servicing smaller communities.

But this is not a book about the economics of the industry. This book is primarily concerned with safety. The key question for this discussion, then, must be: Has deregulation adversely affected aviation safety?

As with most public policy issues, there are differences of opinion. One school of thought believes that safety has not been adversely impacted by economic deregulation. Some base their opinions on the statistical history. Professor Clinton Oster, John S. Strong, and C. Kurt Zorn, state in their book *Why Airplanes Crash* (1992, Oxford University Press, New York, New York), on page 5, "Not only has the airline safety record been better in the years following deregulation than it was before, but the rates of accidents caused by equipment failure, air traffic control error and pilot error, have all dropped."

Supporters of economic deregulation hold to the market theory of safety that goes something like this:

- It is in the economic best interest of airline executives to maintain wide margins of safety because ...
- Accidents reduce the confidence air travelers have in the airline that experiences a crash, which ...
- Causes that airline to lose passenger revenue, which ...
- Hurts profits, which ...
- Reduces the value of the airline stock, which ...
- Leads to a reduction in executive compensation or the loss of their job.

In short, the free marketers believe that airlines will not cut safety corners even during a financial pinch because to do so would risk future business.

We contend otherwise. The safety statistics of the 1980s are not proof of safer flying under deregulation. As National Transportation Safety Board member Dr. John K. Lauber said, the "absence of an accident does not demonstrate that safety has been achieved." (Source: *Air Line Pilot Magazine*, September, 1987.) Moreover, the Ford Pinto gas tank safety matter, among many similar significant problems in the history of capitalism, proves that the invisible hand alone does not do enough to guarantee safety.

A large body of thought believes that safety has been adversely impacted by deregulation. Scholars such as Paul Stephen Dempsey of the University of Denver, leaders of most of the aviation industry's professional unions, such as Captain J. Randolf Babbitt of the Air Line Pilots Association, Christopher J. Witkowski, safety officer for the Association of Flight Attendants, and the leadership of the National Air Traffic Controllers Association (NATCA), the air traffic controllers' union, plus John H. Enders, chairman of the Flight Safety Foundation, share the concern. (A high official of one of the aviation unions went so far as to tell us that the current safety system is a house-of-cards waiting to fall.) In fact, many of the safety problems discussed in this chapter and throughout this book have either been created by or worsened due to deregulation.

Economic deregulation has created the need for stronger safety regulation

"I love to fly but I'm more and more afraid. I buckle up real tight these days."
Official of a major aviation industry professional union, 1992

"There is growing evidence that the cost-cutting, overscheduling, and crowded conditions at airports may be eroding the safety margins and posing a growing threat to the flying public."
U.S. Senator William V. Roth Jr.,
chairman of the Senate Subcommittee on Investigations, March, 1986

During the era of economic regulation, the airlines did not suffer financially when they invested money in safety improvements because CAB permitted airlines to include expenditures invested to improve safety margins into the price of the tickets. (That fact did not stop them from opposing many important safety improvements, such as strengthening the crashworthiness of seats.) Under these conditions, airline executives were not as likely to view safety as a potential drag on profits. As a result, many airlines engaged in activities that brought their operations to a higher level of safety than that mandated by regulations. This added safety cushion has often been called by some the "margin of safety." (Many experts in the field of aviation safety believe the safety record of the 1980s is a reflection of this margin of safety created before deregulation.)

With the advent of deregulation, however, the system changed and not necessarily for the better. The government got out of the business of setting ticket prices for the airlines. The industry was now expected to compete based upon price, whereas before deregulation, the airlines competed based upon service and comfort. The price of many fares dropped. The number of passengers increased dramatically. A cycle of intense competition began where pinching every penny counted. The cost of improving safety has become a potential drag on the bottom line.

Many observers of the commercial aviation industry fear that this economic free-for-all caused a slow degradation of the margin of safety, akin to a balloon slowly leaking air. With the commercial aviation industry in danger of falling into the financial dumpster, safety experts, like John O'Brien, director of the Engineering and safety department for the Air Line Pilots Association, believe that, "all operators can no longer exceed the FAA minimum safety standards in the way they did before, simply because they are unable to absorb the cost."

If that is true, if the FARs are now the ceiling of aviation safety rather than the floor, the question must be asked: Do the current FARs set a sufficiently high minimum level of safety to fully protect the flying public? This is a vital area of inquiry. As long as the airlines operate within the FAR-prescribed minimums, there is nothing the FAA or the courts can do to force them to increase their safety activities; thus, it makes sense to set safety standards at a sufficiently rigorous level to fully protect the public without regard to whether the airlines operate at higher than required safety levels.

Industry critics of deregulation point to many areas where safety has become an increased concern, at least in part, due to deregulation. The impact of deregulation is more apparent upon review of the safety concerns.

Aging of the commercial jet transport fleet
"Under deregulation, the U.S. fleet decayed into the oldest in the developed world."

Paul Stephen Dempsey,
director of the Transportation Law Program at the
University of Denver.
Published in *The Wall Street Journal*,
May 9, 1991

Virtually everyone involved in the airline industry, from the regulators at the FAA, to officials of the Air Transport Association, to the airline operators, to the unions, agree that one of the most pressing challenges facing safe operations in the 1990s is the aging of the U.S. commercial jet transport fleet.

The seriousness of the problem came into sharp focus in 1988 when a portion of the upper fuselage came off an Aloha Airlines Boeing 737 while it was in flight. The jet had been manufactured in 1969 and possessed the second highest number of *cycles* in the entire Boeing 737 fleet. (A cycle is a measure of aircraft age; a single cycle is the combination of takeoff, pressurization and depressurization of the cabin, and landing operations.)

Before deregulation, the airlines were able to regularly replace their older aircraft because those costs were included in the price of tickets as set by CAB. That is no longer true. In recent years, Delta, American, United, Northwest, USAir, TWA, and many other major airlines have made headlines in newspaper business sections, as one after the other canceled or delayed the purchase of billions of dollars worth of new aircraft. That means that many geriatric aircraft are going to be kept in service for much longer than originally intended. Deregulation's destructive progeny of cut-throat competition along with the permissive attitude towards mergers and LOBs during the 1980s, is largely to blame. (Chapter 12 has more information about aging aircraft.)

Increased burden of maintenance

"Money problems do cause reductions in airline maintenance because the cuts are less visible."

Mechanic for a debt ridden U.S. airline, 1992

The effects of deregulation have increased airline maintenance expenses at a time when industry red ink is inhibiting the ability and willingness of many airlines to pay those costs. The increased maintenance costs created by deregulation are caused by two primary factors:

- More planes are flying; thus, by definition, more planes must be maintained.

- Many of the planes in service are aged. Some have already flown beyond their economic life expectancy. The older a plane is, the more maintenance inspections must be performed to ensure safety and the greater likelihood that the plane will require expensive repairs.

Many industry critics fear that airlines, pressed for dollars will skimp on maintenance in order to cut costs. Anecdotal evidence has revealed that this is already happening. Others worry about fraud and the falsification of maintenance records by airlines. In New York, in 1989, Eastern Airlines plead guilty in Federal District Court for falsifying maintenance records and was fined $3.5 million. It is probably not a coincidence that this crime took place when the company was in desperate financial condition.

A July 19, 1988, *The Wall Street Journal* reported that there has been an overall reduction in the number of aircraft mechanics employed by the major airlines. The following chart from that story illustrates the point:

Number of mechanics per aircraft

Airline	1982	1987
American	16.6	15.6
Continental	14.6	13.0
Delta	21.3	14.9
Eastern	22.1	16.9
Northwest	11.6	12.4
Pan Am	27.4	28.2
Piedmont	13.0	9.7
TWA	30.9	25.7
United	17.8	21.2
USAir	12.4	11.8
Average	**18.77**	**16.94**

An increase in the number of independent repair stations might be taking up some of the slack; however, the overall diminution in the number of mechanics per airplane creates a heavy work pressure on mechanics, that when coupled with the pressure they are under to avoid flight delays, can lead to poor maintenance practices.

Commuter flight increases

"I refuse to fly in commuter aircraft."

**Congressman Peter DeFazio,
member of the Subcommittee on Aviation, 1992**

Before deregulation, the airlines principally used linear routes for most flights. That is, a plane might fly directly from Buffalo to Cleveland, or from Sacramento to Phoenix. The aircraft used were generally large transport jets that operated under the highest safety standards established by Part 121 of the FARs.

Since deregulation, that system changed. Now the major airlines operate a scheduling system known as the *hub and spoke* method. A hub is a major airport where a large carrier concentrates its operations. The largest airlines have several hubs around the country. For example, a hub for United Airlines is Chicago O'Hare and a hub for American Airlines is Dallas-Fort Worth.

The hub airports also are served by the smaller regional carriers, mostly operating under Part 135, which has the less stringent safety standards of FAR Part 135. Commuters usually fly smaller airplanes that carry fewer passengers than large jet transport aircraft. The smaller commuter planes fly only the spoke routes of hub and spoke scheduling. (Carriers might still fly jet planes on select spoke routes.) That is, the commuters carry passengers from smaller cities to the hub airport where the major air carrier will then fly them and other passengers that have been "gathered" from other spokes to the final destination—or to another hub, where they will take another spoke route to the final destination. Thus, where once you could fly directly to Phoenix from Sacramento, under deregulation you might have to fly first to San Francisco in a small commuter plane, change planes, and then take a large transport jet on to Phoenix.

Under this system of operations, commuter accident levels have increased. Testimony given March 17, 1992, by Kenneth M. Mead, director of transportation issues at GAO, to the Aviation Subcommittee: "The number of commuter airline accidents increased by almost 50 percent, and the accident rate per 100,000 departures was about 67 percent higher between 1990 and 1991." To say the least, that is a disturbing trend that points to the fact that flight on commuter planes is less safe than on large jets.

The hub and spoke system of air transport created because of deregulation is less safe than the direct route system, for a wide variety of reasons.

Commuter aircraft are not considered to be as safe as large transport jets They carry less safety equipment. They must often fly in weather, rather than over weather.

Passengers must take off and land more often Approximately 80 percent of all aviation accidents occur during landing or takeoff. A typical trip using the hub and spoke system might involve four or more landings and takeoffs.

Commuter pilots generally have less training and experience The military used to be the primary recruiting ground for the commercial air carriers. This is no longer true for a variety of reasons. Now, according to such experts as William Frisbee, former head pilot for Pan American and a former pilot on Air Force One, the commuters are becoming the training grounds for less experienced pilots, before they "graduate" to flying large transport jets. One public official went so far as to tell us he was "appalled" by the low qualification levels some airlines now accept for beginning commuter airline pilots and by the lower training levels they receive vis-a-vis Part 121 pilots. Yet, these inexperienced pilots face greater flying challenges due to a lower level of safety technology in the commuter plane cockpits, the need to fly in weather and the greater number of landings and takeoffs that they must make each day.

Government regulations allow commuter carriers to operate under lower minimum safety standards Part 121 safety standards are significantly higher in important areas such as training, technology standards and maximum duty hours than their counterpart FAR 135 safety standards.

The FAA does not have the resources to inspect all of the commuter air carriers One of the important functions of the FAA is to inspect the operations of commercial air carriers to ensure that they are meeting minimum safety requirements. Unfortunately, the FAA does not appear to have the resources to do this job right, or, if the resources are available, they are not being applied correctly.

Hub airports can be overcrowded during peak periods It's feast or famine at most hub airports. There are periods of intense activity and then hours of slack time. During the peak period, flying might be less safe because of overcrowding and the pressure placed on air traffic controllers, pilots, and other safety personnel.

More planes are in the sky This puts strain on air traffic controllers, pilots, ground control, and the safety system in general.

The push to increase capacity

"In the past, the safety of the traveling public was paramount in FAA's decision to modify procedures or introduce new equipment. Recently, though, we have been disturbed by the growing tendency for an increase in capacity to reduce the safety

margin of a project to an unacceptable level ...."
Captain Henry Duffy,
former president of ALPA, quoted in
GAO symposium, "Aviation Challenges for the 1990s"

Deregulation has created a broad and sustained surge in passenger demand. According to DOT statistics, in 1980, 204.367 billion passenger miles were flown by all certified commercial air carriers. By 1990, that figure had increased to 345.873 billion passenger miles. The increase in demand is expected to continue at a steady rate for the balance of the century.

One reason that many airlines have run into financial difficulty is that the aviation system has not been able to keep up with the increased demand and at the same time maintain safe standards. Airline growth is constrained by the inability of the safety system to absorb the extra business. Delays are also a problem. Airlines are unable to operate at peak efficiency, which adversely impacts profits.

Airline executives and the supporters of deregulation have been pressuring the government to relax safety rules so as to permit an increased number of takeoffs and landings per hour. The FAA has responded favorably, reducing the level of safety in the process. For example, the minimum separation of planes in flight has been reduced and less safe operating procedures are increasingly being allowed, such as jets landing on parallel runways at the same time. (At San Francisco Airport, jets conduct parallel landings on runways that are only 750 feet apart.) This, in turn, puts greater pressure on air traffic controllers, pilots, and ground control. This growing demand by the industry to increase the capacity of the system as a panacea to its economic distress is a serious potential threat to aviation safety and must be watched closely to ensure that safe operations are not significantly degraded.

The FAA has been overwhelmed

"The FAA is understaffed and underfunded and therefore is forced to rely too heavily on the good faith of the airlines to comply with safety regulations."
An independent consultant to the FAA, 1992

Deregulation not only turned out to be poor industrial policy but it was not managed well by the government. The tremendous burst of business activity during the initial stages of deregulation caught the FAA off guard; as new carriers sought certification to do business, more flights created more work for air traffic controllers and the need for inspectors grew at an almost geometric pace.

If the initial creators of deregulation had remained in office to oversee the transition from a regulated industry into a free market, the FAA might have been given the increased resources vital to its ability to perform its safety work. Unfortunately, this was not to be. Ronald Reagan was elected president in 1980 and all of the previous assumptions about government, to borrow a phrase from the Nixon years, were no longer operative.

Ronald Reagan and his administration believed that government regulation had to be reduced so that big business could fly free. Despite the fact that the FAA is an important safety agency, it was not given an exemption from this governing philosophy. Even the Air Transport Association is unhappy with the result. William Jackman, an official of the ATA told us, "Cuts in the FAA during the early Reagan years hurt deregulation." Why did the cuts hurt? At a time when the agency had more work than it had ever had before—more work than it could safely handle—budget cuts forced a reduction in the FAA inspector force by approximately 12 percent in 1982 and 1983.

This, happened at a time when the number of airlines tripled, forcing the FAA to set priorities for the inspectors' workload. Typical of the philosophy of those years, priority was given to conducting new certification inspections at the expense of routine safety programs. As if that wasn't bad enough, the PATCO air traffic controllers strike and subsequent terminations took place during this same period, as did the beginnings of the air traffic control equipment modernization program. The combination of these problems hit the FAA like a hammer blow. The agency faltered and has been trying to recover its equilibrium ever since.

Deregulation is an experiment that is destroying the economic vitality of the commercial aviation industry. If current trends continue, it is likely that there will only be three or four large airlines remaining in business by the turn of the century—perhaps not even three or four. One deeply troubled business consultant to the airlines told us, "I am concerned that the future will see the demise of the air carriers as we know them today because the cost of their product will become too high. The resulting influx of niche-seeking airlines will utilize older, tired equipment and employ improperly qualified personnel at much lower salaries and benefits." That would not bode well for the safety of air travel.

Reform is urgently needed to protect safety of the flying public and to maintain the confidence the American people have in commercial aviation, an attitude that is vital to the financial health of the industry. Throughout this book, in greater detail, we advocate these and other possible reforms to improve aviation safety:

- Increasing the strength of minimum safety regulations.
- Releasing money from the Aviation Trust Fund to finance a growing FAA and safety-related expenditures.
- Structural reform of the FAA.
- Partial reregulation of the airlines.
- Vigorous financial fitness enforcement by the DOT and antitrust enforcement by the Department of Justice.

Part II

The FAA follies

"The FAA has misused its people and its resources. It has not kept up with the evolution of aviation. It has tried to do things it is not equipped to do and paid scant attention to those tasks it is capable of handling."

Aviation accident investigator and safety consultant to the industry

This part takes a close, hard look at the competence and effectiveness of the FAA in performing its important duties. This is an important subject for discussion both domestically and internationally. The world looks to the FAA as the leader in setting safety standards and it is the rare exception when another country's safety rules exceed our own; thus, when the FAA falls short, there is likely to be an adverse domino effect that can impact the safety of flying throughout the world.

Unfortunately, the news is not good. The FAA is troubled—in some areas, deeply troubled. The following few chapters will focus on several areas of concern regarding the FAA:

- The inherent conservatism of the agency and its tendency to allow safety lapses to continue until crashes force change
- The conflicting mandate built in to the FAA by the law creating the agency and the consequential tendency of regulators to be too dollar conscious about the costs of safety

- Its cozy relationship with those it is supposed to regulate
- Its seeming reluctance to aggressively pursue new ideas
- Its many management deficiencies

All these concerns impact the safety of aviation and prevent the FAA from being the effective safety agency it must become if aviation is to grow and safely prosper while flying into a new century.

6

The tombstone imperative

"We regulate by counting tombstones."

Barry Sweedler,
director of safety recommendations,
National Transportation Safety Board,
quoted in *The Los Angeles Times*, **April 11, 1991**

Perhaps our most serious criticism of the FAA is that it is moribund, a reactive agency that usually refuses to mandate safety improvements until accidents take lives. Most of the people we interviewed who work in commercial aviation—from union officials, to airline pilots, to flight attendants, to air traffic controllers, to government bureaucrats—told us they believe the accusation is true.

So do many critics of aviation regulation both here and abroad. For example, Stephen Barley, author of the well-received book *Final Call* (1990, Pantheon Books, New York), which is a critique of international aviation safety, decries the reactive nature of most government safety regulators, including the FAA. Barley claims that authorities who are warned of such potential hazards as the "withering safety cushion" or "too much faith (being) put in human technology," often refuse to act unless blood has been spilled. "They want proof, i.e., accident on a statistically significant scale, to make them sit up and take notice of the 'theories' that they tend to regard as scare-mongering." C.O. Miller, aviation safety consultant, agreed in his own way: "If you need to have an accident to know there is a problem, you are part of the problem."

This is a serious charge. It implies a callous attitude on the part of the people who regulate aviation safety. It makes regulators seem uninspired and indifferent and unable or unwilling to confront unfolding safety issues. Bluntly stated, it approaches the charge of dereliction of duty.

Unfortunately, at least as to the FAA, there appears to be some merit to these criticisms. A Washington consultant to the FAA told us, "I have heard someone at the FAA talk about a rule mandating a general aviation safety improvement that would avert one fatal accident in a million flights at a one-time cost of only about $5 or $10 per plane. But the rule never got passed. There was not a high enough body count."

Ample evidence is available to prove that all too often, it takes dead bodies to induce the FAA to regulate. Not that the people who work for the agency don't care—most regulators do, very much—but with a few notable exceptions, they are deplorably conservative in their approach to their work.

The case of the frozen regulations

One of the most dangerous aspects of flying in winter is what can happen while the plane is parked on the ground. Ice can build up on the edges of wings and other surfaces during a snowstorm or freezing weather conditions. Even a very thin coat of ice can destroy the aerodynamic "lift" of the airplane's airfoil, causing the pilot to lose control, resulting in a crash.

The aviation industry has long recognized this problem and steps are taken, generically known as *deicing*, to counter the accumulation of ice and snow when weather conditions warrant. In deicing, the wings and other important plane surfaces are washed with a solution that destroys the ice and impedes its renewed buildup. This permits normal takeoff, even in very cold weather.

Prior to 1992, the FAA steadfastly refused to update deicing regulations that had remained essentially unchanged since 1950. These rules prohibited takeoff with frost, snow, or ice adhering to the wings, control surfaces, or propellers of the aircraft. The responsibility to comply with the rules was left to sole discretion of the pilot. End of regulations. There were no maximum time on-the-ground standards after which deicing would be mandated, no requirement that airlines submit deicing protocols for FAA approval, and no mandatory guidelines for the flight and ground crews to follow.

This approach simply did not work. Over the last 23 years there have been 16 accidents involving ice or failure to deice. These accidents endangered plane loads of people. Many lost their lives. Despite it all, until November, 1992, the FAA took no action to update mandatory minimum deicing procedures in the FARs and continued to insist on leaving the decision solely in the hands of the pilot.

Meanwhile, lives were lost:

January 13, 1982
National Airport, Washington, D.C.

Air Florida's Flight 95 is parked, waiting approval to push away from the gate. It is bitterly cold. The runways have been closed down for snow clearance. The Boeing 737 is deiced by an American Airlines crew. Their maintenance manual does not provide specific instructions for deicing a 737 and the FARs do not have minimum standards. Unbeknownst to the ground crew, the 737 has unique problems associated with deicing—a propensity to turn newly fallen snow into lethal ice along the leading edges of the wings. They are also unaware that Boeing had issued several warning bulletins about the problem.

Fifty minutes after deicing, the flight is cleared for takeoff.

As the plane taxies to the runway, some passengers see snow on the wings. Pilots in other planes see the snow, too. Amazingly, the pilot and copilot are aware of the snow or they expect it to blow off during takeoff. Perhaps they too are unaware that a deiced 737 has the propensity to turn newly fallen snow into lethal ice.

Takeoff, if it can be called that. The pilots failed to give the engines full thrust, perhaps because the ice affected the instrumentation. Two minutes after the wheels leave the runway, the plane crashes into the 14th Street Bridge spanning the Potomac River. Four people are instantly killed in their cars as they drive across the bridge. Then, the plane plunges with a horrifying certainty into the ice strewn river.

Pandemonium and heroism. No one who has seen the pictures of the daring rescue of the few survivors of that tragedy will ever forget the sight of the brave rescuers in a helicopter hovering over the river and pulling a living human being out of the icy clutches of the river.

Five passengers and a flight attendant survived that ordeal. More than 70 people perished, including three infants.

One would expect that a tragedy almost within sight of the FAA headquarters would stir the agency into action, and it did— but the FAA only went halfway. Rather than mandating strict deicing standards in the Federal Aviation Regulations, the FAA instead published a detailed advisory circular on the subject. The circular's purpose was to provide comprehensive guidance to the industry with information regarding deicing aimed at preventing any further accidents due to ice buildup. That was well and good; however, the FAA action was "advisory." It did not have the force of law. Tragically, the FARs remained unchanged.

February 17, 1991
Hopkins International Airport, Cleveland, Ohio

A Ryan International Airlines DC-9, carrying two pilots and the U.S. mail, lands in Cleveland and is parked on the ground while mail is loaded and unloaded from the hold. A dry snow is falling and the wind is blowing. The temperature is approximately 23°F.

Despite being on the ground for 35 minutes, the pilots do not ask for deicing, nor is it offered by the ground crew. The ground crew's job complete, the plane taxis to the runway and makes its takeoff roll. Takeoff—but not for long. The plane is only able to rise approximately 100 feet, then it rolls to the right and crashes, bursting into a fireball. Both pilots are killed.

After the tragedy, the NTSB conducted a study of the accident's causes and published its usual accident report. Among its conclusions: "... the probable cause of this accident was the failure of the flight crew to detect and remove ice contamination on the airplane's wings, which was *largely a result of a lack of appropriate response by the Federal Aviation Administration,* Douglas Aircraft, and Ryan International Airlines to the known critical effect that a minute amount of contamination has on the stall characteristics of the DC-9 airplane. The ice contamination led to wing stall and loss of control during the attempted takeoff." (Emphasis added.) The NTSB reiterated its previous recommendation (issued after several DC-9 accidents and incidents involving ice) that the FAA establish and legally require specific deicing procedures with the DC-9. The recommendation was not acted upon by the FAA and remained in the NTSB's "Open/Unacceptable" action file.

March 10, 1989
Dryden Municipal Airport, Dryden, Ontario, Canada

The 65 passengers and crew of four wait patiently on the Fokker F-28 for clearance to take off for Winnipeg after its stop at Dryden from Thunder Bay. The weather forecast for the day had predicted lowering clouds and freezing precipitation. In fact, a light snow is falling.

Because of the poor weather and heavy passenger load, the plane has unexpectedly been forced to refuel at Dryden. This has caused a delay in the usual time for departing. The refueling has been complicated by an inoperative auxiliary power unit that has been malfunctioning for a week. The malfunctioning APU has forced the pilot to keep an engine running during refueling, in a procedure known as hot refueling. If the engines were both turned off, the plane could not be restarted.

The plane has been on the ground for just over 30 minutes. During that time, snow has accumulated on aircraft surfaces. No deicing is attempted. It is against operational procedures to deice the plane during hot refueling. The captain has elected not to seek special permission for deicing.

At approximately 12:11 p.m. the plane attempts to take off. Unfortunately, it does not get very far. Ice has formed on the leading edges of the wings. Lift is compromised. The plane is barely able to get its wheels off the ground. The right wing dips and the jet crashes through a grove of trees and breaks apart. Twenty-one passengers, the fight crew and one of the two flight attendants are killed.

In the post-crash recriminations, something quite extraordinary happened. Rather than have the accident investigated by the Canadian aviation regulatory authorities, a Canadian Justice, the Honorable Virgil P. Moshansky, was appointed to head a special commission into the crash.

Justice Moshansky performed an extraordinary service for his country and for everyone interested in the safety of commercial aviation. His commission looked in depth into the accident and the regulatory environment that helped create it, producing more than 1,700 pages of fact-finding, analysis, conclusions, and 191 recommendations for change.

Justice Moshansky told us: "It would have been simple to put the accident down to pilot error and leave it at that. But it was easy to see that the accident involved a widespread safety system failure. It is unfortunate that it takes general public outrage over a preventable accident to generate the atmosphere for reform."

Justice Moshansky's commission issued its *First Interim Report* in 1989. Among its recommendations: that the Canadian Department of Transportation immediately develop and implement a system of mandatory inspection of an aircraft to ensure that the aircraft's critical surfaces are clean of ice before takeoff.

In 1990, the commission's *Second Interim Report* was issued, recommending in part:

- Transport Canada should, on a priority basis, provide, where necessary, enforcement resources to ensure that the clean aircraft regulations are complied with: and,

- Transport Canada require air carriers to produce aircraft deicing/anti-icing procedures and training standards for both flight and ground personnel. Further, that implementation of these procedures should be made a part of an air carrier's operating certificate.

In short, the commission was strongly urging the Canadian equivalent of the FAA to promulgate mandatory deicing procedures in the aviation regulations, as the NTSB was recommending to the FAA.

Back in the United States, the FAA paid no attention to the interim reports and urgent recommendations of the commission. In their defense, FAA officials claim that they were never formally mailed the reports. That appears to be true; however, Justice Moshansky's commission was very big news in commercial aviation circles. Virtually everyone in the aviation community knew of the commission and the publication of its interim reports. Others in the safety community, such as the Air Line Pilots Association had asked for and received copies. An anonymous safety consultant recalls speaking in detail about the report with working staffers in the FAA and NTSB. In any event, a single phone call could have supplied the FAA with the commissions important findings and recommendations.

It's too bad that no one at the FAA thought to make that telephone call—too bad, that is, for the 27 people killed on board an identical Fokker F-28 at La Guardia Airport on March 22, 1992, in an accident eerily repetitive of the tragedy at Dryden. For as Justice Moshansky told *The New York Times* (March 31, 1992), "If the report had been read, there is more than adequate information to have preempted this accident."

March 22, 1992
La Guardia Airport, New York

The weather is ice-cold as the 51 people aboard USAir Flight 405 patiently wait for the plane to take off. Now, the delay is almost over. The plane, which has been deiced twice during the layover has been pushed away from the gate and has waited 30 minutes for a runway to be cleared of snow. But now, the plane is beginning its takeoff roll. Unknown to the pilots, ice has built up on the leading edges of the Fokker F-28's wings.

The takeoff roll seems slow. The runway is covered by slush. Takeoff is attempted, but instead of soaring into the sky with a burst of power, the plane veers and overruns the runway, crashing into the East River, killing 37 people.

The NTSB's accident report essentially said that the FAA's failure to update deicing regulations directly led to the crash. The La Guardia crash created the tombstones that finally broke through the FAA's intransigence on the deicing issue. The FAA vowed to act before the next winter. Even before the NTSB determined that ice buildup was involved in the tragedy, the FAA convened a safety conference attended by experts from around the world on the issue. Soon thereafter, the FAA published an NPRM publicizing intentions to update FAR deicing regulations. The agency was finally acting like a safety agency.

The final interim rules, which became effective November 1, 1992, require the airlines to train pilots and other personnel in the detection and removal of wing ice and establish limits on how long and under what conditions large transport jets can be exposed to snow or freezing rain before they have to be inspected or deiced again. Most of these new regulations had been sought by the NTSB and others for many years and are similar to the recommendations made by Justice Moshansky's commission.

Why had it taken so long for the FAA to update mandatory deicing procedures in the face of so many crashes? Joseph M. Del Balzo, FAA executive director for systems operations and later the FAA's acting administrator, told us: "When you think about the deicing issue, we counted on pilots to do what was expected of them to do. And if every pilot did what was expected, there would not be a deicing issue today. So, we now recognize that you can't count on them, you've got to do something different. There's a safeguard we can build in."

What a shame that it took so many years and deaths for the FAA to acknowledge that it was prudent to build in safeguards and do the right thing. Actually, "partially right thing" would be a more accurate term. The GAO and others complain that the new deicing rules, as promulgated, remain too weak to fully protect the flying public. (*See* chapter 18.)

The case of planes flown into the ground

One of the banes of aviation safety has been the CFIT (*controlled flight into terrain*). A CFIT occurs when a plane is literally flown into a mountain, ocean, or the ground while under the full control of the flight crew, who are oblivious of the pending danger.

CFITs used to be a serious safety problem for large commercial transport jets; however, technology had an answer that would save many lives: the *ground proximity warning system* (GPWS). Recognizing the leap in safety presented by the GPWS, the FAA eventually promulgated rules requiring its installation in large jet transport planes. As a result, CFITs soon became an accident-of-the-past in large commercial jets. The GPWS is one of the reasons the accident rate of FAR Part 121 aircraft fell starting in the late seventies and into the eighties. (According to Paul D. Russell, chief of product safety for Boeing, this is not true of all foreign airlines, many of which do not carry a GPWS when flying overseas.)

When the regulations were passed, the FAA excluded turboprop commuter planes from the GPWS mandate. That might have been because commuter aviation was not considered a major part of commercial aviation. But then along came deregulation. The very nature of the industry changed radically. The hub and spoke airport system stimulated a geometric increase in the number of passengers carried by smaller turboprop planes controlled by the rules of FAR 135. Unfortunately, the number of CFITs involving commuter aircraft increased, too.

The cure seemed simple to the NTSB. It had already proved effective in saving lives for FAR 121 carriers. In October 1986, after several commuter CFITs, including the crash that killed Samantha Smith, the young pen pal of Mikail Gorbachev, the safety board recommended that all commuter airplanes with the capacity to carry 10 or more passengers be required to install GPWS systems.

An idealist would believe that surely the FAA would not need additional tombstones to accept the wisdom of that recommendation. Unfortunately, as Barry Sweedler of the NTSB told us, "Things dragged after that. The FAA thought it would be a nice idea and it went through rulemaking processes and it was just taking forever. So, we decided the time had come to put a little pressure on them." That pressure was placing the recommendation on the NTSB "Most Wanted List," which generated media coverage and congressional attention to the issue.

Still, the FAA refused to act. More crashes had to occur. More people had to die. When the FAA promulgated the final rule that finally requires that ground proximity warning systems be installed on commuter planes, the FAA admitted that the following commuter airplane accidents took place between January 1987 and January 1990—accidents that finally forced the agency to rethink its position about mandating the GPWS on FAR 135 aircraft.

The text supporting the rule published in the *Federal Register* stated (excerpted material):

- On January 19, 1988, a Fairchild Metro III SA227-AC crashed on approach to Durango, Colorado. There were nine fatalities and eight survivors. The NTSB stated that "a ground proximity warning device probably would have alerted the crew to the airplane's increasing proximity to terrain and may have prevented the accident," and that more than "20 seconds advance warning could have been provided" by warning system.

- On February 19, 1988, a Fairchild Metro III SA227 crashed shortly after departing from Raleigh Durham International Airport due to "an excessive angle of bank instantiated at an altitude that was too low." There were 12 fatalities and no survivors. The NTSB stated that approximately "7½ seconds of advance warning could have been provided by a GPWS."

- On August 7, 1989, a DeHaviland DHC-6 flew into a mountain in Ethiopia during a flight with poor weather conditions. There were 16 fatalities and no survivors. The NTSB stated that "a ground proximity warning system may have prevented this accident since it can warn of a projected impact with terrain in time for corrective action by the pilot."

- On October 28, 1989, a DeHaviland DHC-6-300 crashed in Molokai, Hawaii. There were 20 fatalities and no survivors. In the final NTSB accident report dated September 25, 1990, the NTSB stated, "a ground proximity warning system would have provided sufficient warning for the crew to have pulled up and overflown the terrain."

- On December 26, 1989, a British Aerospace Jetstream 3101 crashed during its final approach to Pasco, Washington; the plane had been too high on the final approach and, therefore, required a steep descent. There were six fatalities and no survivors. The NTSB advised that a high descent rate at a low altitude will cause a GPWS warning.

- On January 15, 1990, a Fairchild Metro III SA227-AC crashed during its approach to Elko, Nevada. There were 13 injuries and no fatalities. The NTSB stated that approximately "25 seconds of advance warning time could have been provided by a GPWS."

It took six preventable accidents, 63 fatalities, and 21 injuries to finally convince the FAA of the wisdom of the NTSB's recommendation to require commuter planes to carry the GPWS. This, despite the record of achievement that the GPWS had already shown on commercial transport jets. Once again, the costs of the tombstone imperative were paid in planes crashed and lives lost.

The case of murder in the skies

The FAA has a disturbing tendency to half-regulate. That is, when they do take regulatory action to protect the public's safety, like a teenager that doesn't complete his homework, the agency frequently fails to finish the job. Unfortunately, sometimes only tombstones finally convince the FAA to complete its rulemaking.

One illustration of this tendency concerned airport security. From the day when the first hijacker forced the first plane to fly to Cuba, the FAA has been grappling with security rules designed to prevent people from smuggling weapons onto planes.

One of the rules created by the FAA to interdict weapons requires airlines to screen the public before allowing them access to airport gates. The ubiquitous metal detectors and x-ray facilities at airports were the result.

When the rules were passed, a significant class of people specifically were excluded from the screening rules: employees of the airlines and the airports. This exclusion left a dangerous and gaping hole in aviation security.

Many in the industry urged that employees of the airlines and/or airports also be subject to security scrutiny before being allowed into sensitive airport areas. But the FAA refused. They did not want to force the airlines to spend the money or time on employee screening. They believed that identification badges and other such security measures were sufficient to protect the flying public. Tragically, they were wrong on both counts:

> It is December of 1987. An employee of Pacific Southwest Airlines (PSA) has been fired from his job by his boss, who works for USAir, the airline that has just purchased PSA.
>
> The former employee is enraged. He confronts his former boss and demands that he be given his job back. His boss refuses.

The man is despondent and growing deranged. He decides to take his revenge. He decides to commit murder.

He knows that his former boss flies regularly between Los Angeles and San Francisco. He also knows the flight his boss usually takes. He decides that he will be on the next flight.

Using his PSA identification, which was not taken from him, he gains access to restricted areas of the Los Angeles International Airport and avoids the passenger security screening with its metal detectors. The man is carrying a loaded gun.

The flight is uneventful until the plane is about half way between Los Angeles and San Francisco. Then, he strikes. Later, a note is found in the wreckage of the plane promising the former boss that he would be shown no mercy. Authorities believe he killed his former boss in his seat.

But he is not through yet. There is more bloody work to do. He forces a flight attendant to give him access to the cockpit, where the voice recorder captures the sound of gunshots. The pilot and copilot are murdered. The man turns the gun on himself. The pilots and murderer are lucky compared to the passengers who experience the horror of their jet plunging into a steep dive, racing tens of thousands of feet, and exploding into mountainous terrain. All 43 people aboard are killed.

It is likely that this senseless tragedy could have been prevented if the FAA had required airport and airline employees to be subject to weapons screening and other security measures. Louis A. Turpen, director of the San Francisco International Airport, believes the cause was the FAA's mind-set on issues involving security. He told us, "In matters of aviation security, the FAA responds tactically to events, rather than strategically. They wait until something happens and then they respond, rather than anticipating problems and placing countermeasures into effect before the difficulty occurs."

This tragedy proved to be no exception. After the PSA mass murder, the FAA decided that yes, mandatory security measures should be taken to protect the flying public from airport and airline workers or those fraudulently posing as such workers. Accordingly, they tightened security by ordering that computer card systems be installed at the busiest terminals to keep people who might threaten airline safety from gaining access to restricted airport areas.

The computerized system also can restrict employees to specific areas of an airport and be programmed so that terminated worker's security cards will be invalidated upon termination. Ultimately, 270 airports will be affected by the order. Of course, the airlines complained about the cost (estimated at $170 million in 10 years) but then, as one airport security consultant told us, "The FAA's job is to do what is right, not what is popular. Too bad, they don't understand that truth as well as they should."

There can be little doubt that the FAA is a reactive agency that is often reluctant to fully promote safety until tragedy forces its hand. The three case-histories cited above are merely illustrations of this phenomena. Other examples are found elsewhere in the book.

7

At cross-purposes

"Of course there is a conflict between promoting aviation and keeping it safe. The Department of Commerce should be charged with promoting the industry. Let the FAA be strictly a safety agency."

**Congressman Peter DeFazio,
member of the Committee on Pubic Works
and Transportation: Aviation Subcommittee,
U.S. House of Representatives**

The FAA is charged by law to concurrently promote the aviation industry and foster flight safety. In the aviation safety community, this is often called the *dual mandate*. There is an ongoing controversy about the dual mandate. Many government officials, union leaders, and industry observers who work closely with the FAA believe that in combination with the cost/benefit analysis, the dual mandate is a significant inhibiting factor in the agency's important safety work. These critics point to several cases of apparent FAA foot dragging, some of which are subsequently described.

FAA officials and industry groups such as the Air Transport Association disagree. They do not believe that there is a conflict, but rather see promoting aviation and fostering safety as merely flip sides of the same coin. C.O. Miller, safety consultant, agrees, calling the situation "informed compromise." Joseph M. Del

Balzo, FAA executive director for systems operations, told us in an interview:

> I don't see the conflict when I understand what transportation is all about. There's no question that regulations that we pass cost money. But I look at that money spent on regulations as an investment in safety and I think that what you get in return is passenger confidence and public confidence in the system. And with that comes passenger and public acceptance of aviation as a means of transportation. Just look at the number of people who continue to fly each year and who wouldn't be flying if they did not have confidence in the safety of the system. The first time we do anything that destroys this public confidence in the safety of our air transportation system in the United States, I think you will see airline profitability plummet even more than it has today.
>
> **Question:** But aren't there times when what might be safe for the flying public might also be expensive for the airlines, and under those circumstances, can there not be a conflict and how would that conflict be resolved?
>
> **Del Balzo:** We look at those conflicts in terms of the cost/benefit analysis. I mean, there is a limit to safety. There's a limit to what you can achieve in terms of absolute safety. If one were to focus on absolute safety, they would probably think about flying one aircraft at a time or not flying at all. There is no question that economics come into play and (you have to ask) how much is a safety improvement worth?

These remarks confirm the obvious. Money issues and safety concerns are often at odds. The key question: Which predominates? Money or safety? Too often it seems, the answer is money.

Anthony J. Broderick, associate administrator for regulation and certifications—one of the best known regulators within the agency and frequent point man in the FAA's dealings with Congress—also discussed the issue with us:

Question: Do you believe there is an inherent conflict between your dual mandate to promote aviation and also foster safety?

Broderick: No, not at all. It is rather difficult for me to envision a civil aviation authority anywhere in the world that could think that by promoting safety, it wasn't promoting aviation. That is what people fundamentally look to. I mean, it's the very first thing people ask about an airline. Not what kind of food do they have, but is it safe to fly?

(It is important to note that the FAA does nothing to enable consumers to differentiate among the different airlines on issues of safety. So long as the airlines obey the FARs, the FAA is content to allow the public to believe that when it comes to safety, all airlines are created equal. After all, that false belief promotes aviation.)

Broderick: As a general rule, the amount of promotion we do in the true sense of the word, is largely limited to safety issues. We have asked the people who are arguing with us about this conflict: "Okay, name the things that you'd like to have us stop doing as a promotional thing that you don't think are safety related;" there are indeed, a very few. We consider, for example, our promotional activities to include all of our accident prevention seminars. We give literally thousands of meetings all over the country with literally hundreds of thousands of attendees a year talking about aviation safety issues. That to me is promotion. It's not regulation, it's not enforcement, it's not inspection—it's promotion.

Notice that Mr. Broderick does not directly address the problem. He tries to redefine the issue into a question of the promotional activities that critics would like the FAA to cease performing. But that begs the question. What concerns critics is not what the agency does do, but what FAA fails to do.

The following examples of rules promulgated by the FAA did not sufficiently promote safety because of the agency's concerns for the costs involved.

Survivability standards

"The USAir crash in Los Angeles was a survivable crash. My son and 20 others were alive when the plane stopped. They died because of the post-crash smoke, toxic fumes, and fire. All the USAir survivors escaped within less than 2 minutes. For 21 USAir victims, knowledge [that was] at least 5 years old, about modern cabin linings, accessible exits, and smoke hoods would have saved their lives. We already knew how to give them 60 extra seconds to escape. Sixty seconds would have meant a lifetime for my son."

**Alex Richman MD,
speaking before the International Rally of Endeavors
to Improve Air Safety, August 5, 1991**

According to Mathew M. McCormick, chief of the survival factor division, NTSB, "About 80 percent of U.S. commercial airline accidents are survivable. That is, the crash impact does not exceed human tolerances." A look at accidents in the past decade involving FAR 121 carriers reveals this to be true. With the exception of the PSA flight brought down by the murderer, another jet which crashed because of bad weather and a crash in Detroit where one little girl was miraculously found alive and the sabotage of Pan Am Flight 103, there have been multiple survivors in every large jet transport accident involving U.S. carriers. That is the good news. The bad news is that many passengers have needlessly died in these survivable crashes.

The issue of crash survivability is so important that an entire section of the book is reserved for that topic; however, part of that discussion is relevant here, for it aptly demonstrates that the dual mandate as enforced by the cost/benefit analysis can be the enemy of safety.

Flammability standards

Fire, smoke, and toxic fumes are the primary killers of people who suffer through a survivable crash. In fact, three out of four people who fail to survive those accidents are not killed by the impact, but by smoke, toxic fumes, or fire.

The FAA knew this, and finally after years of urging, the agency has taken steps to compel the airlines to use flame- and smoke-resistant materials in their plane cabin interiors. For example, on October 26, 1984, the FAA published a new rule in the

Federal Register requiring all U.S. airlines to meet specific seat cover flammability standards in all large transport airplanes by a *date-certain,* namely November 26, 1987. The rule applied to jets then in service as well as newly manufactured jet aircraft. According to the FAA, the rule gave passengers an extra 40–60 seconds of time to escape planes before the fire would consume the cabin. The new covers would also reduce the levels of toxic smoke and gasses created by burning seat cushions. The FAA bragged that the rule would "reduce the number of fire-induced fatalities in impact-survivable aircraft accidents by 12 percent to 65 percent." (Source: FAA publication, *Fire-Blocked Seats Increase Aircraft Safety.*)

This rule was a good, if quite belated, start but insufficient. More than new seat covers were needed to protect passengers from the toxic effects of post-crash fires. The NTSB and others in the safety community had previously urged the FAA to pass rules compelling the airlines to use the latest fire retarding and smoke-minimizing materials throughout cabin interiors, including the cabin linings, carpets, and other interior surfaces. Placing such flame-resistant materials throughout the interiors of airliners can further extend the evacuation time for crash impact survivors to exit a plane before the fire and/or smoke and fumes take their lives.

The FAA agreed to issue these regulations, but choked on the timing of the changes. Specifically, it required the cabin interiors of all new planes built after 1985 to be constructed with the new fire-retardant materials.

That was well and good. But what about the jets already in service? Would they be required to be refurbished so as to meet the new fire safety standards? Yes, but the FAA gave the airlines a loophole so huge that a 747 jumbo jet could fly through it. Instead of setting a date-certain by which time all aircraft would have to meet the new rules, the FAA permitted the airlines to wait until an airplane underwent a substantially complete replacement of the cabin interior before making the change. Planes fly for years without having a substantially complete replacement of their interiors. Older planes that are due to go out of service probably never shall be retrofitted. Experts in the airlines and FAA estimate it will be past the turn of the millennium before all domestic jetliners comply with the 1985 cabin safety standards.

It should be noted that the FAA once again refused to heed

the NTSB, which had recommended that a specific date be set for completion of all interior retrofittings. The major unions, including the Air Line Pilots Association and the Association of Flight Attendants agreed with the NTSB. But the FAA, being a majority of one, had the final say. Enhanced survivability standards for much of the fleet will have to wait.

The cost/benefit analysis and the dual mandate had watered down an important safety regulation so as to make the applicability of current safety standards up to the discretion of the airlines. The financial losses that caused many airlines to merge in recent years have also forced the cancellation of orders for new airplanes; therefore, the public faces continued danger from flying in fire-trap planes. (Perhaps if the airlines were forced to retrofit all of their old planes, they would be less reluctant to purchase new ones.)

This issue ceased to be of abstract concern and became a literal matter of life and death.

February 1, 1991
Los Angeles International Airport

The flight had been unremarkable for the 83 passengers and six crewmembers of USAir flight 1493. As the plane is landing at Los Angeles International Airport, it is just after sunset. All seems well. The passengers look forward to arriving at the gate and continuing on to their destinations. No one is prepared for tragedy.

Unknown to those aboard the 737, a Sky West commuter plane has mistakenly been given clearance to enter the runway in preparation for takeoff. It lies directly in the approaching jet's landing path, its presence obscured from the USAir pilots by the lights of the airport.

The collision occurs just as the nosewheel of the USAir Boeing 737 contacts the runway. There is a flash of light and an immediate explosion and fire. The two airplanes, locked in a death grip, slide 600 feet down the runway, veer to the left, and crash into a small outbuilding.

For all 12 people on board the small commuter plane, death is mercifully quick. But the crash is imminently survivable for most of the passengers and cabincrew on board the 737, although the captain and first officer are killed upon impact with the building.

For the passengers, the shock of the crash quickly turns into screaming, crying, pandemonium. The 737 is on fire. Thick, black, toxic smoke begins pouring into the cabin within seconds of the plane's impact with the building. Flight attendants try to open emergency doors and a few people begin to exit. In the center of the plane, panic impedes a passenger from opening the right side overwing exit. Precious life giving seconds are lost. Next, two men briefly scuffle over who will exit first through this exit, until they are pushed out by another passenger.

Then, too quickly, it is too late. The air has become unbreathable. People who have survived the crash, die with the oily taste of smoke in their mouths, their lives suffocated by the poisonous gas that now fills the cabin.

According to the NTSB, it did not have to be that way. Its accident report explained how the FAA had permitted the airlines to delay fire safety retrofitting of their aircraft built before 1985. The report further revealed that the 737 had been manufactured before 1985 and that USAir was only required to refurbish the interior if it had substantially replaced the plane's cabin interior. Unfortunately, that had not been done. The report proceeded to detail the consequences:

> In this accident, all of the cabin furnishings burned except for the carpeting and seats. The overhead bins melted and ignited and then fell on the passengers and the cabin floor. *If cabin furnishings of the type specified for newly manufactured aircraft had been installed in the accident airplane, fire and toxic smoke might not have spread so quickly through the cabin.* The safety board believes that after a specified date, air carriers should be required to use fire retardant materials in all transport category airplane interiors .... (Emphasis added.)

Eleven of the dead, a flight attendant and ten passengers, were found together in the aisle, only 4 to 8 feet from the over-wing exits from which most of the survivors had escaped the burning plane.

These people died as a result of smoke and particulate inhalation, not the impact of the crash, nor the heat of the fire. (Indeed, only one dead passenger was found in their seat with their belt buckled.) It is a reasonable assumption that a retrofitted plane would have allowed the passengers who survived the crash impact an additional one or two minutes of breathable air. Under those circumstances, most, if not all, probably would have lived. It is also reasonable to conclude that if the FAA had followed the NTSB's recommendation about setting a date-certain rather than the airline's whine about the cost of safety, the plane would have been retrofitted because the crash took place more than 5 years after the finalization of the rule.

And still, the FAA refuses to set a time deadline for retrofitting; thus, the real costs of the dual mandate and the cost/benefit rule are tabulated—not in dollars saved but in lives threatened and precious people lost.

Some seats are safer than others

Did you know that you and a friend can buy a ticket on the same flight for the same price and be seated in the same section of the plane, yet one of you might be safer than the other in an accident? Why? Because one of you might be seated in a stronger seat that is better able to withstand crash forces. And guess what? You won't know which of you has the safer seat because the airlines won't tell you.

How did such a ridiculous state of affairs come into being? Blame the FAA. Prior to 1988, most airline seats were required by the FARs to withstand a force of 9 Gs, that is, a force 9 times greater than the force of gravity. That is grossly insufficient because a human body can withstand forces of approximately 20 Gs or more, depending upon the circumstances. People who would have survived a crash impact have died because their 9-G seats ripped apart, throwing them into bulkheads, instead of remaining fixed to the floor.

After years of being urged by ACAP, the NTSB, and others to improve regulations governing seat strength, the FAA finally recognized the need to increase the strength of seats to prevent people from being killed in this manner. (As a result of tests performed in the 1960s, seat upgrades were recommmended, but subsequently were ignored by the FAA for two decades.) Accordingly, it raised the minimum seat standard in the FARs to 16 Gs. The rule applies to all aircraft constructed after August, 1988.

But what about the jets built before that time? As the famous philosopher, Yogi Berra, once said, "It's deja vu, all over again." In promulgating the regulation requiring newly-built transport jets to have 16-G seats, the FAA decided to spare the airlines the cost of retrofitting the seats in their existing fleet to meet the new safety standards. Once again, safety took a backseat to promoting aviation.

As things now stand, the airlines are slowly replacing the old 9-G seats in pre-1988 aircraft with 16-G seats on an as-needed basis. The reason? Manufacturers no longer make the 9-G seats. The surrealistic result: If a seat on a plane has been replaced, it does meet the 16-G standard; other seats on the same plane only meet the older 9-G standard. That means some passengers are safer than others, even though they paid the same price for a ticket and are seated in the same section of the plane.

FAA rule shopping to accommodate airlines

"The FAA will always work hard to find a rule that will allow them to give the airlines what they want."

Union safety officer, 1992

The airlines are ever looking for new ways to squeeze a few extra dollars out of each flight. That is fine, so long as it does not compromise safety. When these practices reduce safety, however, the FAA should step in and prevent abuses.

Instead, the FAA often acts as a facilitator for the airlines, finding the rule to permit them to accommodate airline desires, even when there are other regulations that could be relied on to better promote safety. Here are two examples:

The case of the door that is really a window

The Boeing 757 aircraft is a *narrowbody* jet transport plane, meaning that there is one center aisle between two rows of seats. A *widebody* aircraft, such as a Boeing 747 or DC-10, will have two aisles and three rows of seats. The number and type of exits the FAA requires on a commercial transport jet depends upon the number of people the airline wishes to be able to carry, based upon evacuation tests. All passengers must be able to evacuate within 90 seconds with half the emergency exits blocked in evacuation tests in order for the FAA to certify the craft as flight worthy. (The accuracy of the tests is suspect. *See* chapter 13.)

American Airlines and United Airlines fly Boeing 757s. Both have purchased planes that have oversized door exits when a window exit would technically satisfy the regulations, based upon the number of passengers that they currently fly on the aircraft. Because the large doors are not required, based upon the FARs, the FAA has permitted the carriers to place seats in front of these exit doors and treat the doors as if they were smaller window exits. (Window exits would provide sufficient escape capacity for certification purposes.) The seats block more than 40 percent of the path passengers would take when trying to exit the plane in an emergency. As of this writing, United Airlines partially blocks one exit in this way, adding two seats to the capacity of the aircraft. American blocks two exits, adding four seats.

One American Airlines flight attendant we spoke with, who is worried about the safety effect of these partially blocked emergency exits, told us, "I flew my first 757 two days ago. And I stood by the blocked exits for the longest time figuring out how I could open the doors without being thrown out of the aircraft or trampled by the press of passengers trying to get out. Because of the way the seats are placed, it would be very difficult for me to watch out for my passengers in an emergency."

She is right to be concerned. The potential safety impact of this seat placement is profound:

- Flight attendant stations, usually placed at these doors, have been moved away, despite an FAR rule requiring flight attendants to have their seats as close as is practicable to emergency door exits. In an emergency, the flight attendants might not be able to get to the door quickly to aid with evacuation.

- In a post-crash smoke-filled cabin, terrified passengers might mistake the seat-blocked exit as just another aisle of seats, despite the presence of floor lighting.

- It would be difficult for the passengers to maneuver around the seats to get out of the aircraft, slowing egress from the craft.

- The configuration of the seats makes it awkward for a flight attendant to direct passengers because there is insufficient space for a flight attendant to stand at the door as passengers exit.

Testimony given to the Subcommittee on Government Activities and Transportation by Victoria Frankovich, on behalf of the Joint Council of Flight Attendant Unions, on April 11, 1991, underscores the point:

> Allowing passengers' seats to be situated directly in front of a primary emergency exit door seems to defy logic. It is clear that a flight attendant's ability to access and open this door is severely restricted, and the passengers ability to access this door is extremely limited. But according to correspondence from the FAA, the "exit and its access and egress areas actually exceed certification requirements." Further, the FAA states it has "no reason to doubt that the referenced Boeing 757 R-2 exit arrangement will continue to fully and safely fulfill its designed purpose during an emergency." In contrast, our members continuously express concern over the accessibility of these exits .... A door may be operable during an emergency, but a person must be able to reach the door before it can be opened.

Comments made to the FAA from flight attendants along with Congressman Peter DeFazio, safety consultant C.O. Miller, consumer advocates, and others, decrying the blocked exits on the 757 have been met with a deaf ear. Here's just a small sampling of what flight attendants have overwhelmingly had to say (a flight attendant's primary role onboard the aircraft is safety):

- "It makes it awkward and difficult to open the door. My concern is that (if) crew and passengers have to use those two doors as an egress, I feel the seats would slow down the process."
- "As an American Airlines flight attendant, I have a safety concern regarding our Boeing 757 aircraft. The two seats directly in front of the 2R Exit are a safety hazard and should be removed. American Airlines trains its employees on safety and emergency procedures according to the highest standards. It is astounding that the same airline would sacrifice passenger safety, in this instance, for the sake of saving or making a few dollars on these two extra seats."
- "The existence of (the added) seats on all 757 aircraft is very

unsafe .... If an evacuation was necessary, there would be a lot of chaos at the exit due to the fact that the seats block about half of the exit doorway."

The FAA could legally prohibit American and United from placing seats in front of the doors based upon the rules forbidding the blocking of exit doors and based upon requiring flight attendants to be seated as near door exits as is practicable. Instead, the agency has chosen to apply the FARs to the doors as if they were window exits stating in a letter to Ralph Nader dated Aprill 16, 1991, "We believe the seat installation in the vicinity of the 2R exits ..., to be in compliance with the regulations and that the regulations provide for an acceptable level of safety." In other words, as long as there is enough space between the seats and the bulkhead to satisfy the FAR space rules for window exits, the FAA is willing to let exit doors be partially blocked, which is a shameful example of agency rule shopping so as to promote aviation to the detriment of safety.

The case of the flight attendant who wasn't there

Hugh Wagner, a safety officer for the Association of Professional Flight Attendants, reports that one of his union member's greatest safety fears concerns the Fokker F-100 aircraft as flown by American Airlines. The plane is a narrow body jet that carries 97 passengers. There are six emergency exits on the plane: two doors forward and four over-wing window exits. There are no emergency exits in the rear of the plane. The F-100 may be purchased from Fokker with a small rear door exit and evacuation slide. American Airlines has chosen not to purchase the craft with this added safety option.

The FARs permit the plane to fly with two flight attendants.

As flown by American Airlines, one of the flight attendants is properly seated on landing and takeoff by one of the two forward emergency doors. The other is in a jump seat in the very back of the plane, which allows at least one extra passenger seat to be placed on the aircraft.

The FAA has chosen to permit this practice despite the FAR that requires flight attendants to be stationed as near floor level exits as is practicable. The agency manages to accomplish this by relying upon a different FAR that states that flight attendants should be evenly distributed around the aircraft. The result: one of the two flight attendants would be virtually unavailable to help passengers in an emergency because 40 or so passengers will be between the flight attendant and the nearest window exit and all 97 passengers between the flight attendant and the nearest door.

Hugh Wagner paints a frightening scenario that could result from the FAA permitting this practice: "Imagine that the airline is taxiing and there is a collision with another plane, leading to a fire on the F-100. Smoke begins to fill the cabin. The passengers must be evacuated. But the forward flight attendant has been knocked unconscious by the impact of the accident. The other flight attendant is able bodied, but stuck in the back of the plane, unable to be of any help in the din and panic of the passengers. At that point, it would be up to the passengers to get the doors and window exits open and evacuate, something they (might) not be able to do in the terror of the moment. It is foreseeable that a very real tragedy could develop."

But what do the American Airlines flight attendants who actually work the Fokker F-100 think about the issue? The Association of Professional Flight Attendants took a survey. Here is a sampling of the results, first published by APFA in June, 1992:

- 94 percent did not believe that two flight attendants could safely evacuate a full cabin of 97 passengers during an unplanned emergency.
- 99 percent believed the F-100 is inadequately staffed with two flight attendants on all flights.
- 94 percent did not believe that two flight attendants could complete American Airlines emergency procedures.

Many flight attendants sent comments along with their answers to the survey. They speak volumes about the FAA's decision to allow American Airlines to place one flight attendant in the rear of the aircraft. Here's a sample:

- "I am *terrified* of sitting in the rear of the plane (#2 position). Will I get fired if I refuse to fly it?"
- "Why does the FAA allow an aircraft to have no aft exit? Maybe the USAir tragedy will change this."
- "This aircraft is an insult to our intelligence!"

- "If we were in an emergency situation, I feel I would not have the means to get pax [abbreviation for passengers] out safely and effectively."
- "The aircraft is a 'fire trap' for the #2 flight attendant. It's a violation of safety standards not to have an aft exit!!!"
- "This aircraft is a hazard. I refuse to bid it because it scares me."
- "Get rid of these absolute death traps."

These are not the voices of "white-knuckled nervous-Nellies," but of dedicated professionals who love to fly. If they are scared, passengers should be too. The FAA should put on its "safety hat" and rethink its permissive attitude toward this unwise policy.

American Airlines was contacted for comment but refused to discuss the issue. Questions to the FAA about the topic also went unanswered.

When a rule is not a rule

"By fighting compliance with this rule, some carriers and their representatives are exhibiting a callous lack of regard for the safety of their passengers and crew."

Correspondence by Christopher J. Witkowski, director of air safety and health of the Association of Flight Attendants written to Anthony J. Broderick, of the FAA, regarding a rule that is not being enforced

To the frustration of union officials and others interested in safe airline operations, the FAA will sometimes pass a rule and then fail to enforce it. One such occurrence involved a recent regulation that among other provisions prohibits air carriers from moving an airplane on the surface of an airport while food or beverages are located at any passenger seat. A primary purpose of the rule is to prevent flight attendants from being in the aisle during surface movement where they could be injured in an accident on the ground and be thus unable to aid an evacuation.

The above rules were to go into effect no later than October 15, 1992. Yet, after the effective date, the Association of Flight Attendants had received many complaints from its members that some airlines were routinely violating the prohibition by forcing them to serve passengers during taxi operations and then having them pick up service items as the plane taxied to the runway for takeoff. These complaints resulted in Christopher J. Witkowski's letter quoted above, in which Mr. Witkowski complained of noncompliance by the airlines.

On March 8, 1993, Mr. Witkowski received return correspondence from Thomas C. Accardi, director, flight standards service, for the FAA. Mr. Accardi explained that the FAA was not going to enforce the rule prohibiting flight attendants from picking up service items during taxi because it was to be the subject of further rulemaking. The Air Transport Association, unhappy with the original rule, filed a petition to amend the rule on December 18, 1992; thus, pending the new rulemaking over regulations that had only gone into effect a few months previously, flight attendants are allowed to be out of their assigned seats during taxi, picking up service items.

This is not the only occasion when the FAA has issued a rule and seemingly backed away from enforcement when the industry objected. This, despite the fact the airlines have had full opportunity to comment before rules are adopted.

So, when is a rule not a rule? Apparently when the industry doesn't want it to be a rule and the FAA agrees by allowing its own regulations to be ignored while revisiting the issue that was only recently presumably resolved. Meanwhile, as the FAA jumps to the commands of the industry, years can pass while other worthy safety regulations languish in some bureaucrat's in-box.

8

They have those mismanagement blues

"By any measure of management, the FAA has bitten off more than it can chew."

**David Traynham,
Aviation Subcommittee staff member commenting on the FAA's ATC modernization efforts**

"The FAA allows an awful lot of corner-cutting."

Pilot for a major airline

In addition to its duties as a regulatory agency, the FAA must manage. People are hired, fired, promoted, and transferred. Goals are created, programs are monitored and directed, plans are implemented to achieve the desired ends.

The quality of FAA management has a direct impact on safety. If the air traffic control system is not working at peak efficiency, safety can become impaired. If the FAA mismanages its meager enforcement resources, it might have to rely too heavily on the good faith of the regulated companies to comply with safety rules. If the FAA is unable or unwilling to comply with congressional directives to improve safety, the flying public might be denied important safety benefits.

Unfortunately, the record of the FAA is all too clear. ATC modernization programs are chronically behind schedule, goals are frequently missed, the FAA work force is not adequately supervised and new safety programs often sink into FAA-limbo.

The pervasive mismanagement within the FAA is illustrated in three examples:

- The failure of the FAA to implement the Safety Indicators Program
- The poor supervision of the FAA's inspector force
- The seeming inability of the FAA to modernize the air traffic control system.

The Safety Indicators Program

"After spending 4 years and over $7 million on the Safety Indicators Program, FAA has made little progress on accomplishing its goals of developing a consistent set of safety measures .... Ineffective user involvement and unclear management commitment have contributed to the agency's inability to complete the program."

> **From the GAO report,**
> **"Progress on FAA Safety Indicators Program Slow and Challenges Remain," August, 1992**

One of the principal criticisms of the FAA is that it usually closes the proverbial barn door after the horse has escaped—that is, that it reacts after events rather than anticipate problems before they occur. There is abundant evidence to support this criticism of the FAA ranging from the agency's tragic delay in updating the deicing rules to its failure to order ground proximity warning systems installed in commuter aircraft.

But how can the FAA be given the tools to anticipate safety problems before problems result in accidents? Many people in the safety community believe that the FAA should create aviation "safety indicators"—airline finances, incident reports, near midair collisions, operational errors by controllers and other criteria—to discover weaknesses that might be undermining safety. These safety indicators would be to the FAA what "economic indicators" are to economists. The indicators would prevent accidents by identifying evolving areas of concern so that the FAA could take steps to prevent accidents. In other words, a viable Safety Indicators Program would help the FAA close the barn door before the horse escapes.

There was so much support for safety indicators in the aviation safety community that in 1987, a Senate Appropriations Committee report directed the FAA to develop a "standardized set of safety indicators which can be used with confidence to measure the safety performance of the FAA's air traffic operations on a consistent basis over time." (Senate Committee on Appropriations, "Report on the Department of Transportation and Related Agencies," October 8, 1987.) The FAA responded in January 1988 when it formerly announced the creation of the Safety Indicators Program, with the initial prototype to be up and running by the end of 1988.

From the beginning, the FAA has had trouble getting this important program off the drawing board and into full implementation. By 1989, five categories of indicators had been decided upon: air traffic, flight operations, aircraft certification, airports, and security. Yet, three years later, according to the August 1992 GAO report quoted above, "little had been accomplished ... of the five categories of indicators, only air traffic had progressed ... and even this progress was meager."

One of the reasons for this problem in implementation appears to be a lack of enthusiasm within much of the FAA. Anthony J. Broderick, one of the top officials of the FAA, told us the program was being put together "because of Congressional interest." He also expressed less than wholehearted support for the categories that had been selected (at the time of his interview in August 1992) as measuring standards, stating, "I have a very difficult time in finding those to be fulfilling of the real meaning of the word 'indicators.'"

The GAO also found that management problems had hampered progress. It complained of an "unclear top-level management commitment" and cited as proof the fact that the Safety Indicators Program had "operated for three years on the basis of a pending order that has never been signed." The GAO also criticized "funding uncertainties" that "have made it difficult to keep the system on schedule."

In light of the FAA's admitted difficulties, the question has to be asked whether a true Safety Indicators Programs can successfully be created and put into practice. Professor Clint Oster, coauthor of *Why Airplanes Crash*, has his doubts. "The notion that there are leading safety indicators has not been proven," he told us. "We have looked at indicators such as pilot operational errors and near misses, but we have been unable to find a link between those and overall safety performance."

The fact that there is no objective proof that safety indicators prevent accidents is not surprising. The idea is relatively new and the FAA has not even put the program into practice. Yet, a study in Canada (Sypher: Mueller International of Ottawa), concluded that a number of leading indicators were able to be identified and linked with safety. The indicators included incident reports, financial statements of air carriers, and the individual business characteristics of the carriers and the aircraft they chose to operate. (As reported in the Flight Safety Foundation publication, *Flight Safety Digest,* December, 1991.) Moreover, William Reynard, the well-respected director of NASA's Aviation Safety Reporting System is also a big booster of indicators. He told us, "I feel confident that a safety indicators program can be implemented. When DOD [the U.S. Department of Defense] was putting their safety program in place, I was asked to sit on the advisory board. I was impressed. In the course of two years, the DOD came up with a very effective system."

The system Mr. Reynard refers to is the DOD program that monitors the safety of commercial air carriers that contract with the government for troop transport. The DOD Air Carrier Survey program was created in response to the crash of a charter plane that killed 248 soldiers in 1985 near Gander, Canada. No longer, vowed the Department of Defense, would U.S. troops be endangered by unsafe civilian air carriers. Within a few years, the DOD had the Air Carrier Survey up and running.

It is important to note that the Air Carrier Survey uses a form of safety indicators. The director of the program, Colonel Robert S. Wells, USAF, informed us in an October 1992 letter:

> After 5 years of conducting surveys and performance evaluations, this office formed a set of industry standards that were developed from the firsthand experience of our evaluators. In 1991, these unwritten industry standards were put to paper and published as the DOD Commercial Air Carrier Quality and Safety Requirements (published in the *Federal Register,* July 2, 1991).
>
> These requirements are now the basis for our total inspection process. However, we do look at several areas that were considered important to analyze during the tabletop analysis of each carrier every 6

months. These areas are *maintenance, operations, accident/incident record, service quality, and financial condition.* All five of these areas are analyzed by a sophisticated computer system specially designed for this office.

This system is called the *Air Carrier Analysis Support System* (ASAS). Information is extracted from the system and along with analysts' inputs, the air carrier receives an evaluation of their capability to continue to provide safe and reliable service to the DOD. If indicators point to a *potential problem area that may impact safe operations of the carrier,* a survey team is sent out to take a closer look at the situation .... (Emphasis added.)

Not only does the DOD believe in its program, it actively implements it by withholding business from carriers that are not trusted to carry troops. Colonel Wells continued:

Over the years this office has been in operation, 48 carriers have been denied initial entry into the DOD air transportation program, 8 have subsequently reapplied and been approved, and 42 carriers have been placed in nonuse or suspended, 20 have been reinstated. The majority of these actions were taken because management did not provide the oversight required to assure quality maintenance or operations programs.

Can it be said with certainty that had the DOD allowed the suspended air carriers to carry troops, there would have been a crash? No. It's impossible to prove a negative. Can it be said that soldiers fly safer than the general public? The FAA would say no, but the fact is undisputed that DOD takes immediate action to not fly on airlines that are deemed unsafe, regardless of whether the airline is in technical compliance with the FARs.

Meanwhile, the FAA is satisfied if the minimum safety requirements of the FARs are met. Anthony J. Broderick said as much when he told us, "Department of Defense does not need to rely on the minimum standards that the FAA promulgates because the DOD is buying a service. They could set whatever standard they want, and they do."

The FAA now contends that it has gotten its act together in its attitude toward safety indicators. Darlene Freeman, the FAA's associate administrator for aviation safety told us in early 1993 that the FAA has learned from the GAO report. "I did not take issue with the GAO's criticism," she said. "I agreed that progress had not been as fast as I would have liked. So, I put together a senior level task force and we took a hard look at what it would take to get the program moving."

According to Freeman, she has succeeded in implementing a *System Indicator Program* that is designed to detect changes that "will be of concern to safety," Freeman said. "We are now keeping track of indicators such as operational errors, service reliability of our ATC facilities and traffic delays due to volume. We are keeping track of some indicators we never monitored before, such as large air carrier aircraft incident rates. It is similar in concept to the DOD program but has a different purpose."

The new system indicators program came on-line in November 1992. At the time of this writing, it is too early to tell whether the project is a true safety indicators program; however, one thing is clear: If the FAA is ever to get ahead of the "safety curve," a solid safety indicators program is going to have to be devised and implemented. The flying public deserves no less.

The mismanaged inspectors

"FAA has yet to sufficiently address several fundamental and deeply embedded problems in its airline inspection management and oversight. As a result, FAA still cannot provide sufficient assurance of airline safety and regulatory compliance ...."

Testimony of Kenneth M. Mead,
GAO director of transportation issues, speaking before the
Aviation Subcommittee, February 6, 1992

The FAA can be compared to the small town cop who is also the city council, mayor, and justice of the peace. Not only does it create the rules (the FARs) but it also polices compliance with the regulations and punishes those who fail to meet those minimum safety standards. Punishment can range from a fine to the loss of the privilege to engage in commercial or private aviation.

The effectiveness of the FAA's policing function has a direct and traceable impact on aviation safety. This is simply a matter of human nature. As anyone involved in general law enforcement will agree, the more effective the police department, the more deterrence there is to crime and the safer the community is likely to be. Likewise, the better and more effective the FAA's inspection force, the greater the likelihood that the airlines will comply with the FARs and that flying will be safer.

Unfortunately, the FAA does not have the resources or the inspection force to adequately police the airlines. And those inspectors it does have in place often seem to be misdirected. The result: a partial breakdown in aviation law and order.

The numbers game

As of the end of 1991, the FAA had approximately 2,500 inspectors who were responsible for the oversight of more than 6,500 scheduled commercial aircraft, almost 4,350 repair stations, approximately 550 pilot training schools, more than 170 maintenance schools, not to mention more than 641,000 pilots and nearly 275,000 aircraft. That is an awesome workload for a few thousand people.

From all indications, the FAA inspector force is inadequate to the task. In a November 1991 report, *Aviation Safety—Problems Persist in FAA's Inspection Program*, the GAO found:

> FAA lacks complete and accurate information on its inspection program, a problem we reported in 1987 and again in 1989. Without complete and accurate information, FAA cannot determine whether inspection priorities are achieved, inspection follow-up activities are adequate and timely, and inspection resources are being used effectively. Although inspections are FAA's number one priority, inspectors spent only 23 percent of their time performing inspections, instead of the 35 percent time allocation in fiscal year 1990. Furthermore, although FAA requires at least one operations, maintenance and avionics inspection annually for each airplane, 1,305 of about 3,600 airplanes (36 percent) (including air taxi operators) did not receive the required inspections in fiscal year 1990.

Two years later, the FAA's performance, as measured by GAO, had not substantially improved. Approximately 25 percent of airplanes did not receive the minimum required set of three annual inspections and *50 airlines were not inspected at all.*

Given the finite resources of the FAA, it is not surprising that performance is not up to par; however, understanding how lapses could happen and *accepting* them are two different things.

This is serious business. Passenger lives are at stake. If the executives of a marginal airline know that the FAA might not pay them a visit, they might be tempted to run their operation below the minimum safety standards set by the FAA.

That being so, one would expect the FAA to restructure the inspection schedule, placing more emphasis on airlines with questionable safety practices than those that appear to be performing well. Unfortunately, according to the GAO, the opposite is happening and the lack of an effective safety indicators program seems to be largely to blame. Again, from the November 1991 report:

> FAA does not seem to have a system for assessing airline risk. FAA assigns inspection resources on the basis of airline fleet size. However, DOD's performance evaluation system for scheduled commercial airlines and air taxis shows that airlines can and do pose significantly different risks to the flying public. In this regard, on the basis of DOD performance ratings for 97 airlines that both FAA and DOD inspected during fiscal year 1990, we found that FAA sometimes spent more inspection time on airlines DOD rates as better performers than on poorer performing airlines. For example, FAA spent more hours inspecting six better-rated national airlines than any of the five poorer-rated airlines in this category.

This criticism was reiterated and expanded by Howard E. Johannssen, chairman of Professional Airways Systems Specialists (PASS), the union that represents FAA inspectors. On February 6, 1992, he testified before the House Aviation Subcommittee, stating in part:

> The flight standards [office] work force is negligently understaffed.
>
> The FAA could do more inspections if there were more inspectors. An important concern is not just the number of inspectors or inspections, but that our existing work force is not able to properly utilize the

hours available to conduct its primary function—safety inspections ....

The problem that inspectors face is that they spend as much time on administrative duties as they do on critical safety related inspections .... The inspectors could have easily achieved the required 14 hours per week required to complete the agency's "number one" priority, safety inspections, if not for the current philosophy of assigning inspectors to enormous amounts of nonsafety related duties ....

We agree that the FAA should permit inspectors to concentrate their efforts on the areas that they recognize pose the greatest safety risks. The data to establish the criteria already exists and the *high risk airlines are well-known*. (Emphasis added.)

Well known to the FAA perhaps but not to the general public. Perhaps that's why the FAA resists the Safety Indicators Program—it could force the airlines to compete on issues of safety as well as price and convenience.

Pencil whipping

The shortage of inspectors and the FAA's inability to establish work priorities has resulted in an inspector work force that is insufficiently in the field and over-reliant on reviewing paperwork. Under these circumstances, it is easy for the forest to get lost for the trees.

"The FAA inspectors have become unbelievably good in tracking paperwork errors, but that doesn't have anything to do with real safety," said a union official who is intimately familiar with airline maintenance procedures and FAA oversight policies. This overreliance on paperwork "leads to a great temptation to cheat— that is, airline personnel who are under pressure to get planes out of the shop on time, will fill out the necessary paperwork as if they have performed maintenance when in reality, they have not."

Another source familiar with airline maintenance procedures, who wishes to remain anonymous, said "there is tremendous pressure on dispatchers to have on-time departures. Delays are tracked by the government and airlines, while catching mechanical problems are not. That leads one to skew toward on-time performance over safety. If a foreman delays planes because of maintenance problems, he can lose raises in pay."

The industry has a term for this fraudulent dereliction of duty: *pencil whipping*, which means a form is filled out claiming work has been completed when nothing was done. Pencil whipping is a worrisome problem in the industry and it is unlikely that an inspector who is reviewing paperwork will realize the facts. As a result, the FAA must over-rely on the willingness of workers in the field to report their colleagues who engage in the practice—a doubtful prospect at best. Still, the FAA has established a hotline for such reports and select ethical and safety conscious workers do report their coworkers for pencil whipping. We obtained a copy of a deposition taken by the FAA from a USAir maintenance supervisor—under oath—who was so reported.

The supervisor testified that a flight crew had reported a problem with a plane's *stall* warning light. (*See* glossary definition of stall.) (A stall warning light alerts the flight crew that the plane is in danger of stalling so they can take corrective action. It is a very important piece of safety technology and must be operative for a commercial transport jet to legally fly passengers.) The maintenance crew had been unable to repair the problem in time for the next flight. The plane was due to make one more flight that evening and a second the next morning. Instead of holding the plane or replacing it with another, the supervisor testified that he and the captain agreed to send the plane out, sans the warning system. Here are relevant excerpts from that deposition:

> Q: How did you know there was a stall warning problem?
>
> A: The incoming crew called in with a stall warning problem. I was called to the gate, and when I got to the gate, the outcoming captain was there .... They removed and replaced the overhead module. That did not fix it. They removed and replaced the stick shaker. That did not fix it. The captain and I made an agreement. I felt in my professional opinion that this was something that was not detrimental to the flight. I signed the logbook off, and we dispatched the aircraft knowing it was coming back in the next morning ... and we were going to take care of it the next morning.

In other words, the supervisor filled out paperwork saying the needed maintenance had been performed when the proper maintenance had not been performed and then allowed the plane to carry passengers without the FAA-required safety equipment in operation. When an inspector read the logbook, he would have no way of knowing the record was false. The deposition continued with the witness being asked how long the repair would have taken.

> A: ... It's a lengthy job there ma'am. You're probably looking at a two to three hour job. Then you'd have to rip out the floor and accessory compartment and (testimony offered a detailed description of the repair process). It's a right lengthy job.
>
> Q: The fact that this is a lengthy job, did that fact play into your decision to dispatch the aircraft?
>
> A: Yes, ma'am, it certainly did ....
>
> Q: Was your thinking one of passenger convenience as far as talking with the captain and allowing the airplane to be dispatched, or was it saving the company money? Why did you actually do this?
>
> A: ... It was for the sake of the company ... right.
>
> Q: So, you felt you were saving your company money.
>
> A: Yes.
>
> Q: The financial condition of the airline had a bearing on this?
>
> A: Yes, I would say it did ....
>
> Q: At this time I would like to give you the opportunity to add any statements if you wish.
>
> A: I've been doing this for many years and I've never had an incident before, never had a blemish on my record. Here again, we don't make a practice of doing this on an everyday basis .... It was an unfortunate situation. I felt the aircraft was safe to fly. Captain ___ and I both made a mutual agreement that

we felt the aircraft was safe to fly going to
Jacksonville, coming back the next morning ....

Q: When you say it was an unfortunate incident,
why was it unfortunate?

A: It was an unfortunate incident that my
mechanics turned around and called the FAA hotline
rather than come to me.

Q: Would you have made a different decision if
the aircraft was not going to be dispatched back to
Charlotte the next day?

A: Absolutely. We would never have let the aircraft
go. If we did not feel we could correct it in one day,
we would not have continued to fly the airplane. We
would have taken it out of service.

In other words, it was okay for the plane to take two relatively
short trips without a stall warning system but it was not okay to
allow the plane to fly for a longer period. We wonder if the passengers of those two flights would agree?

Q: Did you think this rendered the aircraft unsafe
or could have rendered the aircraft unsafe?

A: It would depend (on) who was flying it.
Captain ___ had numerous years of experience. You
might not have got experienced pilots that might not
have taken the aircraft. ____ and I made the
agreement to let it go like that, and I knew he would
bring it back the next morning. We would correct the
problem. I don't know who would have taken it the
next day.

Q: In hindsight, if you were confronted with this
situation tomorrow, same exact situation where you
knew the aircraft was going to be turned around the
next day, it was going to be a relatively short flight,
would you do this again?

A: I wish you hadn't asked me that. Given the
situation, the pilot, who it is, *yes ma'am I probably
would.* (Emphasis added.)

We hope this is an isolated case but we fear it is not. Several
sources told us, on the condition they remain anonymous, that

pencil whipping is not uncommon. Some even told us that certain airlines wink at the practice—so long as their people don't get caught. (USAir punished this individual with a 10-day suspension without pay. Our sources tell us the FAA also suspended the man's certification for six months and that the pilot who agreed to fly without a stall warning light was also punished; however, no criminal action was brought.)

Whether pervasive or isolated, pencil whipping is a serious life-threatening practice. If it is to be stopped, individuals who are tempted by company loyalty, laziness, or pressure by superiors to cut corners, must be made acutely aware that the government will be merciless in its pursuit of wrongdoers and that it will criminally prosecute and imprison anyone caught fraudulently filling-out maintenance records. The airlines should fire any employee who pencil whips, regardless of the excuse. The FAA should permanently revoke the certification of any mechanic, supervisor, or pilot who agrees to dispatch a plane that is below FAA minimum safety standards and any airline that engages in systematic fraud, should lose the right to do business.

The government also should modify its recordkeeping priorities. As things stand now, it appears that the DOT cares more about flight delays than about maintenance because the government publishes records about delays, but not on mechanical problems that are caught and corrected. (The CEO of American Airlines has proposed creating an annual award for the airline that does the best job of maintaining its fleet, an idea that has merit and should be pursued.) No matter how difficult the cure, whatever the hardships that might be created in individual miscreant's lives, the job must be done.

The Eastern Airlines embarrassment

The fact that this foreman was caught only because his mechanics blew the whistle to the FAA, illustrates that the agency's overreliance on inspecting paperwork is not sufficient to guarantee that airlines have complied with the rules. This truth was clearly demonstrated in the Eastern Airlines embarrassment.

Eastern Airlines has gone out of business. Eastern did not die a quick and painless death. Instead, it expired slowly, a victim of the era of greed during the Reagan/Bush years when corporate raiders systematically gobbled up and pillaged healthy companies, often leaving them dismembered, unprofitable, and deeply in debt.

What concerns us is the performance of the FAA in monitoring the safety of Eastern during its demise and fall. On that score, the FAA failed the test of competency. Not that it didn't try. As Eastern began its dizzying plunge, the FAA and DOT increased inspections of Eastern to ensure that its maintenance and other safety programs were not compromised by money troubles.

The headlines and media stories of the time said the news was good: the increased government scrutiny had determined that Eastern Airlines was safe, that despite its money problems, it continued to meet all FAR minimum requirements.

There was only one problem. It wasn't true. A large part of Eastern's maintenance program was a fraud. In 1990, Eastern Airlines and many of its executives were indicted by a grand jury in the United States District Court for the Eastern District of New York. The charge was fraud and conspiracy. Count one of the indictment read in part:

> On or about July 24, 1985, through October 13, 1989,
> ... within the Eastern District of New York and
> elsewhere, the defendants EASTERN (and the
> individually named defendants), including the upper
> management at the defendant Eastern's Miami
> headquarters responsible for the defendant EASTERN's
> entire maintenance operation, as well as other
> management employees at Atlanta, JFK and La
> Guardia Airports, did unlawfully, willfully and
> knowingly conspire, combine, confederate and agree
> to defraud the United States by impeding, impairing,
> obstructing and defeating the lawful government
> functions of the Federal Aviation Administration of the
> Department of Transportation to promote the safety of
> flight of civil aircraft and air commerce and (ensure)
> that aircraft are in a safe condition and are properly
> maintained.

For page after page, the 59-count indictment listed the alleged criminal conduct of Eastern and many of its top executives. Included was the installation of "defective or untested" critical electronic components, the falsification of maintenance records, the "disregard" of FAA maintenance requirement that repairs to crucial equipment "examined by a quality control inspector," the falsification of logbooks and work cards, and the creation of false computer transactions to "make it fraudulently appear that required scheduled maintenance and corrective repairs had been completed."

Eventually, in a plea bargain Eastern Airlines and two individual defendants admitted to criminal conduct. Eastern was fined $3.5 million. The case remains pending against other individually named defendants. No thanks to the FAA's inspection program. It had publicly given Eastern a clean bill of health. So, why had the FAA initially missed important information that the Department of Justice caught? And why has no one in the FAA apparently been held to account for their years-long failure to uncover the criminality of Eastern Airlines? (The FAA eventually cooperated with the DOT in bringing criminal charges against Eastern.)

The tragic consequences

The tragic consequences of the FAA's substantial inability to police airline compliance with safety standards is all too predictable: less safety, greater danger to the flying public, crashes, death.

Two recent air tragedies illustrate the high cost of failure. One is the Aloha Airlines tragedy where a portion of the top of a Boeing 737 came off while in flight, leading to the death of a flight attendant who was sucked out of the plane. The second is the crash of a Continental Express commuter plane that broke up while flying because screws were not replaced, leading to a break up of the plane in flight at 11,500 feet; everyone on board was killed. Contributing to both accidents, according to the NTSB, was the poor quality of FAA oversight.

Aloha Flight 243, April 28, 1988 After the Aloha case, the NTSB investigated the quality of the FAA inspection program and found many disturbing deficiencies, most of which the GAO and other FAA critics contend still exist. Among the criticisms were the following cited in the NTSB accident report at pages 63–66. Our comments appear in brackets:

> The investigation revealed that the staffing levels in some (field offices) is insufficient. The PMI (principal maintenance inspector) responsible for Aloha Airlines indicated that he was also assigned as the PMI for *nine other operators and seven repair stations throughout the Pacific Rim* area. (Emphasis added.)

[**Authors' comment:** If the safety inspectors are spread too thin, they will be unable to deter unsafe practices. The NTSB found that the FAA's poor oversight was a contributing cause of this tragedy.]

The FAA has been allocated additional hiring authority and funds to increase the number of air carrier inspectors. While additional personnel will improve the staffing situation, the safety board is concerned about the qualifications of the newly hired inspectors and training of the inspector force ... the new inspectors are not fully familiar with air carrier maintenance programs and practices.

There is *no specific training course for PMIs.* Additionally, recurrent training is sporadic and difficult to attain .... (Emphasis added.)

[**Authors' comment:** Establishing ongoing and effective training procedures is a basic management task.]

Increased staffing levels should help with the manpower requirements necessary to review paperwork .... However, without proper FAA inspection of actual airplane conditions, *less responsible or knowledgeable operators can operate airplanes of dubious structural and mechanical integrity.* The paperwork in the system has become so entrenched in FAA inspections that an *alteration of philosophy is required to create an effective maintenance inspection program.* (Emphasis added.)

[**Authors' comment:** Four years later the GAO still complains that the FAA inspectors are too tied to paperwork and insufficiently in the field. Apparently with the FAA, the more things change, the more they stay the same.]

Evidence suggests that ... in-house evaluation of PMI performance is oriented toward quantity of work and the ability to handle approvals smoothly and quickly.

[**Authors' comment:** In other words, the inspectors are judged on their ability to accommodate the air carriers. Is this an attack on the dual mandate?]

It appears that the current surveillance system can lead to *rubber-stamp approvals* and endorsement of an air carrier's operations and maintenance programs. (Emphasis added.)

It appears that the present system is sustained by the personal integrity and dedication of the concerned FAA inspector personnel rather than by an FAA system that includes adequate oversight and internal review.

[**Authors' comment:** What happens if an inspector accepts bribes or kickbacks from an airline in return for looking the other way when safety hazards are apparent? How will the FAA prevent such corruption if it does not effectively supervise its own inspectors?]

Technically, as stated by the FAA, if an airline complies with the regulations, it is "safe." However, many regulations are subjective in nature and are subject to interpretation. Consequently, even with several significant findings, ... as was the case with Aloha Airlines, the *airline was allowed to continue operations without making immediate changes and without having to set deadlines* for completion of recommended actions. (Emphasis added.)

If an airline is either unable or unwilling to develop and maintain an effective maintenance and inspection program, *the current FAA oversight philosophy will not prevent deficiencies from occurring,* and it will not verify that substantive and timely corrective actions have been taken. Furthermore, the FAA did not intend to actually "inspect" Aloha Airlines' fleet to verify if the airplanes were, in fact, safe. The findings of the safety board following the accident, ... suggests that the *FAA routine and special inspection programs were not effective in verifying that the airplanes were maintained in a safe, airworthy condition.* (Emphasis added.)

In so many words, the NTSB is telling us that the FAA is unable to root out and correct unsafe airline maintenance practices. Under these semiregulated conditions, your safety depends upon the competence and good faith of your airline, manufacturer, and other aspects of the safety system. It seems to be as simple and disturbing as that.

But, you say, perhaps the FAA's failings with Aloha Airlines is an isolated situation. Perhaps elsewhere, the inspectors are more effective. No such luck ....

Continental Express Flight 2574, September 11, 1991

Nearly three years after the Aloha Airlines tragedy, Continental Express Flight 2574, carrying three crewmembers and 11 passengers, was flying an uneventful Texas commuter run between Laredo and Houston. The cockpit voice recorder (CVR) transcript picked up the following:

Time & source	Content
1001:32 Pilot	... Winds are zero two zero at five thirty ten and they're gonna bring everybody in on two six or two seven.
1001:45 Copilot	Okey dokey.
1001.46 Pilot	Alrighta.
1001:46 Copilot	Thanks.
1001:55 Copilot	Captured on the right
1002:10 Copilot	Push'n this descent, making like the space shuttle.
1002:14 Pilot	Uh huh.
1003:07	Sound similar to objects flying about the cockpit.
1003:08	Sound similar to a human grunt.
1003:09	Sound similar to a fluctuation in prop rpm (decrease and then increase)
1003:11	Sound similar to three warning tones and aural warning, "oil."
1003:13	Sound similar to three warning tones, decrease in prop rpm, aircraft breaking up, depressurization and aural warning ... oil and stall warning clacker
1003:23	Fire warning tones
1003:36	Last recorded sound—aural warning, "aural unit one channel," and stall warning clacker

Without warning, in 30 short seconds, Flight 2574 had suddenly veered into a dive, burst into flames and broken apart in flight: 14 dead. Weather was not a factor in the accident. The performance of the flight crew also was not a factor in the accident. How could such a thing happen? How could an airplane suddenly crash in midflight?

The answer was disturbing. The accident should never have happened. The maintenance personnel of Continental Express had removed the upper row of screws from the left horizontal wing stabilizer and for a variety of reasons had failed to return them into place. As a result, as the plane was descending during the approach, the stabilizer broke away from the plane. That caused the plane to immediately go out of control, dive, and break apart.

The NTSB issued its report on the tragedy and found that the probable cause of the accident was "the failure of Continental Express maintenance and inspection personnel to adhere to proper maintenance and quality assurance procedures ...." The contributing causes were the failure of the Continental Express management to ensure compliance with the approved maintenance procedures and the failure of FAA surveillance to detect and certify compliance with approved procedures.

How did the FAA fail in its oversight duties? The NTSB reported:

> FAA oversight of the airline failed to find safety problems (with the Continental Express maintenance operations), such as those found during the safety board's investigation. This oversight included routine monitoring by a principal maintenance inspector (PMI) and a special National Aviation Safety Inspection Program (NASIP) team inspection following the accident.
>
> In the case of the routine inspection, the PMI indicated that he was *subjected to tremendous workload that limited the effectiveness of his safety monitoring* .... He indicated that the *workload considerably limited his time for on-site inspection.* He stated he could keep up with the number of required inspections but that *the depth and quality of these inspections were limited by lack of time.* (Emphasis added.)
>
> The PMI who assumed responsibilities one week before the accident, characterized his workload as "extremely full." He stated that he *worked evenings and weekends to fulfill all his responsibilities.* Maintenance personnel at Continental Express indicated that they saw the FAA personnel in the hangar infrequently, providing estimates of "perhaps a couple of times a month at maximum ... once every 2

months ... every 2 or 3 months ... once every three
months ... and the last visit may have been *6 or 7
months before.*"

It is clear to the safety board that the PMI's limited
visits to the hangar floor would make observations of
deviations from GMM (general maintenance manual)
procedures difficult, forcing the PMI to rely *exclusively
on paperwork records* that might not have reflected
actual conditions .... (Emphasis added.)

Out of the accident, the NTSB reiterated its previously issued
recommendations that the FAA "Enhance flight standards (inspection) program guidelines, ... to *emphasize hands-on inspections* of
equipment and procedures, *unannounced spot inspections*, and
the observation of quality assurance and internal audit functions,
in order to evaluate the effectiveness of air carrier maintenance
programs related to aircraft condition, the adherence to approved
and prescribed procedures, and the ability of air carriers to identify and correct problems from within." (NTSB Recommendation
A 92-7)

Subsequently, the FAA responded favorably to the NTSB recommendation. Yet, as late as the end of 1992, the GAO continued
its decade-old complaint that the FAA is still doing an inadequate
job inspecting the nation's airlines and that FAA inspectors spend
too much of their time on clerical and other tasks rather than on
checking planes.

And the beat goes on ....

Regulators relying on the regulated

The FAA has attempted to supplement its inspection force with
two self-monitoring programs designed to assist the airlines in
policing themselves. The programs are the *self-audit program* and
the *voluntary disclosure program.*

The self-audit program encourages airlines to develop improved internal management mechanisms to evaluate basic areas
of safety, ranging from maintenance, to flight operations to security. In other words, the airlines take their own safety pulse as
guided by the FAA. The voluntary disclosure program allows the
airlines to "turn themselves in" when they breach safety standards
and in return, receive amnesty against fines or other penalties.

Human nature and corporate enterprise being what they are, we have little faith that these programs could ever take the place of vigorous regulatory oversight by the FAA; however, because vigilant policing by the FAA does not seem likely during current fiscal and management circumstances, these programs could be worthwhile if well managed and the airlines gave their wholehearted cooperation.

Unfortunately, neither good management nor airline cooperation has occurred. Despite announcing the programs in 1987, the FAA still has not been able to effectively implement them. Moreover, it appears that the airlines have mostly refused to cooperate in the undertaking. A March 1992 GAO Report, entitled "Aviation Safety; Progress Limited with Self-Audit and Safety Violation Reporting Programs" concluded:

> Of the four major and six smaller airlines we visited, only one believed it met, or planned to meet, FAA's self-audit guidelines. These 10 airlines carried about 57 percent of the flying public in 1990. Similarly, as of September 1991, voluntary disclosures were limited to 292 reports from 96 airlines, or about 3 percent of the 3,031 airlines eligible to participate.

According to the GAO report, the airlines are uncooperative with the FAA's self-monitoring programs for three reasons:

> First, the airlines are skeptical that the program benefits outweigh their costs .... The airlines doubt that the programs will provide more than a marginal increase in safety and are concerned that any benefits could be overshadowed by extra staff and other costs associated with the self-audit program.
>
> *They also fear the potential losses in revenue if FAA cannot protect voluntary disclosure of safety violations from release under the Freedom of Information Act.* (Emphasis added.)
>
> [**Authors' comment:** The airlines talk a big game of freedom of choice in the deregulated marketplace but are horrified at the thought that you, the flying public, could gain access to information that would allow you to make an informed choice about which airline to fly based upon issues of safety.]
>
> Second, shortcomings in FAA program administration have resulted in confusion among

airline officials and FAA inspectors alike and compounded airline doubts about the programs. Ambiguously written guidance still in draft form does not clearly answer basic airline questions ....

(Third), the FAA is viewed as taking a "hands off" approach to oversight. *FAA does not plan to monitor or approve airline self-audit programs and has assigned few staff to analyze voluntary disclosures and determine trends in safety programs* .... Without more FAA commitment, these programs will have little chance of significantly affecting aviation safety. (Emphasis added.)

In other words, the FAA talks a good game but won't get behind its own programs. The seeming inability of the FAA to execute its own programs and the airlines' haughty refusal to participate, bodes ill for aviation at a time when the threats to safety have rarely been so acute or the challenges so formidable.

Modernizing air traffic control

"The big problem with the air traffic control system isn't the people, it's the junk equipment we have to work with and Washington doesn't seem to be able to do anything about it."

Air traffic controller who asked to remain anonymous, 1992

"The (modernization) project has become a runaway train and controller anticipation has been replaced with fear; fear derived from the knowledge that we could end up with a system that is less reliable, more cumbersome to operate, and no better than what we have now."

**Barry Krasner,
president of NATCA, testifying before the
Aviation Subcommittee, March 3, 1992**

In 1981, the FAA embarked on an ambitious effort to modernize its air traffic control equipment. This program was and is necessary because equipment in use at the time was obsolete and much of the equipment has not been replaced more than a decade later. Worse yet, the outdated equipment is increasingly subject to malfunction.

The modernization effort consists primarily of developing and purchasing new ATC equipment, including radars, computers, and communications networks. The expense of the program is huge. The appropriations for ATC modernization have increased from $260 million in fiscal year 1982 to the almost $2.7 billion amount requested by the FAA for fiscal year 1993. (Source: GAO report, "Status of FAA's Modernization Program," April, 1992.)

It could be expected that with all of the time, effort and billions expended by the FAA on the modernization program for more than 12 years, that the system would be the envy of the world. One would expect the new computers to be on-line and the computers' operation to be virtually flawless. New state-of-the-art radar should be in place keeping track of every commercial plane in the sky. The efficiency of the system should be at its peak. A new day should have dawned in the history of aviation.

Oh, if that were only true. The skies would be safer. The system would be more efficient. Capacity would have been safely increased. The safety and economics of the industry would both have benefited.

Unfortunately, the reverse has occurred. The FAA has largely performed incompetently in its efforts to modernize ATC. Most of the programs have experienced long delays and huge cost overruns. Much of the equipment that has been installed has experienced severe technical difficulties. There have been repeated design flaws. Virtually everyone agrees that the modernization program has been seriously mismanaged and bungled. Some go so far as to call it a fiasco.

To be fair, the FAA took on a daunting challenge when it undertook to modernize its ATC equipment. Joseph Del Balzo, executive director for systems operations for the FAA, told us: "It's a very complex program. I would tell you that it is the most complicated undertaking that any civilian agency has ever undertaken. More complicated than Apollo (the U.S. moon program); Apollo had a single mission in mind. If one thing didn't work, you could wait until tomorrow. If an error occurred, that was okay, (we'd fix it before takeoff). In a traffic control system, you can't do that. Whatever you do, whatever you install, it's got to work the first time because we're making the change in real time. It's much more complicated."

Fair enough. But if the equipment is going to be installed in a dynamic, open, functioning system, preplanning has to be the key to success. Does the agency have the people with the experience to manage the modernization? How should the equipment be designed? What are the needs of the personnel who will be working the equipment? How does the installation of one piece of new technology impact the rest of the system? How much testing should be conducted prior to installation? What problems can be anticipated?

According to most of the people we spoke with about the FAA's failed ATC modernization efforts, the FAA jumped in where wise men fear to tread causing the program to go awry from the very beginning. "The FAA oversold the modernization program and its ease of accomplishment," David Traynham, professional staff member for the House Committee on Public Works and Transportation, told us. "It was sold as a low technical-risk program that could be accomplished with off-the-shelf material. That assessment was flat-out wrong. Every system had to be invented. The systems they were putting in place had never existed before."

Joseph Del Balzo admitted as much when he told us that the FAA engaged in deceptive practices at the outset of the program; however, his justification shows that there is plenty of blame to go around:

> We really had to market (to Congress) a really
> substantial increase in capital investment money. How
> do you do that? We put together a plan that we say is
> going to cost whatever you think we can get. So, we
> want to aggressively underestimate because we need
> Congressional approval. So, we'll say $12 billion. How
> long will it take? It can't take long because nobody
> will be interested in giving you the money. So, you
> develop aggressive and optimistic schedules, not
> unreasonable but very optimistic .... We built the plan
> on the assumption that everything would go precisely
> right. Everything would go exactly to our cost
> estimates, no surplus held aside, everything would go
> exactly to our cost estimates and we got approval of
> that plan.

In other words, the FAA intentionally understated the cost and difficulty of the task to Congress because agency officials believed that elected representatives are so short-sighted that they would never approve the program if it were accurately depicted. That is outrageous and probably true but not surprising in the dysfunctional governing culture that exists in Washington, D.C.

(David Traynham, a professional staff member of the Aviation Subcommittee seems to support Del Balzo's claim that the system is to blame for the agency's disingenuous approach. When asked about the agency's failure to modernize ATC, he said, "The FAA can be faulted for poor projection. In hindsight, they were genuinely optimistic, but they needed to sell the system to get the funding. They needed to get people on the Hill committed to the project.")

Perhaps the FAA can be forgiven for simply "working the system." If they hadn't, there might not be any ATC modernization effort at all. Still, with that kind of start, it's no wonder the program shortly foundered.

The FAA soon compounded its conceptual falsehoods with managerial incompetence. The people in the FAA were not high-powered technical experts well versed in the intricacies of creating new systems from scratch. They were regulators. Their failing was one of pride. One insider, intimately familiar with the modernization effort told us of the FAA: "They tried to do what they were not equipped to do. They didn't have the knowledge or expertise to modernize the ATC system. Only they refused to admit it."

The truth of at least the first part of that statement can be seen by the current status of the modernization program. In 1981, the FAA developed a long-term strategy for modernization called the National Airspace System Plan (NAS). The program originally was to take 10 years, cost $12 billion and was comprised of about 80 projects. Yet, nine years later, little had been accomplished. An April 1990 GAO report entitled "Air Traffic Control: Status of FAA Effort to Modernize the System" detailed the sad truth. (Excerpted.)

> All of the major modernization projects in the original NAS Plan have experienced significant schedule delays since the inception of the plan. In November 1988, we reported that implementation milestones had slipped an average of about 2½ years between 1983 and 1987 NAS plans. Delays in first-site implementation—when the first system becomes operational in the field— ranged from 1 to 4 years. These delays have continued—8 of the 12 major systems we reviewed experienced a delay of at least 200 days during the

past year .... Although approximately 32 percent of the
NAS Plan projects are now complete, they account for
only about 4 percent of the FAA's $15.8 billion
estimated NAS Plan cost.

The FAA responded to the problems with the NAS Plan in
time-tested Washington style—if at first you don't succeed, try to
expand the program and increase the price. It worked. Despite
nine years of failure and incompetence, Congress agreed to increase the size and cost of the modernization effort.

In 1990, the original NAS Plan was converted into a new and
improved version of modernization and renamed the Aviation
System Capital Investment Plan (CIP). (Here's another time-tested
bureaucrat's trick—if a program doesn't work, rename it and go
on as before.) CIP added about 150 new projects to the uncom-
pleted NAS Plan to include some 200 projects now estimated to
cost $31.9 billion.

The FAA has not done much better managing the CIP. Delays
and cost overruns continue to be the order of the day. Year-after-
year, the GAO details depressing reports on the FAA's lack of
progress. For example, an April 1992 GAO status report revealed
that:

- 56 of the 80 projects in the 1983 NAS plan should have
  achieved their last-site implementation by the end of calendar
  year 1991. In fact, only 28 were implemented.

- 10 of the 12 major modernization projects reviewed in detail
  by the GAO had experienced either cost increases or schedule
  delays in the previous year. Four of the 12 had cost increases
  combined with schedule delays.

- Six of the delayed projects were expected to generate the
  majority of the benefits for users.

- CIP costs continued to escalate.

- Completion of modernization projects had been delayed from
  as little as one year to as many as nine years between the 1983
  NAS Plan projections and the 1991 CIP projections.

How could so much go so consistently wrong? Simply stated,
the FAA still does not have managerial resources to oversee a
technical improvement project the size and scope of the CIP Plan.
The GAO, members of Congress, and other FAA critics, have re-

peatedly complained that the FAA fails in basic management tasks, that it:

- Does not set incremental goals and time lines that would lead step-by-step to a completed project.
- Enters into contracts with vendors before system capabilities have been determined, leading to significant performance delays.
- Does not sufficiently consult with personnel who would actually use the technology, forcing the equipment to be redesigned.
- Does not have a system of accountability that punishes incompetence and/or mismanagement. Programs founder, prices skyrocket, systems malfunction, and as far as we could determine, only one person in FAA suffered any job sanction due to the ongoing failure of the modernization program—and that was a simple transfer to another department.

Some will say, the past is past. What counts is the performance of tomorrow. Officials of the FAA claim that they have learned their lesson and are prepared to move forward in a prompt and competent manner to complete the modernization program. They speak forcefully of their new resolve to consult with the people in the field, of designing a new "building concept," where the FAA builds a little, tests a little, and moves forward step-by-step to completion. The FAA's more vigorous approach is confirmed by congressional staffer David Traynham: "The modernization program is in much better shape. They now take a 'fly before you buy' approach."

There is cause for skepticism here, having heard that tale before. We also worry about the potential of the FAA to cut corners to get critics off its back. Barry Krasner, president of NATCA, fears that such pressure might "force the FAA to accept less than perfect systems, hoping that corrections or modifications can be accomplished during the operations phase—in other words, 'the controllers will make it work.'"

That would be a threat to safety. And given the FAA's history of failure, we believe that the principle of "trust but verify," should apply. Congress, the Department of Transportation, and the GAO must increase their oversight of the FAA to ensure that its modernization program improves and that shortcuts are not taken.

One FAA official who is worried about the quality of the program told us, "People's lives are at stake. We don't have the luxury of putting something in the field that we're not absolutely certain is going to work the first time, every time."

The many failings of the FAA that have been detailed are disturbing and worrisome. The failings tell a story of an FAA that is overwhelmed by its mandate, that is unwilling or unable to effectively carry out its responsibilities, that too often seems more concerned with carrier profits rather than public safety concerns.

That is not to say that all of this is the FAA's fault. The FAA was also a victim. It suffered from the myopia of the Reagan Administration that cut the agency's budget just at the time when deregulation created an explosion in its workload. FAA lost most of its experienced controllers in the PATCO debacle and has had to rebuild the controller force. FAA's hands are tied by the bureaucratic ways of Washington, D.C. FAA has had a failure of continuity of leadership, having had a new administrator on the average of about once every two years. Moreover, FAA has chronically been underfunded by a Congress that prefers to use the nearly $7 billion surplus in the Aviation Trust Fund to hide the true size of the national budget deficit rather than spend that money paid by you, the flying passenger, on aviation safety.

The FAA can be saved. Aviation can be made safer; however, the effort is going to require substantive reform, increased participation and involvement by airline passengers, an infusion of resources, a willingness to change, and a depth of soul searching that those within the agency might find difficult to accept.

Part III

Air traffic control

"Air traffic control is a balancing act. There is an awful lot of strain and burden in the system right now. The controllers are being pushed to the limit."

William A. Faville,
NATCA director of safety and technology, 1992

Operating the air traffic control system might be the FAA's most important function. Air traffic control is essential to safety and to the viability of commercial aviation. Without it, people would be afraid to fly. No one would feel safe getting on an airplane. The financial base of commercial aviation would collapse.

Today's air traffic control system is troubled. It is undergoing a precarious transition. Current technological systems are outdated and increasingly subject to breakdown. As described in chapter 8, the pace of the modernization effort is interminable. At the same time, the sky is becoming more crowded. Controllers are becoming more strained because the amount of separation between aircraft being controlled has been reduced to increase capacity. (The noteworthy instance is airplanes flying closer together when lined up for approach and landing.)

The questionable performance of new cockpit technologies to avoid midair collisions have controllers and pilots, who need to work in partnership and mutual trust, at loggerheads. Meanwhile, the air traffic controller work force continues to suffer in the aftermath of the disastrous 1981 air traffic controller's strike and subsequent firings.

Yet, the news is not all bleak. Success stories are to be found. The FAA's Central Flow Control System, while constraining the capacity of the system, has done a good job of maintaining safety. Despite the stress and strains, the ATC system continues to keep planes from colliding in flight. And there is no doubt that the controller work force is dedicated to safety and committed to "moving metal."

The discussion starts with a tour of the Oakland Air Traffic Control Center and the Central Flow Control headquarters on the sixth floor of the FAA and NTSB building in Washington, D.C.

9

Flying from here to there

"At the end of the day, air traffic control still works."

**Louis A. Turpen, director of
San Francisco International Airport, 1992**

To enter the hushed and darkened control room at the Oakland Air Route Traffic Control Center (ARTCC) is to be impressed. The room is huge, perhaps half the size of a football field. The subdued light reveals 30 or 40 people around their individual stations, intensely concentrated on radarscopes. Some of the controllers speak quietly into their headset microphones. Others watch intently. The atmosphere is one of diligent work and quiet efficiency.

A closer look at the radar terminals shows 15 or so *blips* on each screen. The blips have minuscule letters and numerals underneath. Each blip is moving. It is like watching bees fly in slow motion. To the untrained eye, all is chaos. But to the trained air traffic controller, each blip represents an individual aircraft, the flight identification, the altitude of the aircraft, and its speed.

Two blips merge. The visitor's heart leaps into his throat. Is something wrong? Has there been a collision? Are people dying a horrible death? But then they separate. A controller explains that the planes were never closer than 1000 vertical feet apart.

This is the quiet, intense world of the air traffic controller, whose job it is to guide planes safely from takeoff to landing. It is an intense job and a crucial one. Air traffic controllers literally have your life in their hands every time you travel aboard a commercial aircraft.

How air traffic control works

Air traffic control is a collaborative safety system involving technology such as radar, aircraft transponders, computers, and radio, and people, primarily pilots and air traffic controllers. All pilots flying commercial and military planes are subject to some form of air traffic control as part of their responsibility to abide by *instrument flight rules* (IFR). Pilots flying under IFR must file a flight plan in advance of departure, the aircraft must have the requisite technical equipment on board to be managed by the ATC system, and the pilots must fly in the direction (compass heading), at the speed, and at the altitude as directed by the air traffic controller. Typically the cruise altitude is prescribed in the flight plan, but might change for reasons such as weather that makes for a bumpy ride; other altitudes during climb and descent are determined by a prescribed procedure or by the controller.

Controllers maintain the safe distance between controlled aircraft by radioing instructions advising pilots what altitude, speed, and heading they are required to fly. These instructions are based upon the controller's view of the three-dimensional parcel of airspace under their authority. The parcel of airspace is called a *sector*. Controllers also advise pilots about other controlled aircraft in their immediate vicinity and act as traffic cops keeping all aircraft at a safe distance from each other.

Controllers also direct pilots to a specific heading for landing that typically places the airplane in a position to receive an airport runway's *instrument landing system* (ILS). The ILS sends out two radio beams to a receiver and indicator on an aircraft. One beam gives the pilot left-right guidance; the other beam gives the pilot the correct angle of descent to the runway. This permits smooth landings and pinpoint accuracy even in inclement weather.

All aircraft do not fly under IFR. General aviation planes are typically flown under what is known as *visual flight rules* (VFR), unless they are flying in the vicinity of an airport terminal or other airspace that requires contact with ATC. Depending upon the classification of controlled airspace, a general aviation aircraft is handled by the controller precisely as if a commercial airliner; the general aviation pilot is consequently flying as if an airline pilot, expected to respond with identical professionalism. Beyond controlled operations, VFR flying is much as it was in the early days of aviation where the separation between aircraft and the safety of a landing or takeoff depended largely on the judgment of the pilot based upon what was seen from the plane cockpit. See and be seen is still the first line of defense for all pilots, whether general aviation or air carrier, in cooperation with sophisticated ATC equipment and experienced controllers.

Central Flow Control

"There are 3739 IFR flights currently in the air (over) the Continental United States."

**Information obtained from the
FAA Central Flow Control computer,
October 15, 1992, 17:35 hours**

Imagine a map of the continental United States depicted on a large computer screen. A controller pushes a computer key and suddenly, the entire map is covered by white dots. Each dot represents one plane in the air. The effect is that of a gigantic blizzard covering the entire country.

The controller keys another set of instructions into the computer and the display now depicts every plane heading for San Francisco International Airport. With the click of computer keys, specific information about a specific flight is depicted. It is October 15, 1992, at approximately 17:35 hours: United Airlines Flight 31 is flying between New York and San Francisco at 35,000 feet at a speed of 411 knots. The equipment in use is a DC-10. At that moment, the flight is approximately 136 minutes from its destination.

All of this activity and much more takes place on the 6th floor of the FAA building in Washington, D.C., in an area known as Central Flow Control. Central Flow Control manages the nation's entire air traffic control system. Air traffic control for every commercial flight begins in flow control. The facility does not communicate with individual planes, but no commercial airplane takes off without Central Flow Control's approval.

According to Richard Stafford, FAA public affairs officer, "The purpose of Central Flow Control is to manage the air traffic of the entire nation based on the circumstances of the day. We do not allow any more planes into the air than can be safety controlled and landed, based on conditions. The more complex the situation, such as bad weather or technical problems with the system, the less traffic can be handled and the fewer planes we will allow into the air."

The Central Flow Control system looks ahead to anticipate problems and makes decisions based on what it can forecast. "We can project three to four hours in advance," Stafford says. "Every morning and afternoon we will have a conference call and brief the carriers on what to expect. If things look to get complicated, we will slow up the system."

For example, if there is a severe thunderstorm system expected over Miami beginning at about 3 p.m., flow control might delay planes on the West Coast heading for Miami in the morning because fewer planes will be able to land at Miami during the severe weather. At the same time, planes might be permitted to leave from airports within a couple of flying hours from Miami without delay, until midday.

Anyone who flew on a regular basis more than 10 years ago might remember the frequent flyer's lament, "I was stacked-up for an hour over Chicago." Stacking planes, known as *holding* in aviation circles, is the practice of having planes fly in an oval race track path near an airport until able to land. Stacking has been substantially reduced and in some areas of the country eliminated by flow control. Now, instead of holding in the air, flights are held on the ground and are not permitted to take off unless it is reasonable to expect that they will be able to fly directly to their destination and land with little or no delay. When a sudden change in weather occurs at an airport, after a flight has departed, holding might be required.

The flow control system is safer than the unmanaged air traffic control system it replaced. A plane sitting at a gate cannot be in a midair collision. It is also more fuel efficient because a plane on the ground is not burning fuel as if at cruise altitude.

The FAA contends that flow control permits maximum system efficiency. Some critics disagree ("Air Traffic Control Deficiencies: Death of an Industry?" ACAP, July 10, 1992). They contend that the centralized management of flow control has been used as an excuse by the FAA to keep from building a sufficient cadre of experienced air traffic controllers. This, critics believe, has suffocated commercial aviation and contributed to the financial difficulties of the industry.

Central Flow Control has made for safer flying, but that does not mean that the critics are incorrect. Subsequent chapters discuss understaffing at the FAA's ATC facilities, which restricts the number of planes that can be safely permitted to fly.

From takeoff to landing

"In 1989, controllers at the (New York City radar approach control) facility worked 1.7 million aircraft operations (takeoffs and landings) in their airspace, a 70 percent increase over 1981."

Performance Magazine, Issue Two, 1990, as reprinted by the FAA

Fly with us now on an imaginary flight from Los Angeles to New York on Consumer Airlines Flight 111. Flow control has not delayed the flight. Actual hands-on air traffic control of our flight begins with the airport tower. The controllers in the tower are responsible for giving our plane permission to push off from the gate, taxi toward the runway, and enter the runway for takeoff. This is a vital area of flight safety because most accidents occur during takeoff, landing, or on the ground.

When Flight 111 is in the air and about 5 miles away from the airport, the tower air traffic controller will *hand off* responsibility for our safety to the next ATC step in our flight: a *terminal radar approach control* (TRACON) facility. To initiate the handoff, the tower controller imforms the pilot of Flight 111 to establish radio communications with the TRACON on a specific frequency and subsequently the TRACON controller will take responsibility for the flight. (Before entering the TRACON airspace, TRACON controllers received a computer printout advising them to expect Consumer Airlines Flight 111 to come under their responsibility. The printout is the flight *strip*. The strip will be kept at the ATC workstation responsible for the flight until 111 leaves the airspace under that workstation's control.)

TRACON controllers manage the "approach airspace" surrounding several major airports in their area of jurisdiction and generally have responsibility for airspace up to 10,000 feet. For example, from its location on Long Island, the New York TRA-

CON, controls airspace that covers 21,000 square miles (based upon a ground reference) and controls the path of aircraft flying in and out of airports such as La Guardia, Kennedy, Newark, Westchester County (Liberty), and MacArthur Field (Islip).

In addition, TRACONs will control general aviation and other aircraft that fly through TRACON airspace. In 1989, the New York TRACON handled more than 600,000 transients that did not involve landings or takeoffs.

After our plane climbs above 10,000 feet, control of our flight is passed off to one of the 24 air route traffic control centers, usually called a *centers* or abbreviate ARTCC. Like the TRACON, each center that takes responsibility for our flight will have received a computer printout announcing our pending arrival into its airspace. The centers will control our flight while en route and ensure that our plane is separated by at least 2000 feet vertically and 5 miles horizontally from all other aircraft, as we fly across the country—approximately 7 miles up in the air.

As we approach New York, the center in charge of our flight will give our pilot permission to begin the descent, giving instructions as to the headings, speed, and altitude to take. As we descend to 10,000 feet, the New York TRACON will guide our approach to the airport, passing it off to the airport tower when we are about 5 miles from the airport. Upon landing, the ground controller (who is in the tower) will guide our plane safely to the gate.

All of this is not as simple as it appears. Controllers have to be able to look at a two-dimensional screen and mentally translate the information on the screen into a three-dimensional reality. They also must anticipate where the blips will be in the minutes— even seconds—to come and be ever alert to warn planes to change the aircraft altitude, speed, or heading, as conditions warrant. "Air traffic controllers walk a fine line," Ed De Valle Jr., a controller at the Oakland Center told us. "The planes are flying hundreds of miles an hour. They are flying at different altitudes, and many are merging targets (planes going in different directions). A controller might have 5 planes on his scope and be busy as heck or might have 25 and not be busy at all. It all depends on what the planes are doing."

Air traffic controllers are important people performing a vital function. Their work is difficult and complex and largely out of sight of the passengers. It is in the national interest that controller recruitment, training and job conditions be top notch and that enough *experienced* controllers remain on the job to keep the system functioning smoothly and safely. Chapter 10 reveals why the FAA has been remiss in maintaining that kind of atmosphere for its controller work force for the last dozen years.

10

The controller's unhappy decade

"Current controllers do not know how to hold aircraft in the air because they have no experience at it."

Bill Taylor,
publisher of the newsletter, *PATCO Lives*, 1992

A former FAA controller, now working as a tower controller for the Department of Defense, wrote to tell us of his fears that the current crop of air traffic controllers is not performing as well as it should. "I think it is fairly safe to say that the (today's) controllers are no less diligent or bright than their predecessors. The difference in performance and execution lies solely in the fact that these people have never seen things done the 'right way.' "

Is this merely sour grapes from a man who was a member of the Professional Air Traffic Controllers Association (PATCO), the former air traffic controllers' union, and who was fired by the FAA? Perhaps. But he is far from alone in his opinion. Another veteran controller who works ATC for the FAA in the Los Angeles area told us in September 1992, "I am working with a new breed of controllers. There is a distinct difference in ability. The new controllers, on the West Coast at least, do not know how to hold [stack] aircraft. That skill was lost in the strike." That was an oft repeated sentiment from many veteran controllers.

Former PATCO controllers are not the only ones grumbling. John Thornton, senior director, legislative affairs for the National Air

Traffic Controllers Association (NATCA), the current air traffic controllers' union, stated at a conference on aviation challenges for the 1990s, "There is a disagreement between FAA and the NATCA on the number of controllers in the ATC system today. FAA will tell you that there are more controllers now than there were in 1981. NATCA, on the other hand, contends that there are 2000 fewer controllers than there were in 1981 .... FAA seems to believe that more can be done with less and that a portion of that 'less' can perform on a part-time basis. NATCA completely disagrees with these assumptions. We believe the system has gotten past the point of being able to survive on best wishes and sacrifices."

Notice the language used to describe the state of the air traffic control system: "1981," "the strike," "the new breed of controllers," the "current crop," and a system surviving "on best wishes and sacrifices." These terms and phrases speak of an air traffic control system that is deeply divided and troubled. Despite assurances by FAA officials and field supervisors that the system is working well, most observers with whom we discussed the issue spoke of an air traffic control system plagued by low morale and growing internal tension.

This malaise did not arise in a vacuum. Its source can be traced back to the disputes the FAA had with members of PATCO and the union's final, fatal political battle with President Ronald Reagan. That epochal event created all that followed.

The PATCO strike

"I have been thoroughly briefed by members of my staff as to the deplorable state of our nation's air traffic control system. They have told me that too few people working unreasonable hours with obsolete equipment has placed the nation's air travelers in unwarranted danger. In an area so clearly related to public safety the Carter administration has failed to act responsibly."

Excerpt from a letter that presidential candidate Ronald Reagan wrote to the president of PATCO, 1980

In 1981, PATCO and the FAA reached an impasse after months of negotiating the terms of a new contract for the controllers. PATCO wanted higher wages, but the main thrust of its negotiation strategy was to win better working conditions. "Money was way down the list of what we were after," one former PATCO member told us. "We were more concerned with forced overtime, equipment going down the 'pooper,' and other working conditions that were detrimental to controllers' health and (aviation's overall) safety."

Ironically, the union thought it had the support of President Reagan in much of what it wanted to accomplish. As a presidential candidate, Reagan had expressed sympathy for PATCO's position, writing a letter to Robert E. Poli, president of PATCO—now derisively known in controller circles as the "I pledge letter." In the letter, Reagan promised to "take whatever steps are necessary to provide our air traffic controllers with the most modern equipment available and adjust staff levels and workdays so that they are commensurate with achieving a maximum degree of public safety." Reagan then added, "I pledge to work closely with you to bring about a spirit of cooperation between the President and the air traffic controllers. Such harmony can and must exist if we are to restore the people's confidence in their government." The controllers took Ronald Reagan at his word and thought he would use his good offices to help resolve PATCO's dispute with the FAA. The controllers were very mistaken.

The previous contract had expired in January 1981. Former PATCO members claim the FAA never negotiated in good faith—that the agency sought a strike to break up the union based on disputes between the agency and PATCO that went back years. The FAA claims that every reasonable effort was made to accommodate PATCO's demands, even going so far as to offer wage increases in excess of raises being received at that time by other government employees. What is not in dispute is that PATCO and the government reached a bitter impasse.

On August 3, 1981, PATCO went out on strike, an action that threatened to shut down the nation's aviation system. President Reagan took a very hard line against the controllers. As public employees—Reagan cited the Civil Service Reform Act—PATCO did not have the legal right to strike; therefore, its job action was illegal. Four hours after the commencement of the strike, Reagan issued an ultimatum: Go back to work within 48 hours or be fired.

Both parties to the dispute were adamant, insisting that right was on their side. Each hoped the other would blink. Neither did. Some 875 controllers returned to their jobs joining nonstriking personnel, but most refused to cross picket lines. True to his threat, Ronald Reagan fired all PATCO controllers who continued on strike. Out of a work force of about 16,200 controllers, 11,345 were terminated. The air traffic control system was in danger of imminent collapse.

The FAA scrambled into emergency mode. "We knew that we could only supply 25 percent of the ATC demand with supervisors and the nonstriking controllers," the FAA's Richard Stafford recalled. "So we set priorities. The first priority went to the president. Then, medical flights. Third were FAA flights transporting maintenance personnel and finally, any flight more than 500 miles in length, on the supposition that the public could make transportation arrangements for shorter trips." The FAA took other action. Working controllers were put on extensive overtime. Military controllers were brought in to assist the FAA and retirees were called back to service. General aviation's use of ATC was cut back with a reservation system. (General aviation flights that did not require any ATC were not restricted.) The length of separation between planes was increased and the aviation system was otherwise slowed to maintain safe conditions.

Three days later, the FAA found that it was operating at nearly 75 percent of the then existing capacity. "We were astounded," Stafford recalls. Still, it would take the FAA more than three years to get the system back to what it would claim, and critics dispute, is an ATC system operating at full capacity.

Out of the dark cloud of the emergency, recalled Stafford, a bright silver lining was discovered. "We were using our computers to advise the controllers in the field. After a while, we realized that we could actually manage the air traffic flow for the entire nation." Thus, out of the turmoil of the PATCO strike, was born one of the FAA's main safety success stories of the last decade, the Central Flow Control facility in Washington (chapter 9). (There is some dispute about this. PATCO activist Bill Taylor suspects the FAA had created Central Flow Control before the strike so that the agency could safely break PATCO.)

The government wasn't finished with the striking controllers. It soon took PATCO to court and obtained a court order decertifying it as a union. Moreover, members of PATCO were blackballed, permanently barred from working for the FAA or for consultants to the FAA. More than 10 years afterward, that ban remained in effect, although the Clinton administration indicated within the "first 100 days" that it would lift the ban.

The issue of who was right and who was wrong in that dispute remains a matter of emotional controversy. Bill Taylor, a for-

mer PATCO official who was active in the strike, is still bitter. "The
FAA had a sick, dysfunctional system," Taylor proclaims. "They
were burning the controllers. People were getting sick from all
the work and stress. They were retiring in their 40s. We had to try
and do something." On the other hand, a consultant to the FAA on
issues of air traffic control disagrees. "When PATCO went on
strike," he told us angrily, "they violated their oath. They thought
they were indispensable and it made them arrogant. Everything
that happened, they brought on to themselves."

At the time, the majority of the public approved of Reagan's
tactics, viewing the firings as supportive of the rule of law and
promoting of respect for authority. A minority saw it as sheer
union busting, a signal to private enterprise to take a hard line
against its unions. Despite the controversy and draconian termination sanctions, the PATCO firings proved to be one of Ronald
Reagan's most significant political triumphs.

But all of that is history. The important questions for this discussion are these: Was the Reagan victory over PATCO purchased
at the price of aviation safety? And, if so, does safety remain compromised today?

The FAA says no to both questions. It claims that the adoption
of central flow control and the agency's decade-long effort to rebuild the air traffic controller work force now meets all national
ATC requirements. Critics contend otherwise. They charge that
FAA remains qualitatively, if not numerically, understaffed. Moreover, these critics contend that the new air traffic controllers do
not possess many important controlling skills once possessed by
the long lost members of PATCO.

These disturbing thoughts are reinforced by a NATCA official
who told us that during the years following the strike, "Too often
people were being certified because they needed the controllers,
not because they possessed the requisite skills."

Based upon how air traffic controllers are trained, these critics
have a point.

How controllers are trained

*"The heart of the system is the seasoned air traffic controller, the
FPL, not just one who has qualified, just made it last week or
yesterday, but the one who has been an FPL and been on the
boards for quite some time and knows how to handle a situation*

when weather has built up, traffic has built up, the sector is
overloaded, and you get people up there in the air who are in
trouble and this person knows how to get them out of trouble."
   Representative James Oberstar,
   Aviation Safety-Investigations and Oversight Subcommittee,
   March 17, 1986

The first step to becoming an air traffic controller is to apply with
the FAA for initial training at the Mike Monroney Aeronautical
Center in Oklahoma City. Not everyone who applies is accepted.
According to Roland Herwig of the FAA, "It takes special skills to
become a controller; the ability to think three-dimensionally, the
ability to anticipate future moves, much like a champion chess
player, the ability to make decisions and to handle stress." Thus,
applicants are tested to determine if they have the aptitude to perform the job. The testing process once took nine weeks of acad-
emics and testing. It now takes five days and is performed with
the use of computers.

Next comes three months of intensive training at Oklahoma
City, where students learn the basics of air traffic control, the rules
controllers must follow and a general overview of the aviation
system, although this system will be changing. Herwig explains,
"Soon we will be separating the training into different tracks. For
example, future tower controllers are going to be on one mode
and future center controllers will be on another. We expect that
will help make on-the-job training of controllers go much easier
and quicker."

Controller trainees who make it through the academy are next
sent to an air traffic control site, be it a tower, a TRACON, or a
center, for hands-on education and training. At the Oakland
Center, newly trained people undergo six weeks of intensive
work before they ever reach the control floor. "We teach them
where the towers are, where flight service stations are located [A
flight service station is a primary source of weather information
for all pilots. Among other services provided is flight plan tracking for the aforementioned general aviation VFR flights; failing to
close a VFR flight plan prompts a search for the aircraft.] and
things of that kind," one trainer told us, "The point is to give them
knowledge of the details they will need to work the Oakland
Center airspace."

Trainees who pass tests proving they have absorbed the in-

formation become known as *assistant controllers* and are assigned part-time to the control floor as they continue their off-the-
floor education and training. Assistant controllers rip off the
computer printer strips and deliver the strips to the appropriate
workstation and otherwise work with all of the information they
need to understand how to control planes. This might seem like
"go-fer" work, but it provides an important comprehension for the
trainees of how the intricate system operates.

Eventually, assistant controllers achieve the status of a *developmental controller* and then *operational controller.* The FAA considers a developmental controller as one who has *checked out* (passed
a proficiency test) on one or two operational positions. An operational controller has checked out on up to four positions. Both
work under the direct observation and supervision of a fully certified controller, known as a *full performance level* (FPL) controller.

The FPLs are controllers who have been certified (passed the
proficiency tests) on all positions for which they are responsible;
FPLs are the backbone of air traffic control. (In Oakland, an operational controller must certify in six different sectors to become
an FPL.) FPLs are a vital part of the air traffic control system because of the depth of their hands-on experience and the flexibility they bring to their duties, having the ability to work many
different controller stations without direct supervision.

The creation of an FPL air traffic controller is primarily a mentoring process. "Most of the really important work comes from the
FPL teaching the new developmental kid the tricks of the trade,"
one experienced controller told us. "It is like handing down trade
secrets from father to son. It is where the 'art' of controlling is
passed from generation to generation. You can't get that out of a
book." Another controller expanded on the point. "FPLs proudly
take the new controllers under their wing, not only at the work-
place but beyond. After-hour 'debriefings' take place where many
years of experience are transmitted from journeyman to fledgling.
That's where the real learning takes place."

The quality of this all-important mentoring process deterio-
rated after the strike. One former FAA controller, who now works
as a tower controller for the Department of Defense, told us,
"Little or none of this (mentoring) is possible under the current
circumstances because most of today's controllers were run, indeed rushed, through the mill at the same time." According to
these "old hands," the new generation of controllers never

learned many important skills they would have received if the fired controllers been had around to teach them.

First and foremost among these, is the art of holding planes, also known as stacking (chapter 9). "PATCO controllers used to be able to safely hold scores of planes over an airport at one time," one former PATCO member claims. "The new guys can't do that because they were never taught the skill by the older guys." Several current controllers we spoke with agreed, as did at least one official of NATCA, who said, "Unfortunately, holding is fast becoming a lost art, except in the eastern part of the United States."

Holding skills are especially important in light of the growing pressure on the FAA to increase capacity of the number of airplanes permitted to fly in order to improve the economics of the industry. To do that, the FAA would have to ease up on flow control restrictions. If the FAA accedes to these demands, the chances of planes having to circle an airport until there is room to land will increase. If "stacking planes over O'Hare," once again becomes a common practice, the ability to hold planes will be as important to protecting safety as it was before the PATCO strike.

Another safety area former PATCO members worry about is the ability to control the airways for a period of time without using radar. A former PATCO controller now working for the Department of Defense, says, "One of the important parts of being checked out (to be an FPL) used to be learning to control planes without radar, just in case the equipment went down. That isn't true anymore. Today's crop would be lost if that happened." NATCA told us the emphasis is on radar training and nonradar training is being de-emphasized based on the belief that the new equipment will be more reliable." (To which we state, remember the *Titanic*.)

John H. Enders, chairman of the Flight Safety Foundation, told us in May 1993 that "there is no question that the controller work force has less experience holding aircraft. That's okay because of managed control procedures. More planes should be able to fly as our ability to accurately predict weather improves. In the meantime, I'd hate to see a rush toward reestablishing holding patterns as a matter of policy. I believe that would not be as safe as the current system."

Of course, the FAA denies that there has been any diminution in the training, quality or skills of post-strike FPLs, a sentiment echoed by the "official" NATCA position.

FAA tries to rebuild the system

"... The aviation industry is still 3000 full performance level air traffic controllers shy of the 1981 prestrike level. Controllers on the job handled 12 million more operations in 1989 than in 1981; thus, the number of full performance level controllers has decreased by about 20 percent, while the number of operations has increased by almost 50 percent."

Congresswoman Barbara Boxer, February 25, 1991

The FAA was dealt a severe blow with the PATCO firings. Gone were more than 11,300 air traffic controllers who, like Rome, are not built in a day. Gone was the expertise they had gained from years on the job to be passed on to the next generation of controllers. The FAA had a rebuilding job to do that would have tested the mettle of any agency.

From the beginning the FAA had troubles getting back on its feet. Remember, this whole debacle occurred during the early powerful years of Ronald—"the government is the problem"—Reagan, who did not spare the FAA from his budget-cutting axe. At the same time, the FAA was gearing up to modernize the ATC system. This, while the impact of deregulation was changing the entire aviation system of the country, greatly increasing the number of people who fly and the demands on the agency to certify new airlines. To say the least, the FAA's plate was full.

The FAA tried to rebuild the controller force, but to do so, it had to cut corners.

Training

In order to make it appear as if the controller work force was more experienced than was the case, the FAA reduced the time and on-the-job training required to become an FPL. A 1986 GAO report found, "Before the strike, it took four to five years to qualify as an FPL. Since the strike, the Office of Personnel and Management has waived time in grade requirements so that controllers can become FPLs in about half the time ...." The FAA admitted as much in the March 1990 congressional testimony of Norbert Owens, FAA's deputy associate administrator for Air Traffic, who acknowledged that the number of positions that a controller had to certify on in order to become an FPL had been reduced.

Staffing standards

A June 1988 GAO report showed how the FAA altered its staffing standards to meet the reduced level of available controllers. "Before the strike, the FAA provided a staffing cushion to protect against 'hard times.' With the strike, FAA management decided that staffing before the strike was too high. In 1982, FAA shifted to providing a staffing level that would cover average system requirements. FAA accomplished this shift by reducing the number of sectors and terminal radar positions upon which staffing was based. FAA then assumed that overtime would be used to cover traffic peaks, prime annual leave periods and other special requirements." In other words, the FAA would compel fewer controllers to work harder and make up any shortfall with forced overtime, in much the same way that a rider might whip a horse to keep it running past the point of exhaustion.

FPL levels

The FAA now has about the same number of air traffic controllers working for it as it did when PATCO went on strike. But, according to a September 1991 GAO report, FPL levels remain 2400 fewer than before the strike, even though the training and experience required to become an FPL has been reduced. This at the same time that levels of air traffic have dramatically increased.

Clearly the FAA's controller work force needs to increase in size and experience to meet growing capacity levels. According to Joseph M. Bellino, executive vice president of NATCA, "Lower staffing of controllers not only makes it difficult to find qualified replacements, it adds to the overall early retirement problem by increasing stressful work place conditions, resulting in some controllers retiring due to stress-related medical problems." Moreover, a dramatic increase in experienced controllers is going to be needed to safely accommodate the expected increases in air traffic anticipated by the year 2000 and to allow controllers to certify on the new ATC equipment that will be coming on-line if the modernization effort ever bears fruit.

But how to do that, especially in light of the fact that, according to NATCA, almost 50 percent of current controllers will be eligible to retire by 1995?

Rehire the fired controllers

"Of the 11,300 PATCO members who were terminated, between 3000 and 4000 would be interested in returning to the FAA as air traffic controllers."

Bill Taylor,
publisher of *PATCO Lives*, August, 1992

The time has come to let bygones be bygones, and rehire any former PATCO controllers who still want to work ATC and who still possess the ability to do the job. If this were simply a matter of humane consideration for the thousands who lost their professions, it would be worthwhile. But rehiring the controllers would do more than help individuals, it would promote the national interest and improve the aviation safety system. Here's why:

• The PATCO controllers are a national resource. According to Bill Taylor, between $175,000–$200,000 of taxpayers' money was spent to train and provide on-the-job experience for each fired controller. The knowledge they possess and the experiences they have had are invaluable and need to be passed on to the new crop of controllers.

• The current controllers would not resent a rehiring of PATCO people. We spoke to many controllers about this issue: NATCA officials, former PATCO controllers who were not fired, and controllers hired after the strike. Not one said they would resent a rehiring of qualified PATCO controllers. Most enthusiastically welcomed the prospect.

• The FAA is the only government agency refusing to hire former PATCO members. It is ironic that while civilian aviation was being denied their expertise, the military wisely pursued a different policy. Moreover, many foreign countries have employed former PATCO controllers. Indeed, many PATCO members worked ATC in support of the Persian Gulf War.

• PATCO controllers very quickly would add to the FPL work force. According to several controllers we spoke with, it would only take a few months for most PATCO controllers to get recertified as FPLs. Many who have worked for the military would not need that amount of time. How better to upgrade the quality of the air traffic controller work force than to hire experts who will not need a lot of additional schooling or training?

There might be those who would say that rehiring PATCO people would reward unlawful behavior. But that attitude is a cutting off of the national nose to spite the controllers' faces. Most PATCO people have rebuilt their lives after suffering financially and emotionally for the choice they made back in 1981. But it is our safety that might be compromised by refusing to allow the most qualified people to sit at the ATC workstations. Surely, there must be a place in our national heart for forgiveness and redemption—especially when the national interest would be so well served.

Let us hope that President Clinton's stated desire to eliminate the ban on fired controllers can be drawn up and implemented. Then let us hope that FAA will accept back those controllers who remain qualified to work ATC so that they can be retrained and recertified, thereby increasing the number of FPL controllers available to the FAA and hopefully increasing the level of safety of the ATC system.

11

Troubled technology

"The unhappy fact is that our air traffic control system was not designed to handle today's volumes and it was not designed to handle the very closely grouped flows of aircraft that hub and spoke systems generate."

Robert Crandall,
president of American Airlines, speaking before the
Committee on Commerce, Science, and Transportation,
Subcommittee on Aviation, 1989

Traditionally, the ATC system has operated as a symbiosis of the technological and the human. People have always been the heart and brain of the ATC system. Ultimate decisions have rested with humans—air traffic controllers and pilots—who work as a team to keep planes apart and whose experience and skill often make the difference between a little-noticed near miss and a tragedy that makes headlines around the world. At the same time, technological systems, such as radar and computers, have served as the eyes and ears of air traffic control, perceiving far more than any human possibly could detect about emerging flight patterns and the potential for impending collisions and issuing warnings so that human solution-making could occur.

Just as the human element of air traffic control has experienced significant problems over the last decade, so too has the technological element. As the FAA's technological modernization program has foundered, much of the equipment currently in use has grown old and obsolete, increasingly subject to malfunction and breakdown. At the same time, there have been cutbacks in the number of technicians employed by the FAA to keep the equipment up and running. Meanwhile, emerging technologies in which great hope is placed by the FAA to increase the safety of the ATC system, have experienced a rocky break-in period that might be endangering the flying public.

This chapter examines both areas of concern. First, some of the problems with existing equipment will be outlined. Then, the ongoing controversy between pilots and air traffic controllers over the safety of TCAS (pronounced tee-kas and explained in this chapter), the latest technology designed to avert midair collisions.

System breakdown

"You want to know how well the equipment is working? No comment."

**Answer of an air traffic controller
when asked about systems breakdown**

Much of the current equipment on-line in air traffic control facilities is increasingly subject to breakdown and malfunction. This is happening at a time when the FAA is attempting to squeeze more efficiency out of the system. William A. Faville Jr., director of safety and technology for NATCA stated, "The space between aircraft in terminal areas is being reduced from 3 miles to 2½. Under ideal conditions, it is harder to make a hole for takeoffs. But with the equipment increasingly having trouble, that adds to the pressure on our controllers." (When asked on January 28, 1993, whether separation standards between aircraft were being degraded, Hank Price of the public affairs office of the FAA avoided the query by stating, "There are many variations of separation requirements. You'll have to ask about specific airports during specific flying conditions for me to answer that question.")

Laura E. McGrath, an official of PASS, the union which represents the technicians who maintain and repair ATC equipment, said in the summer of 1992 that "Much of the equipment that is used is well past its projected life expectancy. There's more bad news." she adds. "There are more problems being experienced with the equipment than shows up in the FAA statistics. For example, if an entire system experiences an outage that lasts less than a minute, it is not reportable. But that minute can be crucial when airplanes are flying at hundreds of miles an hour."

Ms. McGrath also gave another way in which the FAA's statistics paint a too rosy picture. "If a component of a system fails but not the entire system, it may not make it onto the government's statistical data which keeps track of the national rate of equipment problems." In other words, the FAA uses selective recordkeeping to make the equipment appear to be more reliable than it really is.

This concern was confirmed by the GAO in August 1991. It reported that the FAA does not generate performance indicators for failed component equipment that make up part of an entire ATC system. Yet a partial failure of a system can have a significant adverse impact on safety.

As an example, the GAO described the danger that was created at an air route traffic control center when one radar display screen malfunctioned, even though the radar equipment for the rest of the center continued to operate: "Another controller temporarily had to assume responsibility for the airspace served by the failed radar display in addition to his assigned airspace. The sudden increase in volume and complexity of air traffic for this controller contributed to the controller's not maintaining the minimum required separation between aircraft—two aircraft got too close together, creating a potentially dangerous situation in the air."

The GAO checked to see if a record of this serious equipment failure made it into the FAA's national data base (the National Airspace Performance Reporting System), which keeps track of serious equipment failure for purposes of measuring the reliability of ATC equipment. It had not. Instead, the record was kept in a different data bank, maintained at the location where the failure occurred (the corrective maintenance data base). This form of recordkeeping makes the system appear more reliable than it really is. During a 12-month period at one center alone, the GAO reported that there were 1935 failures or malfunctions of equipment, such as controller radar displays and control panels. Of these, only 170 made it into the national data base.

The GAO and others have investigated additional reported problems with ATC equipment and technology as follows.

Software malfunctions

The FAA has replaced its old computer hardware system with new equipment known as the *Host*. Host hardware is intended to increase safety and efficiency until it can be replaced by an entirely new system in the late 1990s (the *Advanced Automated System*). Unfortunately, new hardware is being used with a modified version of old computer program software created in the 1960s. Because the software has been rewritten many times, it has become unduly complicated and increasingly difficult to maintain.

So many software difficulties have occurred in recent years that there is a long backlog of unresolved problems. As of June 30, 1991, there were 1662 reported problems that were not resolved. Of these, 74 percent were considered by the FAA to have the potential to adversely affect the air traffic system by causing system interruptions or otherwise disrupting the flow of information to air traffic controllers. Some of these interruptions might only last seconds, other interruptions might last minutes. Whether for a long or short period, the outages might impede the air traffic controllers' ability to track aircraft.

The FAA attributes its backlog of software problems and the agency's continued need to rely on temporary fixes to a lack of necessary resources. This is a valid complaint and another reason for the Congress to release the current surplus in the Aviation Trust Fund to allow that money to be put to its intended use.

Airport surface detection equipment (ASDE)

ASDE is designed to help ground controllers prevent planes from colliding while taxiing at airports. An advanced system, known as ASDE-3, is currently in development and testing. ASDE-2 is in use in many airports.

ASDE is most important during inclement or foggy weather and at night when the tower controller cannot visually keep track of planes. According to the testimony of R. Steve Bell, president of NATCA, given before the House Government Operations Subcommittee on July 10, 1991, ASDE-2 and ASDE-3 suffer from significant technical problems. With regard to ASDE-2, Bell testified: "Sometimes it splits one large target into two .... During bad weather, when it is most needed, ASDE-2 is unreliable. Controllers lose approximately 25 to 35 percent of the display when it rains."

The new system being developed also has problems. According to Bell, "The principal problem associated with ASDE-3 is that of split targets. Large targets, especially aircraft with high T-tails [stabilizer and elevator at the top of the tail section, forming a T], such as an MD-80, often produce two if not three targets. There is usually one large target and then one or two other smaller targets surrounding it like small moons, which could easily be confused with a (car or truck), person, or small aircraft .... We certainly do not need controllers trying to differentiate between real and phantom targets, or make assumptions that certain aircraft will give off additional targets." The split target problem is not expected to be resolved until the turn of the century.

William Faville of NATCA told us that ASDE has another problem. "The screen is small and, worse, there is no color enhancement for any air traffic tower display. The scopes and blips are green-on-green. If there is any type of alarm, warning of pending trouble, there is no color differentiation between traffic that is normal and those planes which are in danger. There is a bell and a flash, but the time it takes to find the trouble may be more than the time it takes for vehicles to collide."

Communication outages

Most ATC facilities depend upon regular telephone lines to communicate. That leaves the controllers vulnerable to telephone outages. According to a September 1991 House Subcommittee on Telecommunications and Finance report, there were 114 major outages averaging 6.1 hours, between August 1990 and August 1991. (A major outage was defined in the memo as one that had a significant "operational impact, including air traffic delays, increased air traffic workload, and safety concerns.")

In 1991, a major telephone outage in the New York area created havoc in the area's air traffic control. First, imagine the horror of being an air traffic controller and losing the radar image. You'd have to establish a visual image in your head as to where the aircraft were and try to keep the planes in your sector apart based upon where you think that they have moved to. In an instant, you'd be back to the level of control available in the 1930s. Second, imagine being the pilot responsible for the lives of several hundred people who discovers that your plane and others like it are, for all practical purposes, flying blind.

The FAA has a plan to solve its problem of having to rely on local phone company service in its ATC functions. The *Leased*

Interfacility National Airspace Communications System (LINCS) is designed to be the FAA's private communication system, designed to make the FAA independent of general-service telephone lines. LINCS is being installed by MCI Telecommunications Company and is expected to be on-line nationwide by 1995. Given the record of the FAA's modernization program, there is room for skepticism that the time goal will be met; however, as of February 1, 1993, the program was not behind its installation schedule. William Faville of NATCA told us that as of January 28, 1993, the controllers had not seen enough of the system to evaluate its performance.

The current ATC system is too reliant upon outdated technology, obsolete equipment, jury-rigged software, and telephone services that are not within the control of the FAA. The modernization effort is designed to cure these problems, but as we have seen, the modernization effort is proceeding at an agonizingly slow pace. Even when new technology comes on-line, there is no guarantee that it will work properly.

It is hard to have confidence in a safety system so vulnerable to the often-hear lament: "We are sorry for the interruption in service but we are experiencing technical difficulties beyond our control."

The TCAS controversy

"The individual pilots and controllers we interviewed gave mixed reviews of TCAS. A number of pilots said they believed that TCAS is a good system or told us of incidents in which TCAS had helped them avoid other aircraft. Some pilots, however, were less complimentary, stating that TCAS interrupts normal flight operations. Most of the 38 controllers who we interviewed agreed that TCAS is a good concept, but stated that problems exist."

GAO report, March 1992

One would think that a *traffic alert and collision avoidance system* (TCAS) would be the last technology to be the subject of heated and protracted controversy. Its purpose is laudatory: to warn pilots of impending midair collisions, so that they can take immediate evasive action. Yet, air traffic controllers insist the technology as functioning is potentially a deadly hazard; pilots are equally adamant that it is a valuable safety tool.

Three different types of TCAS are classified -1, -2, and -3. TCAS-1, issues oral traffic warnings when other planes are nearby, but does not direct pilots on how to avoid them. TCAS-1 will be required on all commuter planes with 10–30 seats by February 1995. TCAS-2, is currently in use in most commercial transport planes that carry more than 30 passengers. It warns pilots of an impending collision and gives *resolution advisories* (RA) on whether to descend or climb to avoid a collision. TCAS-3, still in development, would warn pilots of an impending collision and in addition communicate RAs telling the pilot to climb or descend, would also be able to tell the pilot to turn left or right. TCAS-3 is years away from installation.

In a nutshell, here is the problem. The pilots claim that TCAS-2 is already saving lives by averting midair collisions. The air traffic controllers claim that TCAS-2 is issuing false alarms, causing pilots to take unnecessary avoidance action without advising ATC, thereby increasing the chance of a midair collision. Both sides are adamant that they are correct.

The pilot's case

The pilots are very vocal in their support of TCAS. J. Randolf Babbitt, president of the Air Line Pilots Association told us, "What you have with TCAS, is a device that is monitoring for (air traffic control) mistakes. We've had too many cases where the controller, through a flaw in the software or a new controller, made a mistake. They're people. They make mistakes. They didn't see something happen. Thanks to TCAS, lives have been saved."

In August 1992, the ALPA publication *Air Line Pilot Magazine*, published a chilling true-story account of two planes that might have collided but for TCAS.

(From an abridged version of the article, "TCAS Warning Averts Disaster," by Jim Portale, first published in *Air Line Pilot Magazine*, August 1992. Used with permission of the author and the magazine.)

"USAir 000, traffic at ten o'clock, five miles, southbound at seven thousand feet," said approach control.

"There he is, Steve, beneath us and converging," I said.

"Yes, I see him."

"USAir 000, traffic twelve o'clock, less than a mile," said Approach.

Steve keyed the mike. "Approach, USAir 000 has traffic in sight."

"USAir 000. Maintain visual separation from the traffic."

Steve responded: "Unable to maintain visual. We can take a vector to the west."

After a short silence, approach said, "Roger, USAir 000. How about a vector to the east? Turn left heading one five zero and maintain eight thousand. I'll advise."

"Approach, USAir 000. We're showing thunderstorms ahead on this heading. We'd like to get a vector back toward the west."

By this time, the traffic had flown under our aircraft and was once again visible.

"I've got him over here, Steve," I said as I departed 8000 feet for 7000 feet; however, something just didn't look right. So, I kept my eye on the traffic as I leveled at 7000 feet. Now I was sure.

"Steve, take a look at this guy. What altitude did approach say he was?"

"Six thousand feet. Why, what altitude is he at?"

"It sure looks like our attitude," I said as the twin-engine commuter flew away into the haze.

"USAir 000, traffic at two o'clock is at six thousand feet. Maintain seven thousand."

As our aircraft was turning toward a heading of two three zero, I began searching hard for that commuter traffic.

Steve asked, "Do you see that guy?"

"No, not yet, but wait—there he is. We've got a pretty good closure on him and he sure looks at our altitude."

"TRAFFIC, TRAFFIC!" signaled TCAS, confirming what we already knew.

"We're flying straight into him, Steve. Let's get another altitude."

"Keep an eye on him."

"No problem." I responded.

"Approach, USAir 000. That traffic is co-altitude. We—"

"DESCEND! DESCEND! DESCEND!" commanded TCAS. My eyes met Steve's for a split second, and we both glanced at the TCAS scope as I started a descent out of 7000 feet.

We had a visual on the traffic, and I knew we weren't going to hit him. I felt very uncomfortable departing an assigned IFR altitude without a clearance. The maneuver was smooth and gentle—no one in back suspected anything unusual. The traffic flew directly over the top of us, and we had a good 500 to 700 feet of vertical separation.

Short silence from approach control: then, "USAir 000, descend and maintain five thousand feet. Fly heading two-seven zero."

"USAir 000. Turn right heading three four zero. Descend and maintain four thousand feet."

I felt relieved that we were once again on an assigned IFR altitude as I descended through 5000 feet. We had entered the clouds at about 6000 feet. The visibility was near zero and it was instrument meteorological conditions [very poor, perhaps virtually no, visibility] all the way to the ground.

I shook my head slowly and said sarcastically, "Well, that was fun."

Steve replied. "Makes you wonder, huh?"

"TRAFFIC! TRAFFIC!" came from TCAS.

Steve and I were trying to make sense of the TCAS scope.

Why was TCAS still reporting the commuter plane and what were the odds of a second, independent traffic conflict? All this took place in a period of not more than 10 seconds.

Steve was obviously feeling as uncomfortable as I when he keyed the mike. "Approach, USAir 000—"

Silence.

"DESCEND! DESCEND! DESCEND!" commanded TCAS.

Here we go again, I thought.

Only this time there was a huge difference—we were in near zero visibility. Departing an IFR altitude without a clearance is one of the most uncomfortable decisions you'll ever deal with in peacetime aviation.

"INCREASE DESCENT!" screamed TCAS at a volume I'd not heard before.

No time for smoothness—I pushed hard on the yoke, rolled in a little right bank, and applied bottom rudder in an effort to achieve the TCAS-commanded rate of descent.

"There it is!" yelled Steve.

I looked up and could not believe what I saw— the illuminating lights of a Boeing 757. Our closure rate was 500 knots, and we had absolutely no time to react to the visual.

The huge jet roared past as I found myself bracing for the impact. We looked straight into its left engine. The engine cowl width exceeded the width of our windscreen—it was close!

We were now heading toward the ocean. We had departed an IFR altitude without a clearance and under the control of an FAA controller who was having a worse day than we were.

"I need an altitude, Steve."

"Approach, USAir 000. You just turned us directly into an aircraft!" Steve's voice revealed he was less than happy.

"Yeah. We just got a good look at USAir," said the pilot of the other jet.

Silence from approach control.

I picked 4000 feet for level-off. I found the TCAS scope was now a vital part of my cross-checks. The information that TCAS supplied replaced what a controller normally provides.

A new and different voice responded from approach. "USAir 000, fly heading zero niner zero."

"Approach, I'd like you to save the tapes on this near miss."

"USAir, roger."

And so it went.

Controllers are just people, and like all people, they sometimes make mistakes. To point an accusing finger serves no purpose. Far better instead is emphasizing the positive side of this incident—TCAS technology saved hundreds of lives this day.

Pilot unions contend that incidents such as this are not isolated, that at least 10 collisions have been averted based upon information from TCAS-2 equipment on board commercial jets. The pilot's primary complaint is that the development of TCAS-3 has been delayed by the FAA, which has instead spent TCAS development money attempting to correct TCAS-2 problems.

The controllers' position

The air traffic controllers are equally insistent that TCAS performance flaws represent a potential hazard to commercial aviation. On August 4, 1992, Barry Krasner, president of NATCA, testified before the Aviation Subcommittee, stating in part:

> I wish I could come before you today and tell you TCAS is working as originally conceived and the air traffic control system is safer as a result. Unfortunately, I cannot do so with a clear conscience. We have documentation ... that shows TCAS has not only been a disappointment, but highly disruptive to the safety of the air traffic control system. If allowed to continue without proper oversight, our next testimony before this subcommittee might very well be that which claims the National Airspace System is no longer safe ....
>
> NATCA's major concerns with TCAS are:
>
> One, TCAS causes pilots to take unnecessary deviations because of false TCAS alerts. From the start, we have experienced problems with TCAS issuing Resolution Advisories which are followed even though traffic is appropriately separated .... When a pilot responds to an RA generated by a false TCAS warning, the results can be catastrophic if his plane strays from a controller-directed altitude into the path of another aircraft ....
>
> Two, TCAS is incompatible with new high-performance aircraft. New high-performance aircraft

climb at a higher rate than anticipated in TCAS logic. For example, a departing aircraft climbs out rapidly and is cleared by ATC to level off at 1000 feet below another aircraft. Unfortunately, TCAS on an arriving aircraft, approaching from the same fix from an opposite direction, does not know that the departing aircraft will level off. The RA is given, causing the pilot to deviate from a safe altitude without prior knowledge or consent of the controller.

Three, TCAS interferes with ground-based radar ....

Four, ghost targets are still appearing. In the month of May 1992 alone, there were 22 false RAs reported due to ghost targets .... (In one case) a United Airlines (pilot) was warned by his TCAS that he had a flight of four aircraft head-on at the same altitude (37,000 feet). The pilot, following the RA, climbed 800 feet to 37,800 feet before the controller could advise him that he was responding to false targets. The United jet descended back to 37,000 feet but had already compromised separation with traffic in the opposite direction at 39,000 feet. The minimum separation at these altitudes is 2000 feet.

Five, TCAS causes pilots to second-guess directions given by controllers .... When TCAS sounds, which it does far too often in normal traffic sequencing situations, the pilot probably thinks the controller 'missed one' and he takes evasive action. Such evasive actions not only wreak havoc on the system, but the pilot's false perceptions of controller error denigrates the critical working relationship between controllers and pilots ....

Other groups will assert to you today that TCAS has saved us from 10 midair collisions this year alone. I would like to make two points about such a statement. One, are we to believe that without TCAS we would have had more midair collisions this year than we have had over the past 20 years? And, two, If (that) is true, then we have dramatic core safety problems that signify the total collapse of this nation's air control system.

To support its position, NATCA has published statistics compiled from reports received from U.S. air traffic controllers; the reports were submitted May 1991–July 1992 to the FAA through the TCAS II Transition Program office:

TCAS Report
Separation lost due to action taken by invalid RA: 56

	Number	*Percent*
Controller reports filed	2781	100
Reports from terminals	1854	67
Reports from enroute	927	33
Invalid TCAS RA occurrence (Approved separation existed before RA)	1741	63
Valid TCAS RA occurrence	203	7
Undetermined validity	837	30
Unnecessary missed approaches (Only tabulated since May 1992)	54	8
Ghost or phantom targets	132	19
TCAS RA was the same maneuver cssontroller would have issued	256	9
ALTITUDE AT WHICH RA OCCURRED		
Surface to 2500	350	13
2500 to 10,000	977	35
10,000 to 18,000	607	22
18,000 to 29,000	329	12
29,000 and above	336	12
Not reported	182	7
ALTITUDE DEVIATION AMOUNT		
0 feet	182	7
Less than 300 feet	224	8
300 to 500 feet	475	17

Continued on p. 154.

Continued from p. 153.

500 to 700 feet	514	18
700 to 1000 feet	215	8
More than 1000 feet	272	10
No report	899	32

These statistics, if true, paint a disturbing picture. During the the 13 months covered by the statistics, 63 percent of all TCAS RAs were in error. Also, 48 percent of all TCAS RAs occurred during airport approach, landing, or takeoff—up to approximately 10,000 feet, the area with more traffic and a reduced margin of error for altitude and heading deviations compared to higher altitudes. Moreover, according William Faville of NATCA, who discussed these statistics with us, 10–12 percent of the unauthorized flight deviations caused a plane to leave one controller's airspace and enter another controller's airspace without a formal handoff or other coordination.

That is dangerous. The controller responsible for airspace that the plane unexpectedly enters, will be unprepared to take control of the flight and might not notice the intrusion. That could lead to real trouble, including a midair collision.

Who is right?

Pilots and the controllers seem to have rightness and safety on their side. A March 1992 GAO report on the issue, stated:

> TCAS is now installed in a substantial portion of the U.S. commercial fleet, and both the Air Line Pilots Association and FAA believe that the system adds a margin of safety to air travel.
>
> However, problems that have emerged prevent the system from reaching its full potential. The aviation community is nearly unanimous in recognizing that TCAS needs to be improved because it issues too many unnecessary alerts, causes excessive altitude deviations (over 1000 feet), and causes pilots to miss landing approaches. Pilots and air traffic controllers stated that these problems reduce users' confidence in TCAS and the margin of safety that the system provides.

In other words, *both* sides are right.

So, what is to be done? Some people, such as Paul D. Russell, chief of product safety for Boeing Commercial Airplane Group, would prefer to take TCAS off-line until it is perfected; however, a compromise between the controllers' and pilots' positions—a compromise that will permit TCAS to avert potential midair collisions while not creating the threat of accidents caused by uncontrolled deviations—might be the better way to go. After sorting through the recommendations of the pilots and controllers and discussing the issue with the Air Transport Association, and others, it would seem prudent that the FAA:

- Quickly, increase the number of FPL air traffic controllers, using former PATCO controllers to increase the reliability of ATC. That should reduce the number of controller errors that lead to a TCAS cockpit alert.

- Establish a maximum permitted deviation of 500 feet in response to a TCAS RA. That should be sufficient to resolve conflicts without the danger of straying into another plane's path.

- Alter TCAS software so that alerts are triggered only when planes violate air traffic control separation standards. Currently, TCAS alarms can ring even when planes safely exceed minimum separation standards. According to the GAO, such a change would not require significant software modifications because no new functions are being introduced.

- Mandate TCAS alerts in pilot flight simulator training so that pilots have experience in reacting to them.

- Release money from the Aviation Trust Fund to fully test and perfect the TCAS system so that pilots and controllers can feel comfortable that safety is not compromised.

Unquestionably, TCAS offers the aviation system a significant opportunity to increase the margin of safety by virtually eliminating midair collisions—in much the same way that the ground proximity warning system has made controlled flights into terrain an accident of the past (on Part 121 flights). But we have not yet traveled from here to there. The need to develop an effective and operationally safe TCAS system is an unfinished task that urgently needs to be completed if, as projections predict, there will soon be more planes flying in an already overcrowded sky.

Part IV

The equipment

"The FAA does not and cannot serve as a guarantor of aviation safety. The responsibility for safe design, operation and maintenance rests primarily and ultimately with each manufacturer and each airline."

Leroy A. Keith, manager of FAA's transport airplane directorate aircraft certification service, speaking at the Flight Safety Foundation 43rd annual International Air Safety Seminar, 1990

This part investigates the most pressing safety issues involving the equipment used in commercial aviation. Chapter 12 describes the aging aircraft crisis. The U.S. civilian transport fleet is the oldest in the Western world. These geriatric planes present significant challenges to safe flying and quality maintenance practices. The FAA and the industry have energetically responded to the issue but the question remains: Are their efforts sufficient to maintain safety levels?

Crash survivability is another pressing issue. In addition to establishing improved cabin fire safety standards (while falling short in requiring retrofitting, as discussed in chapter 7), the FAA has also required that lighting be installed on cabin floors to guide passengers to an exit during an evacuation, has required smoke detectors to be installed in lavatories, and ordered automatic fire extinguishers to be placed in lavatory trash cans. As laudatory as these steps are, they have not gone far enough to protect passenger safety. Safety equipment such as escape (smoke) hoods and child restraint safety seats need to be mandated by the FAA to be part of every airplane's minimum equipment list (MEL).

Chapter 14 briefly covers issues of aircraft certification and the contention of critics that airworthiness tests are stacked in favor of the airlines. The chapter describes attempts to make transport aircraft less vulnerable to explosives that are smuggled on board.

12

Aging aircraft

"The aviation community was debating the issue (of multiple site damage on aging aircraft) as part of our increased understanding of how aircraft structures behave ... when, in fact, multiple site damage occurred on the Aloha Airline aircraft. It was a tragic and startling demonstration that one side of the argument had been proven dramatically correct."

Anthony J. Broderick,
FAA associate administrator for
regulation and certification, August 1992

Aging aircraft and what to do about them is one of the great challenges facing commercial aviation in the 1990s. The airlines are faced with a fiscal conundrum: they can continue to fly geriatric aircraft, which use more fuel, require more maintenance, and are generally more expensive to operate, or they can buy new, technologically advanced and more efficient aircraft that are expensive to purchase. Either decision causes airlines to continue to hemorrhage red ink all over profit and loss statements. This at a time when most major airlines are already financially anemic and burning up with debt-fever after years of excess capacity, the costly merger mania of the eighties, and the fiscal after-effects of the recession.

The Aloha Airlines tragedy

The philosophy about aging aircraft can be divided into two eras:

- B.A. Before Aloha (Airlines accident)
- A.A. After Aloha (Airlines accident)

April 28, 1988
Hawaiian Islands

Aloha Airlines Flight 243 has just leveled off at 24,000 feet en route to Honolulu, Hawaii, from Hilo. The aircraft is on its seventh flight of the day, having already flown one round-trip flight between Honolulu and Hilo, Maui and Kauai. Every aspect of each flight has been routine.

The plane, a Boeing 737-200, was delivered to Aloha Airlines on May 10, 1969. In April 1988 it is the second oldest operating 737 in the world, as measured in landings, having flown 89,680 cycles. A 737 is considered "high time" by the aviation community when it has flown 60,000 cycles.

Suddenly and with no warning, both pilots hear a loud clap and then a whooshing sound. This startling noise is followed by the surrealistic sound of wind. This shouldn't be happening. Wind can't be heard in a cockpit. The alarmed pilot turns in his chair and barely believes the horrific sight—the cockpit door has disappeared. Through the portal, he can see blue sky where the first-class ceiling should be. Unbelievably, the top of the fuselage has violently ripped off the plane.

The pilot begins an emergency descent.

In the passenger cabin, an explosive decompression has occurred.

(Fortunately, at the time of the incident, the seat belt sign was lit and all of the passengers were restrained in their seats. Tragically, Clarabelle Lansing, the No. 1 flight attendant was standing in the aisle in first class. As the roof ripped off the plane, to the horror of those around her, she was immediately swept out of the cabin through a hole in the left side of the fuselage. Her body will never be found. The

No. 2 flight attendant was thrown to the floor. She crawled up and down the aisle of the wind-swept cabin, rendering assistance and calming the passengers. The No. 3 flight attendant was struck in the head by flying debris and was unable to perform her duties. She suffered a concussion and severe head lacerations.)

After some difficulties communicating with air traffic control, the first officer switches to the Maui tower frequency and declares an emergency. Maui acknowledges and begins emergency notifications based upon the first officer's report of rapid decompression.

The flight to Maui is harrowing. The pilots cannot communicate with the flight attendants. The plane is becoming less controllable as the pilot slows down in preparation for landing.

As the plane approaches Maui, the nose gear does not come down. "We don't have a nose gear," the crew warns the Maui tower. "We'll need all the equipment you've got." After much effort, the nose gear is manually extended. Then, the captain senses a yawing motion. The No. 1 engine has failed. He tries to restart the engine without response. The plane is shaking and rocking. But the pilot is able to land.

The plane is evacuated. Fortunately, 94 out of 95 people on board the flight escape with their lives. Eight of those are seriously injured and 57 suffer minor injuries.

Approximately 18 feet of fuselage had ripped off the B-737 flying as Aloha Airlines Flight 243. What could have caused such a horrifying and unexpected occurrence? Fuselage failure caused by metal fatigue.

It's a simple matter of physics. Take a steel paper clip and re-peatedly bend it back and forth. Eventually, the clip can be broken in two when metal fatigue has sufficiently weakened the integrity of its structure. Similarly, but on a far larger scale and over a much longer period of time, metal fatigue can weaken a jet fuselage. If not discovered and repaired, the weakened structure can cause accidents such as Aloha Airlines Flight 243.

The primary culprit causing metal fatigue is the pressurization process that permits commercial plane passengers and crew to breathe normally at an altitude where the air is too thin to support life. This pressurization reacts with the lower pressure in the outside environment causing an inflating and deflating type of stress that is applied against the metal fuselage; aircraft are engineered to be stressed by normal pressurization and depressurization. Eventually, this might lead to cracking in the metal skin. If the cracking is not repaired, or the cracked fuselage section replaced, these cracks can enlarge and expand, and become dangerous to the flight integrity of the plane. Add the problem of corrosion around rivets that often occurs to aircraft that operate over or near oceans, and older planes become potential flying death traps.

This is not news. The danger of fatigue cracking has been known for years. What the Aloha Airlines accident did was challenge the industry's entire approach toward preventing fuselage cracking associated with aging aircraft from becoming a safety hazard.

The government and industry react

"The 'graying' of America's civil aviation fleet has changed forever not just the way aircraft maintenance is conducted—but more importantly, it has radically changed our thinking about maintenance—our philosophy, if you will, regarding the conduct of maintenance."

Congressman James L. Oberstar,
Chairman, Subcommittee on Aviation speaking before the
Second annual Aging Aircraft Conference, October 1989

The news of Aloha Airlines hit the commercial aviation community like a thunderbolt. Entrenched attitudes were forced to give way to a new, frightening reality. Regulators and the industry were galvanized as they rarely had been before.

The before-Aloha philosophy of aging aircraft
Prior to the Aloha tragedy, the gurus of aviation believed that regular and ongoing maintenance inspections could prevent Aloha-type accidents. Years of experience and extensive studies have long enabled the FAA, manufacturers, and airlines to predict where fuselage cracking is likely to occur as an aircraft ages. The B.A. belief

was one of "inspect and repair." Under this philosophy, when cracks were discovered, they would be monitored until they reached a certain size, whereupon a repair would be made. The Aloha Airlines tragedy revealed the fatal flaw in this maintenance philosophy: Inspections do not necessarily discover all cracks.

The government's response

"(Before Aloha) we always worked on the assumption that said an aircraft is not like an automobile," Joseph Del Balzo, the FAA's director of systems operations told us in August 1992. "Aircraft are essentially rebuilt during their lifetime, (so, it was believed that) it is as good today as it was 20 years ago." With Aloha, this attitude was shaken to its very core.

The FAA and the commercial aviation industry suddenly had a real problem on their hands. If inspections could not be relied upon to discover and correct metal fatigue cracking, the FAA might have to promulgate a rule requiring mandatory retirement of aircraft from service after reaching a certain age, based upon cycles. Otherwise, safety would be compromised. The public would lose faith in flying. The industry would be devastated financially.

Acting with uncharacteristic promptness, a month after the accident, the FAA convened an International Conference on Aging Airplanes to reevaluate the agency's and the industry's approach to the issue of aging aircraft. Approximately 400 representatives of airlines, manufacturers, and regulatory authorities from 12 countries participated. The Conference made 27 recommendations to the FAA and to the industry advising changes in regulatory philosophy, increased reliance upon nonvisual inspection techniques, improved maintenance recordkeeping, and new directions for research. A second conference was held in October 1989, which resulted in additional recommendations.

Congress also became involved in the issue; bills were introduced; hearings were held; votes were taken. The Aging Aircraft Safety Act was passed and was signed by President Bush, becoming law in 1991.

The after-Aloha approach to aging aircraft

The Aging Aircraft Safety Act compels, among other mandates, that the FAA create rules "to assure the continuing airworthiness of aging aircraft" by requiring airline operators to demonstrate that "maintenance of aircraft's structure, skin and other age-sensitive parts and components" have been adequate and timely enough to ensure the highest degree of safety on all aircraft age 15 years or older.

The general mandate of Congress resulted in a specific approach that upheld the FAA's desire to avoid mandatory retirement for aging aircraft. Under the new approach, safety is not dependent upon inspectors discovering cracks and the airlines repairing them when they grow large enough to require repair. In Congressman James L. Oberstar's words, maintenance was changed to a new philosophy of terminate and replace sections of planes at specific intervals.

Here's how the new system works: The FAA maintains an ongoing committee to oversee issues involving aging aircraft; the Airworthiness Assurance Task Force is made up of a coalition of manufacturers, airlines, and regulatory agencies. The FAA also has issued mandatory airworthiness directives requiring that approximately 1400 of the oldest of the nation's 4100 transport aircraft fleet, undergo extensive structural modification to guard against metal fatigue cracking, *regardless of whether any actual cracks have been detected.* These repairs also are mandatory for aircraft that are considered "aged" after that date based upon a threshold of cycles set for each individual model of aircraft flown. The idea is to replace suspect portions of a fuselage at a specific age whether the section, in fact, actually needs the repairs or not.

The FAA also instituted the Corrosion Prevention Control Program, which has created minimum procedures to fight corrosion if the airline's own program is unsuccessful in preventing corrosive damage. Any alternate means of preventing corrosion, other than that established by the FAA, must have the agency's specific approval.

The mandatory repair program instituted by the FAA and the industry is a welcome step forward in protecting the safety of the flying public. (The new rules are especially welcome in light of the growing industry practice of leasing planes, thereby tempting the leasing airline to delay major maintenance when a plane is due to be returned to its owner at the expiration of the lease.) Compliments for the program have come from many quarters, even sectors of the aviation safety community that usually disagree with each other. For example, when asked about the aging aircraft program, William Jackman, of the Air Transport Association, answered, "There has never been anything that worked as well in my 25 years in the field." Public Citizen attorney Cornish Hitchcock, former director of Aviation Consumer Action Group and a long-time industry critic, is also complimentary, stating, "This is the best example I can think of where the industry believed that it was in their enlightened self-interest to make hard and important changes."

Still, an important question remains: does the aging aircraft program go far enough in protecting the public's safety? Unfortunately, we have our doubts.

First, the industry continues to cling to the belief that properly designed and maintained planes need never be taken out of service for safety reasons. In his presentation to the Flight Safety Foundation's International Air Safety Seminar in 1990, Leroy A. Keith of the FAA stated, "The underlying philosophy ... to aircraft continued operational safety is that an airplane is capable of operating safely indefinitely if properly designed, inspected, and maintained .... Through all the technical reevaluations and soul-searching that followed the Aloha accident, we have found no reason to abandon this philosophy."

Is there not a degree of hubris in the belief that humans have the ability to use technology to solve every problem and overcome all safety hazards? If nothing else, the *Titanic's* sinking and the *Challenger* shuttle explosion prove that. Moreover, the philosophy that a plane can be flown indefinitely assumes that all planes are properly designed and will be adequately maintained, inspected, and repaired. That assumes an awful lot, especially in these times of industry financial straits. If philosophers and theologians the world over agree on anything, it is that man is imperfect. Mistakes are built-in to the human program. To assume that this reality somehow does not apply to the issue of aging aircraft is shortsighted.

With this caveat in mind, we spoke with several maintenance experts, pilots, and other experts about the aging aircraft program. All agreed that an old airplane, even one that has been properly maintained and inspected, is not the same thing as a new airplane. There was also broad agreement that the regular purchase of new planes is a safer practice than keeping geriatric aircraft in service past their *economic life expectancy*, a time when maintenance costs can outweigh the financial benefit of keeping the plane in service.

There are also ancillary safety benefits that are being lost because planes are not retired as they grow old. Recall the discussion in chapter 7 about the rules requiring newly built planes to have fire retardant materials in cabin interiors and 16-G passenger seats. These important safety improvements do not apply to older aircraft unless a complete interior retrofitting is performed. If geriatric planes had to be retired, the airlines would have to purchase or lease new planes.

That would diminish a myriad of safety problems.

Good-bye aging aircraft crisis.

Adios, the current cabin fire safety problem.

Auf wiedersehn, 9-G seats.

Hello, increased survivability.

Entrez quieter jets.

Bienvenidos, increased efficiency.

There is another potential problem. The FAA and the industry have agreed upon a time for aircraft "old age" at approximately 15 years, depending upon the specific model of aircraft in question. What if this age underestimates the time when metal fatigue first becomes an acute concern?

An accident that happened in August of 1981 in Taiwan, Republic of China, brings this concern to mind. A Far East Air Transport Boeing 737 experienced a sudden decompression and in-flight breakup. The Republic of China's Civil Aeronautics Administration, China's equivalent agency to the FAA, conducted an accident investigation and determined that the probable cause of the accident was:

> ... Extensive corrosion damage in the lower fuselage structures, at a number of locations ... corrosion penetrated through pits, holes and cracks ..., and in addition, the possible existence of undetected cracks because of the great number of pressurized cycles of the aircraft ... interaction of these defects and the damage had so deteriorated that rapid fracture occurred ... resulting (in) rapid decompression and sudden break of the passenger compartment floor beams and connecting frames, cutting control cables and electrical wiring. And eventually loss of power, loss of control, midair disintegration.

(As translated and quoted in the NTSB Aloha
Airlines Flight 243 accident report, page 13.)

What was the number of cycles that ill-fated plane had before
falling apart in flight? Only 33,313. That's more than 50,000 fewer
than the 737 involved in the Aloha Airlines accident and almost
30,000 cycles beneath the 60,000 level that is considered excessive in aviation circles.

There are other concerns about the aging aircraft rules. The
GAO, for one, has questioned the ability of the industry to complete the required repairs of its aged aircraft by the 1994 FAA-im-
posed deadline. In a May 1991 report, "Additional FAA Oversight
Needed of Aging Aircraft Repairs," the GAO stated:

Although the current recession and the recent war with Iraq
have decreased air travel demand and, in turn, airlines' demand
for repair services, GAO believes that demand for repairs eventually will rebound. However, on the basis of the following factors,
some of the U.S. fleet (might) not be repaired before the 1994
deadlines:

- The 1994 deadlines (might) not provide enough time to do the
  AD (airworthiness directive) work.

- Some replacement parts are still scarce, airframe mechanics
  are in short supply, and hangar space has been marginally
  sufficient.

- Although 13 of 17 carriers GAO visited had written plans for
  complying with FAA's new rules, lack of action by (nine
  carriers—including four) major airlines—shows that they
  (might) not comply with the deadline.

- Almost 30 percent of the U.S. airline market is under financial
  stress due to debt, the recession, and high fuel costs and
  cannot afford to repair or keep many of their older planes in
  service.

The GAO report describes the "rock-and-a-hard-place" that
the FAA would be between if the carriers fail to comply with all
aging aircraft airworthiness directives, stating: "Grounding planes
could affect air carriers' flight schedules and some carriers' financial survival; not grounding them has safety implications."

Congressional hearings were held by the House Aviation
Subcommittee in the wake of this disturbing GAO Report where

the industry and FAA response to the conclusions of the GAO were "animated." Joseph D. Vreeman, vice president of engineering and maintenance for the Air Transport Association called the GAO "irresponsible" for using what he called "survey data (that) was not current." He further testified:

> The 1994 deadlines that are incorporated in many of the airworthiness directives that require aircraft modifications are indeed very challenging for our industry to meet. However, despite the complexity, U.S. airlines intend to fully comply with the mandatory modification work. They have a high degree of confidence they will succeed, based on the additional information that has become available in just the past few months.

Anthony J. Broderick of the FAA also testified, stating in part:

> We have had an opportunity to review the newly released Government Accounting Office's report on aging aircraft, dated May 1991. While much of the data in the report is very useful, the overall message sent by the report is off the mark ....
> In its report, GAO concluded that the availability of parts, maintenance space, and mechanics will now prevent compliance with the 1994 date. Information available to the FAA, however, suggests that problems of parts have, for the most part, now been resolved and should not substantially affect efforts to comply with our ADs (airworthiness directives). There remains an industry-wide shortage of maintenance technicians and facilities, but a wide variety of programs and new business ventures are rapidly closing these gaps; therefore, we believe that GAO's information is somewhat outdated. More recent information indicates to us that timely compliance continues to be an attainable goal.

It is certainly to be desired that the airlines comply with their 1994 deadline and thereafter, that they repair every plane that reaches its mandatory refurbishment date; however, when we asked Mr. Broderick in August of 1992 whether he held to his optimistic testimony about the compliance of the airlines with aging aircraft advisory directives, he told us, "Things aren't going as well as they were in 1991 because the economy has continued to suffer and as a result, there are fewer airplanes that have been modified. Now, on the other hand, those that are not modified are going to end up sitting out in the Mojave Desert. [The Mojave, California, Airport in the desert northeast of Los Angeles stores planes not in service. The arid climate limits corrosion and other damage to an aircraft and its components.] We still don't see a substantial problem in the industry's ability to conduct the work we're talking about." (Mr. Broderick was unavailable for a further update on the progress of the program.)

The GAO has expressed a further fear: that FAA will not know how well the airlines comply with the aging aircraft ADs. On August 4, 1992, Kenneth M. Mead, GAO director of transportation issues, complained in testimony to the Aviation Subcommittee:

> Although FAA's associate administrator for regulation and certification told this subcommittee last year that FAA would develop a data base by December 1991 to track aging aircraft compliance, FAA officials now say they plan to collect airline compliance plans only once and report to the Congress in September 1992 .... A one time report, while informative, is shortsighted because it will only provide a snapshot of compliance as of the summer of 1992. The usefulness of the report will be limited further because at the present time, FAA headquarters officials told us that neither FAA nor inspectors will be provided the results from the individual airlines ... (that data) would be extremely useful to provide continuous tracking and oversight in an ever-changing situation.

In other words, the FAA believes in the honor system for airline compliance. We, like Mr. Mead, do not believe in it.

The success or failure of the FAA mandatory aging aircraft maintenance program will not be known until 1994 and the years that follow; however, this much is true: In the words of a memo by the House Aviation Subcommittee staff, in a memo to the members of the committee on April 12, 1991:

> The number of aircraft 20 years or older, and their proportion to the total fleet, will increase dramatically over the next 10 years. In 1988, the world jet transport

fleet contained 2440 aircraft 20 years or older or 28 percent of the total. It is projected by the FAA and the industry that in 1995, 4100 aircraft, or 35 percent of the total, will be 20 years or older, and in the year 2000 more than 5700 aircraft, or 40 percent of the fleet will be this old.

The average age of the U.S. airline fleet in 1993 was 12.7 years, with 20 percent of the fleet between 15 and 20 years, and 26 percent older than 20 years. The average age of the U.S. fleet is expected to increase through the balance of the century.

Those are disturbing statistics. Anyone who flies on a regular basis has a high probability of flying on a plane that is geriatric and subject to the FAA's mandatory repair orders. It shall be difficult to obtain information on the age of the specific aircraft that you are flying in; however, when you enter the aircraft, depending upon the door being used for boarding, you might see a plaque in the door that would provide the information. Of course, at that point there is nothing you can do about it, except perhaps refuse to fly—an act not currently warranted by the risk involved.

Airline passengers are depending upon the FAA to enforce the public will as expressed by Congress in the Aging Aircraft Safety Act. The FAA must not allow the airlines any compromise or delay in implementing its aging aircraft advisory directories. Any aircraft that does not comply should immediately be decertified upon passing its threshold date of compliance, even if it puts an airline corporation in financial peril and even though an inspection fails to reveal cracks in need of repair.

As Anthony J. Broderick told us, "What we have to do, basically, is hold these people's feet to the fire." To do less would be a violation of the public trust and grounds for the Congress to take the matter out of the hands of the FAA and compel mandatory retirement of all aged aircraft.

13

Crash survivability

"Many people are still dying in survivable crashes."
Matthew H. Finucane,
director of air safety and health for
the Association of Flight Attendants,
quoted in *The Washington Post*, February 10, 1991

The subject of aviation safety, we are told, is too complex and arcane to be digested by ordinary people. But that isn't true. Peel away the veneer of the policy debates, research, position papers, and regulatory proposals (not to mention the book writing), and two basic and fundamental safety issues would remain:

• Preventing accidents
• Surviving when an accident does occur

Both are vital. When accidents do not happen, by definition people are not killed or injured, and property is not destroyed; thus, the preponderance of emphasis in this book, and in the field of aviation safety, focuses on prevention. That does not mean, however, that survivability should be given short shrift. To the contrary. Accidents happen. That being true, emphasis must also be given to maximizing the survivability environment of those aircraft that are involved in accidents.

A review of the major aviation accidents of the past few years reveals that most crashes have survivors. In fact, seven accidents in the United States since 1988 have left four times more people alive than dead:

Date	Location	What happened	Mortality
8/31/88	Dallas-Ft. Worth	Delta Boeing 727 crashed on takeoff	14 killed 94 survive
7/7/89	Sioux City	UAL engine exploded on a DC-10 in-flight leading to a crash landing	111 killed 187 survive
9/20/89	La Guardia	USAir 737 crashes on takeoff	2 killed 61 survive
1/25/90	Long Island	Avianca 707 runs out of fuel and crashes	73 killed 85 survive
12/3/90	Detroit	Ground collision between Northwest 727 and DC-9	8 killed 34 survive on burned DC-9
2/1/91	Los Angeles	USAir 737 crashes into Air West plane on runway	34 killed 67 survive
7/30/92	Kennedy (NY)	TWA L-1011 crashes on takeoff	0 killed *292 survive*
		TOTAL:	242 killed 820 survived

Those are eye-opening statistics. They disprove the belief held by many passengers that being in a plane crash inevitably leads to the grave. Such unfounded fatalism can in itself be a safety hazard if it permits regulators to believe that it is politically safe to establish crash survivability rules less stringent than are necessary to adequately protect passenger safety.

Everyone who travels by air has a fundamental stake in the crashworthiness of aircraft and in having lifesaving equipment on board that will enhance their chance of surviving a crash. This topic extends well beyond the issues of fire retardant materials in cabins and stronger G-force-resistant seats discussed in previous chapters.

Child safety seats

"The agency requires everything on an airplane to be safely tied down except babies and toddlers. I don't understand the rationale in protecting parents and luggage or cargo, but not children."

U.S. Senator Christopher S. "Kit" Bond, September 16, 1991

When it comes to assuring the safety of all airline passengers, the FAA is guilty of age discrimination. Infants receive less protection in the FARs than do older children and adults. Adults and children over age 2 must be restrained in their seats during takeoff, landing and during turbulence. Infants under age 2 do not benefit from the same protection. Instead, the FAA allows them to be held unrestrained in the arms of an adult.

This is folly. The forces generated in an accident or during severe in-flight turbulence, make it literally impossible to hold on to an infant. This has led to the death or injury of lap-held infants, who would not have been hurt or killed if they had been properly restrained.

For years, warnings have been issued that permitting babies to be held in laps is a dangerous practice that unnecessarily endangers the safety of these young children and infants—as well as other passengers who might be injured by a blow to their head or body from the unrestrained infant. As far back as 1982, the FAA did not finalize a proposed rule requiring infants to be secured in infant safety seats during flight. Then, the 1989 Sioux City tragedy aboard UAL Flight 232 brought the issue once again forcefully into the public consciousness.

On May 30, 1990, the NTSB issued a recommendation requesting the FAA to promulgate a rule requiring that babies be secured in infant safety seats during takeoffs, landings, and times of turbulence in flight. In doing so, the board recounted the harrowing experience that lap-held infants and their parents experienced aboard Flight 232:

> During the preparation for the emergency landing, parents were instructed to place their "infants" on the floor and to hold them there when the parent assumed the protective brace position. The four "in-lap occupants" were held on the floor by adults who occupied seats 11F, 12B, 14J, and 22E.

Investigators do not know what happened to the 26-month-old child at 12B during the impact sequence. Investigators do know that the child sustained an abrasion to his left hand and that his father was not injured. The 11-month-old infant at seat 11F was pulled from her mother's grasp during the impact, and the parents were unable to find her when the plane stopped. She was found by a passenger who reentered the cabin when he heard a baby crying. The infant sustained an abrasion under her left eye; the mother was not injured.

The woman in 14J said there were two extremely hard impacts before the airplane rolled to the right. She stated, 'My son flew up in the air and I managed to grab hold of him around the waist. He struck his head [on the side of the cabin wall] several times before the plane came to a stop and several times I had to pull him back into my arms as he slid out of my grip.' Her 23-month-old sustained a scalp contusion, and she sustained a contusion to her right ear.

The woman seated in 22E stated that she assumed the brace position with her 23-month-old infant on the floor between her legs. During the impact, she was jolted to an upright position and she saw her son's body 'flying' down the right aisle toward the rear of the cabin. When the airplane stopped, she could not get to the back of the cabin where she thought her son was. Smoke immediately entered the cabin and hindered her breathing; she was urged by other passengers to exit. She was not injured, but her son died of asphyxia.

In each instance cited in the NTSB report, the parent was unable to hold on to the child. In each instance, the infant suffered more severe injuries than their parent. In one tragic case, the infant died while his mother survived. If these children had been seated in infant safety seats, they probably would have been injured less seriously and the one who died probably would have escaped such an early and tragic death.

The Sioux City crash is not the only accident or incident

where lap-held infants suffered because they were not restrained in infant safety seats. Among the others are:

- In January, 1972, a National Airlines B-747 hit turbulence and an unrestrained 6-month-old infant flew out of its parent's arms and struck an overhead compartment, suffering a facial contusion.
- On May 28, 1985, an Eastern Airlines flight hit turbulence. An 8-month-old infant was thrown from the seat and hit the cabin ceiling, then fell to the floor and was injured. On the same flight, a second baby was thrown from the mother's arms and landed on the floor. That child was not injured.
- On July 13, 1986, an Eastern Airlines A-300 encountered turbulence as it descended for landing at Miami. The seat belt sign was on. An unrestrained 7-month-old child was propelled upward and fell on an armrest on the seat in front of the parents, sustaining a contusion to the left temple.
- On November 25, 1987, a Continental DC-9 crashed during takeoff from Denver, Colorado. A six-month-old in-lap infant died of multiple injuries from the blunt force of the impact. His mother survived with serious injuries.
- On June 6, 1989, a United Airlines DC-10, hit severe turbulence. A lap-baby was lost by the mother and ended up underneath garment bags that piled onto the cabin floor when the garment bag closet door broke. According to the flight attendants on the flight, the mother yelled, "My baby! Where's my baby?!" The child was found injured and required medical assistance.
- On January 20, 1990, an American Airlines DC-10 encountered turbulence near San Juan, Puerto Rico. The seat belt sign was on. An unrestrained 7-week-old infant sustained serious head injuries and was hospitalized with a fractured occipital bone, subdural hemorrhage, and intra-cranial bleeding. The infant was the only passenger on the flight to sustain serious injuries.
- On January 25, 1990, an Avianca Airlines B-707 crashed on Long Island. A 4-month-old lap infant was killed. Six other lap infants, who were between the ages of 4 months and 18 months were seriously injured. The NTSB report stated on the accident stated, "Surviving passengers who held infants reported that during the impact the infants were ejected from

their grasp and that they were generally unable to locate them in the darkness after the impact. The safety board believes that the problems experienced in this and other accidents illustrate the impossibility of parents holding on to infants during a crash. If the infants had occupied AA-approved restraint systems, injuries most likely would not have been as severe."

- On January 5, 1993, an American Airlines Boeing 767 hit clear air turbulence shortly after takeoff while the seat belt sign was on. It is reported that a lap infant was ripped from his mother's arms but was caught by the mother before he could be injured.

These occurrences and other incidents in this country and around the world have created an amazing coalition within the aviation community calling for the FAA to mandate that all passengers be suitably restrained at appropriate times on commercial aircraft. The Air Transport Association, flight attendant unions, Air Line Pilots Association, NTSB, ACAP, Flight Safety Foundation, and crash family groups are all in agreement on the issue. The coalescence is a remarkable occurrence considering how often the industry differs from consumer groups and unions on other safety issues.

On July 12, 1990, Susan Bianchi-Sand, national president of the Association of Flight Attendants, testified in favor of requiring the use of infant safety seats, stating in part:

> Our job as flight attendants is to ensure that passengers are properly restrained prior to crash, and to assist them in immediate evacuation. *We simply cannot do this job when it comes to an unrestrained infant.* If a child is placed on a parent's lap, the child may break free from the adult's arms as the plane decelerates and strikes objects on the ground. If the child is placed and held on the floor in front of a bulkhead, the child may also fly about the cabin during the jolting surface movement of the aircraft. Another serious problem is turbulence. In 1974, an infant on a turbulent flight was strangled when it fell out of a seat and its neck was caught by a seat belt .... Members of the subcommittee, there is absolutely nothing in the Federal Aviation Act that allows the

Federal Aviation Administration to provide one level of safety for adults, and another level of safety for children under two. (Emphasis added.)

Yet the FAA remains unmoved. Reluctantly, because of the mounting pressure for rules protecting infants, the FAA has promulgated a rule requiring airlines to permit child safety seats if the parent pays for the seat or the airline otherwise makes the seat available for that purpose. But, the FAA refuses to ban lap-babies on commercial flights. The reason? The FAA contends that forcing parents to pay for a seat for their infant will induce them to drive rather than fly—and driving is statistically more dangerous than flying; therefore, the agency contends, such a proposed rule would actually be detrimental to infant safety.

Anthony J. Broderick, one of the FAA's principal safety officials and a moving force behind the FAA's position, expressed his strong opinion to us on this issue:

> **Broderick:** It would be a terrible thing to do to the low-income families because what you're now doing is saying to a mother and an infant who want to visit a GI in Germany or something like that ... "We're going to force you to buy a seat and pay for an international ticket for the infant because we think that the danger associated with not buying a seat is too great to allow you, a mother or father, to get away with that."
>
> **Question:** What I got from your (congressional) testimony was that you thought there is actually a negative benefit because you thought that the lives saved would be few, but the lives lost—because people were driving in their cars—would be greater. Is that an accurate summary of your position?
>
> **Broderick:** I think that's a fair statement. That's certainly the argument that we put forth and certainly what the studies indicated.
>
> **Question:** There is an irony though in reading your testimony. You began your statement by saying "We urge all parents to use safety seats because it will make the baby safer when they fly ...."
>
> [On July 20, 1990, Mr. Broderick testified about the issue of child safety seats before the House Aviation

Subcommittee. He began his testimony by stating: "At the outset, I want to make clear that the use of approved child safety seats for infants provide a greater level of safety in the event of an airplane crash. Parents should be aware that the use of a child safety seat can increase the likelihood of their child surviving a crash (that) is otherwise survivable. There should be no debate about that point nor should there be any question about whether the FAA believes that child safety seats should be used. We do. *We strongly urge parents to use approved safety seats for their children*." (Emphasis added.)]

Broderick: We do urge that.

Question: But then you are saying, while we say it is safer for them to do it, we don't want to make it mandatory, because if too many people follow our advice, more infants will be killed on the highways.

Broderick: Wrong! That's completely twisted logic. People who follow our advice can afford to follow our advice. We are urging people to do something that is ... a free choice and ... presumably they are going to do if they can afford it. If they can't afford it, we are absolutely not telling people, "Don't fly because it's too dangerous for the child without a safety seat." In fact, we're saying just the opposite. The additional risk borne by the infant is very, very tiny .... I think it is wrong for us to require people to either spend money for the additional seat, or—if they can't do that—get off the airplane. And that's what that rule would have us do if we were to enact it and that's why we said no, it's a bad idea.

Question: If I, as an adult, have to be restrained during takeoff, landing and turbulence, why should my infant be given less protection by the government?

Broderick: There are two answers to that question. The first is, if we do what you suggest, more infants whose parents didn't have the ability to earn money to contribute to their ticket purchase are going to die. It's as simple as that and that was the heart of our testimony .... The second point is that when you do the analysis that I do in terms of the number of

infants per year that would be saved by the child restraints, without the seat belt, it comes out to 1 or 2 per year. How many adults, do you think would be lost per year if we didn't require seat belts?
Question: I have no idea.
Broderick: Lots. Because there are a lot of survivable accidents. And you can't survive if you're not protected ....

Pay close attention to what Mr. Broderick told us. The FAA mandates less protection for infants because far fewer infants fly than adults. He said as much when he admitted that adults are required to be suitably restrained because to do otherwise would cost too many lives. That is age discrimination, pure and simple. There is no other way to describe it.

But what about the argument that forcing parents to buy a seat for their infant would force the parents to travel by automobile, which would lead to an increase in infant deaths? Christopher J. Witkowski, then director of the Aviation Consumer Activist Project (ACAP), testified before the House Aviation Subcommittee on July 12, 1990, stating in part:

I would like to address briefly two recent reports that predict a net safety loss if cost-conscious parents choose to drive rather than fly with their infants. Both are based on assumptions that ACAP believes lead to unfounded conclusions.

A paper cited by the Competitive Enterprise Institute predicts that a child restraint requirement would push many families back on the nation's highways, where travel would be more hazardous than by air; however, this report ... relies on FAA estimates that airlines will charge half-fare for all infants and also experience an 18 percent drop in infant boardings. We find it doubtful that airlines would set fares so high as to force away the adults attached to nearly one-fifth of all infant boardings.

The paper also uses national statistics on highway accidents, injuries, and deaths that include high-risk groups such as unmarried young men and intoxicated drivers. This fails to recognize that accident statistics are likely to be considerably lower for parents traveling with young children ....

ACAP has received many letters from consumers advocating mandatory child seats. As one woman so eloquently wrote, "This is a country of choice. As adults, we choose ways to keep ourselves safe. But until our children can decide for themselves, it is up to us to keep them safe."

Susan Bianchi-Sand also addressed the FAA's reasoning in her testimony of July 12, 1990, stating with appropriate sarcasm:

If the government really wants, as a matter of safety policy, to promote air travel over car travel, why not put a halt to all proposed air safety improvements, since the increased cost of these improvements might show up in ticket prices and force some individuals to drive instead of fly?

The argument in support of the FAA's resistance to the NTSB recommended rule mandating child safety seats is unreasonable on its face, and ridiculous in its justification. It protects theoretical children from driving in cars at the expense of real flesh-and-blood infants whose safety is unquestionably compromised when flown as a lap-baby. Moreover, the airlines *want* a rule requiring infants to be restrained. Flight attendants are emotional in their support for such a rule because they have experienced the horror of watching infants torn from their mother's arms in turbulence and crashes. The NTSB continues to recommend that all passengers, regardless of age, be restrained during takeoff, landing, and times of turbulence. (Its recommendation to that effect remains in the "Open/Unacceptable Response" list.). Only the FAA continues to resist.

The time has come for the FAA to give up its stubborn intransigence on the issue and to perform its job of fostering the traveling safety of *all* passengers. If the FAA refuses to change its official position, Congress should intervene and pass legislation forcing such rulemaking. (Such a bill has been introduced in the House of Representatives.) The airline corporations could help by offering substantial discounts for infants, thereby eliminating the fear that more infants will be injured or killed in automobile accidents. The most helpless and innocent among us, our infants, deserve no less.

Passenger protective breathing devices

"Smoke hoods would reduce panic and keep people conscious long enough to get out of the plane. I would have used one instantly if it had been available to me."

David H. Koch,
survivor of the crash of USAir Flight 1493 at
Los Angeles International Airport

Another piece of crash survival equipment that many safety advocates want air carriers to provide for every passenger is passenger protective breathing devices (PPBE) more commonly known as smoke hoods, smoke masks, or escape masks. Smoke hoods come in many varieties, sizes, and shapes. Their purpose as mandatory equipment on an airliner would be to provide passengers with several minutes protection from smoke, toxic fumes, and the gasses that can cause asphyxiation during a post-crash fire. This would allow those who survive the impact of a crash extra time to escape rather than die inhaling poisoned air.

The FAA, the Civil Aviation Authority (CAA) (Britain's FAA), and the airlines resist mandating smoke hoods for passengers. These nay sayers contend that smoke hoods actually would delay the evacuation of planes because they would increase panic, slow egress, and increase the difficulty of evacuation through exits.

The argument over whether to compel airline companies to provide smoke hoods for all passengers caught the limelight after a tragic accident at Manchester Airport, in Britain, on August 22, 1985. "Manchester," as it is known in the aviation safety community, began like any other flight:

> The British Airtours Boeing 737 begins its takeoff roll. Suddenly the captain hears a "thump" and fearing a bird might have been ingested into an engine, decides to abort takeoff.
>
> As the plane is being braked, a fire breaks out in the No. 1 engine. The captain is informed by the tower that there is "a lot of fire" on the port side of the aircraft. He is told by the tower to evacuate the plane from the right side, away from where the fire appears to be.

The pilot gently, perhaps too gently, decelerates the craft and brings it to a smooth stop. Approximately 45 seconds have been lost stopping the plane. Unfortunately, the plane is parked in such a way that the wind blows the engine fire toward the back of the fuselage. Fire soon breaks through windows at the rear. Within seconds, thick black smoke begins to fill the cabin. Passengers are screaming in panic, some climbing over the seats to get away from the flames. People begin to choke from the smoke, their knees buckle from the toxic gas, their soot-covered eyes can see only inches in front of their faces.

A flight attendant finds the starboard exit door jammed. He opens the port exit and people began to crush forward, desperately seeking to get out. At about the same time, a young woman, seated at the window exit seat, has panicked. Instead of pulling the exit handle, she pulls at her seat arm rest. Another woman manages to open the hatch but it falls inward, on top of the woman next to the window. A man finally moves the 48-pound door and people begin to escape. But nearly a minute of precious lifesaving time has been lost.

Within a few minutes, it is over. All who are going to escape, have escaped. One dead passenger literally dies half in and half out of an exit, only inches from life. But the smoke has killed him before he can make the final effort of escape.

Manchester's tally: 82 people survived but 55 people died, 46 due to the toxic smoke and fumes. No passengers were killed by fire. The accident was eminently survivable. A few extra minutes protection against the smoke might have saved every life that was lost due to smoke inhalation.

Manchester was certainly not the first accident where should-be survivors died because of smoke and toxic gases, such as hydrogen chloride, hydrogen fluoride, cyanide, and carbon monoxide, that are generated by aircraft fires. Other accidents also are on the smoke tragedy list:

- 1973: A Boeing 707 landed in Paris, France, eight minutes after a fire broke out in a lavatory; two people survive, 124 passengers and crew were killed by smoke and fumes.

- 1978: In Los Angeles, the captain of a DC-10 rejected a takeoff, the landing gear collapsed and a fuel tank ruptured. Fire broke out. Four people were killed, two by fire and two by smoke.
- 1983: A fire started while in flight. The plane made an emergency landing at Cincinnati, Ohio, 17 minutes later. Twenty-three people died due to smoke and toxic fumes.
- 1988: An L-1011 crashed because of a wind shear during approach to landing at Dallas-Fort Worth Airport. Thirteen of the dead were killed by smoke and toxic gas.
- 1989: The Sioux City crash: 37 of the 111 dead were killed by smoke inhalation.
- 1990: A ground collision between a 727 and DC-9 caused the DC-9 to catch fire. Eight people were killed, 7 by smoke.
- 1991: At Los Angeles International Airport, a landing Boeing 737 crashed into a commuter plane; 22 of the 34 who died in the crash were killed by smoke and toxic gas.

Supporters of mandatory PPBEs disagree with the FAA that smoke hoods would delay emergency evacuations. They believe that PPBEs would protect passenger respiratory systems by permitting passengers to maintain their consciousness and mobility. (Smoke hoods that would be used on planes contain filters to keep smoke, toxic gasses, and soot away from sensitive body tissues.) That should also mitigate panic and could protect passengers' eyes, increasing their ability to see, depending upon the type of hood or mask used. David Koch, survivor of the 1991 USAir accident at Los Angeles International Airport is a voice of experience on this subject. Mr. Koch described the effects of toxic smoke during a post-crash evacuation:

> The impact of the 737 against the stone building caused an enormous fire-ball to shoot up past the windows on the left. The cabin lights immediately went out and people began to scream hysterically and rush down the aisle toward the rear of the plane. A few seconds later the interior of the plane began to fill with intense, heavy black smoke, which was extraordinarily painful to breathe and very toxic.
>
> I reached for my suit jacket, which had been on the chair to my right, but could not find it. My thought

was to use it as a face mask to protect my lungs from the smoke. I was on my hands and knees attempting to crawl down the aisle toward the rear of the plane. Several people stampeded over me. It quickly became pitch black in the cabin from the heavy smoke, in spite of the bright light from the fire on the left side of the plane. I could only make out the vague outlines of people directly in front of me. As I moved down the aisle, I encountered a mob of fighting, frenzied people jamming the aisle.

At that point I stood up on my feet, choking heavily from the smoke and walked back toward the first class section. My state of mind was objective about the condition I was in. I had a real sense of curiosity about what it would be like to die.

Suddenly, an inspiration came over me as I realized that the heavy smoke must have come from an opening in the fuselage somewhere. I walked forward in calm desperation to the front of the plane behind the cockpit. I looked to my left at the entrance door through which passengers enter the plane, and saw a terrible inferno through the porthole of the door. The doorway to the cockpit was closed and I sensed heavy smoke coming from the cracks around the door. I next turned to the right and felt my way to the service door in the galley. To my astonishment, I detected an opening between the door and its frame on the right side of about several inches width. It was possible to see light on the other side.

By this time, I was feeling very faint and I later guessed I only had about 15 to 30 seconds of consciousness left. Every breath caused me to convulse and was extremely painful. I put my fingers in the opening and pulled. The door moved somewhat, which enabled me to put my head out and take a deep breath of fresh air. A tremendous feeling of strength came over me and I felt like Superman. I revived somewhat. With this added energy, I pulled the door more and it moved to the left a couple of feet. This permitted me to step into the doorway and jump to the ground below.

I crawled and stumbled away from the plane and ran about 30 yards before stopping. My lungs hurt terribly and I coughed and choked badly for about 5 minutes before I could breathe normally again.

In the hospital, I was examined by a lung specialist and he determined that there might be some lung damage. The doctor advised me that smoke inhalation can take between 12 to 40 hours to fully develop all its harmful effects. The lungs respond to smoke damage by swelling and filling with fluid. If the injury is serious enough, one can suffocate in one's own fluid. An additional danger is contracting pneumonia because bacteria can enter the body very easily through the damaged membrane tissue of the lungs.

After treatment in the hospital, during which I remember writhing in agony on the operating table while a bronchoscope was inserted in my lungs, I continued to cough up blood and mucous filled with black smoke particles. That continued for some time after my treatment.

(From "Recollections of My Survival of an Airplane Crash" by David H. Koch, published and abridged with Mr. Koch's permission.)

David Koch is an enthusiastic supporter of mandating smoke hoods on all commercial aircraft. He believes a face mask device, protecting the nose and mouth with a filter that screened out soot and carbon monoxide for 5 minutes, would be best. (He worries that fearful passengers might not be willing to don a full over-the-head hood if they already felt suffocated.)

The opposition to smoke hoods being a better form of protection comes from the contention that fire blocking materials would save many lives now lost in crashes due to the effects of fire. (This ignores the fact that most aging aircraft might never be retrofitted to meet updated fire safety standards.) Opponents also contend that passengers will be unable to put on the hoods in a crisis situation and, therefore, will lose precious escape time. One report conducted for the FAA found that a 15-second donning period would result in a protective breathing device safety "disbenefit." Anti-smoke hood advocates also point to studies that indicate it takes longer for passengers to evacuate a plane wearing smoke hoods than it does for passengers who are not wearing the devices.

However, another study (DOT/FAA/AM-89/12) commissioned by the FAA, found that the time it took test passengers to evacuate a plane while wearing one test model of smoke hood (manufactured by Sabre Safety Limited) was fundamentally the same as when wearing no smoke hood at all. Moreover, this study found that the *size of the exit* was the most critical element in determining the speed of plane evacuation, regardless of whether smoke hoods were used.

Assuming that opponents are correct in their contention that smoke hoods delay evacuation—a contention that is questionable—that argument loses sight of the purpose of the PPBE. Smoke hoods or masks *buy extra time* for passengers to evacuate a plane, assuming that a fire does not engulf them.

The history of survivable crashes shows that most people who survive the impact are killed by smoke, not fire. It might be minutes after people have collapsed from the smoke, before the fire flashover through the cabin makes further survival impossible. Those extra minutes could be used to escape by people wearing smoke hoods, who would otherwise succumb to smoke and toxic gas.

Most smoke hood supporters suspect that the real reasons for FAA and airline opposition to mandating the safety devices on planes are a combination of public relations and financial considerations. The airlines fear the public's reaction to a flight attendant demonstrating how to don a smoke hood. That would highlight the potential in passenger's minds that there could be an onboard fire. Then there is the financial aspect. Manufacturers of smoke hoods—clearly nonobjective sources—claim that money should not be a major problem.

According to one study, a PPBE that costs the airlines $55 per seat would have a total initial price tag of approximately $22 million (based upon 400,000 seats). Because smoke hoods come wrapped in airtight pouches and do not need replacement very often, the manufacturers assumed a five-year shelf life and predicted that the total cost per year would be fewer than $5 million, or approximately $11 per passenger seat per year. That figure might not be accurate, but it is unlikely that cost alone would be a reason for turning a thumbs-down to smoke hoods.

In resisting the call for mandatory PPBEs, the FAA seeks to boost its position by comparing its inaction to the refusal of Britain's CAA to mandate smoke hoods. Indeed, the CAA has also refused to issue a smoke hood rule. But it is important to note that the manager of the CAA's smoke hood research issued a statement on December 16, 1988, stating in part:

> I know that this decision (not to mandate smoke
> hoods) will disappoint individuals and organizations
> who have argued passionately that smoke hoods
> should be made mandatory now. To them I would say
> that if a fully adequate smoke hood capable of doing
> everything we believe to be necessary was available
> from manufacturers and ready for production, I think
> we would have decided to introduce it.

In other words, bring us the right smoke hood and we'll require it to be placed on planes.

Talk about a classical catch-22. The manufacturers will not invest the money necessary to fully develop a suitable airline PPBE that would be easy to distribute in the cabin and easy for passengers to don unless the manufacturers know that there is a reasonable chance to reap a substantial market—profit—from the airlines. At the same time, regulators will not mandate the availability of smoke hoods because regulators claim more research needs to be done.

The time has come to break this impasse. While reasonable people differ on the advisability of a rule requiring that smoke masks be available to all passengers, the only way to know whether an appropriate mask and delivery system can be created is to try and create one. Surely private enterprise would find the way to make a PPBE that would be simple to use and provide effective protection without substantially increasing evacuation time, plus meet all reasonable criteria established by aviation regulators. If a rule were made that by a specific date, all airlines would have to carry a smoke hood for each passenger-seat with a defined minimum performance capability—leaving the method of providing the hoods to the airlines, subject to FAA approval—private companies would find a way to get the job done.

Evacuation time

"A modern airliner ... generally has a higher occupancy density than any fire marshall would permit for a fixed structure with comparable floor space."

Paul G. Rasmussen,
FAA Aeromedical Institute Evacuation Research Unit,
speaking at a Flight Safety Foundation workshop on
cabin safety, December, 1984

Segue now to the important issue of evacuation time. The time it requires for passengers to evacuate a plane in an emergency is dependent upon many factors: the number of people on the plane, the size and number of exits available, the presence or absence of smoke or fire, whether passengers are orderly or in a panic, and the ability of the flight attendants and/or passengers to open emergency exits and to direct the escape.

The FAA's rulemaking and aircraft certification roles have significant impact on the escapability of an aircraft during an emergency. The agency's record in this area of promoting safety, is decidedly mixed. Here are some examples:

Evacuation testing

The number of exits required on an aircraft depends upon the results of evacuation testing. In essence, FAA's aircraft certification requires that a planeload of passengers must be able to be evacuated (during a test) through half of the available exits in 90 seconds. That sounds reasonable, but many critics contend that the tests are rigged in favor of the airlines in that the tests do not involve the effects of smoke, fire, panic, or the shock of a crash. (Even so, in October 1991, 44 people were injured, and one woman paralyzed, while participating in an evacuation test of a McDonnell Douglas MD-11. If that can happen in simulated evacuation, imagine the problems that occur in a bona fide emergency.) Without those factors, the 90 second escape capability is essentially bogus and permits fewer exits to be installed than might actually be required to evacuate a planeload of people in a timely manner. (The fewer the exits, the more seats can be replaced in the aircraft.) The minimum test standards should be reduced to 60 seconds to make up for the differences between a test and a life-threatening emergency. (A move afoot that would limit evacuation testing should be resisted.

Emergency exits

For years, pressure was put on the FAA to widen the rows at window exits and to make sure that exit doors can be opened quickly in an emergency. (Each accident at Manchester and LAX involving 737s had a passenger who was unable to open the window exit, which wasted precious lifesaving time in the evacuation of the planes.) Subsequent to those accidents, the FAA did take some welcome rulemaking action that will make future plane evacuations easier and quicker:

Lighting installed in the cabin floor In an emergency, these lights will direct passengers to the nearest exit.

Aisles widened at window exits The Tombstone Imperative finally stimulated the FAA to engage in rulemaking about the accessibility of window exits. After Manchester, Britain's CAA required all British aircraft to remove one seat adjacent to each overwing emergency exit to ease egress. The FAA also has acted, but has given the airlines a choice: either remove the window seat or increase the space between the exit row and the row in front to 20 inches, thereby allowing for easier passage.

Passengers must be able to operate the exits Carriers have the legal obligation to ensure that the person who sits next to an emergency exit has the physical and mental capacity to operate the exits. That is, they must be able to: find the exit; see if there is fire or an obstacle outside; be able to open the door; see, hear, understand and relay instructions for evacuation of the plane; unfurl the slide; and select a safe path away from the plane.

This requirement does not go far enough. Each passenger seated at an exit should be given a brief hands-on training session with a mock-up of an exit so they will know exactly what to do and how to do it if the exit needs to be opened during an emergency. Or, frequent flyers could volunteer for limited emergency evacuation training and then be given a computer code that would place them at or near exits when they fly. Either way, passenger training could make a big difference in how quickly and how well emergency exits would be opened.

Flotation devices

Deplorably, the FAA does not require airlines to carry passenger life preservers on aircraft unless the flight is deemed an "extended overwater flight," that is, a plane that travels more than 50 nautical miles from the nearest shoreline. Yet, according to a 1985 NTSB safety study, at least 179 airports operate within 5 miles of a significant body of water. Anyone who has ever flown in or out of Los Angeles, San Francisco, Boston, New York, or other coastal airports, or has flown over the Great Lakes or other significant bodies of water, knows that planes regularly fly miles out over water, even when not technically an overwater flight. Moreover, most survivable crashes involving water have happened close to shore, or in a lake or river.

The NTSB safety study also criticized the emphasis the FAA put on preparing for the rare incident of "ditching at sea" versus preparing for the more common accident close to shore or in a lake or river. Accordingly, it issued recommendations that life preservers be on every commercial aircraft and that all predeparture briefings include a full demonstration of correct life preserver donning procedures and that any unwarranted regulatory differences be eliminated. To date, the FAA has not followed the NTSB's recommendations. (The recommendations remain on the NTSB Open/Acceptable list, meaning that the FAA is working on the proposals but has yet to accede to the NTSB request.)

Additional survivability factors deserve further study:

- Limiting carry-on luggage. Carry-on luggage has been found to be an impeding factor in the emergency evacuation of aircraft because it piles up in the aisles during a crash and because people often stop to retrieve their luggage, which slows the evacuation of the plane. Luggage that breaks loose in turbulence or in a crash might also cause injuries to passengers. The government and the people will have to decide whether the increase in safety that would be achieved by restricting carry-on luggage to one piece is worth the time delay and inconvenience of having to check more luggage with the airline. (European airlines restrict passengers to one carry-on bag.)

- Installing a sprinkler system. Retarding fires with an onboard sprinkler system is being studied. The weight of the water is a big problem here but if that could be overcome, sprinklers could be a valuable tool in increasing the survivability of accidents involving fires, especially those occurring in flight.

- Fuel lines and fuel content. Research is ongoing to reduce the risk of fire in an accident, perhaps with automatic shutoff of fuel lines, changing the fuel mixture to retard the chance of fire, and other such studies. More should be done on creating fuel lines that are resistant to breakage. Those efforts need to be continued because fire and its side-effects are the biggest cause of death in survivable crashes.

- Backward facing seats. Many safety experts believe that passenger safety would be enhanced with seats that face backwards. The idea behind this theory is that the momentum in a crash is forward and thus the seat could absorb much of the impact stress of a crash and prevent impact trauma. Other safety experts discount this theory, pointing out that flying debris in a crash would become a hazard to passengers facing backwards.

Other factors ultimately determine the likelihood that passengers will actually come through a survivable crash. The factors include flight crew training and the steps passengers can take to increase their own chance of survival. These issues are addressed in subsequent chapters.

14

I dotting &
T crossing

*"Investigation ... revealed that the DC-10-30/40 brake wear limits
in effect at the time of the accident were adequate only for
normal airplane operations. Brakes at or near the brake wear
replacement limit did not have the capacity to stop a DC-10
airplane during a high energy takeoff."*

**NTSB report regarding the
cause of DC-10 crash on May 21, 1988**

Many other safety issues involving equipment need to be addressed: FAA airworthiness certification, protection against terrorist bombs, and the persistent questions of the safety of the DC-10.

Certification and testing

*"When it comes to airworthiness certification, the FAA tends to
stack the deck in favor of the manufacturers and airlines.*

**Pilot with many years of experience
who flies for a major U.S. airline**

Worries about airworthiness certification

On May 21, 1988, the pilot of a DC-10 attempted to abort takeoff
at the Dallas-Fort Worth airport. Eight of the plane's 10 brake systems failed, despite the fact that the brakes were within FAA cer-

tification standards. The DC-10 ran off the end of the runway. Luckily, there were no fatalities or serious injuries in that incident.

The NTSB cited the FAA for the inability of the plane to stop. The board found that brakes—adequate to normal operations—were not up to stopping a plane attempting to abort a takeoff and found that the FAA's inadequate requirements for brake testing were to blame. Thereafter, the FAA took corrective action to better ensure that brakes on planes will operate in stressful situations.

This little remembered event shows how vital it is for the FAA to make sure that sufficient and accurate testing is performed to make sure planes are not only airworthy for normal flight, but able to adequately perform in emergency situations.

Faulty FAA certification procedures have also been partially faulted for several crashes involving the DC-10. As originally built, the DC-10 had an apparent design defect. The placement of its hydraulic control systems, plus the fact that the separate lines—designed to create redundancy—were located too close together, made the hydraulic systems vulnerable to rupture if other parts of the plane were damaged. (Recall that the hydraulic system allows the pilots to control the ailerons, rudder, and other aerodynamic control surfaces.) If all the lines are ruptured, the plane can become uncontrollable. Critics contend that the poor placement of the hydraulic lines created a lethal hazard.

A series of deadly accidents and other incidents involved hydraulic system damage on board the DC-10:

- Windsor, Canada 1972: In June 1972, an American Airlines DC-10 suffered in-flight damage when a cargo door blew off, which caused a sudden depressurization of the craft. (By May 1972, McDonnell Douglas had received numerous reports of door latch failures and had issued a nonbinding service bulletin (SB) suggesting additional safety measures be taken. This was especially serious because the FAA took no action to issue an airworthiness directive (AD) that would legally require that the additional measures be taken.) The depressurization caused the cabin floor to collapse between the cabin and the cargo area. Hydraulic lines, placed in the floor, were damaged and many of the flight controls for the craft went dead. Fortunately, the crippled plane was able to limp to a safe landing.

After such a near tragedy, one would resonably have expected the FAA to jump into action to make sure that all DC-10 aircraft were modified to prevent a recurrence of the mishap which would, in all likelihood, lead to a crash and a significant loss of life. But that was not to be. The then administrator of the FAA, John Shaffer, agreed to accept oral assurances from the manufacturer that it would issue yet another service bulletin and provide repair kits to the airline to modify planes and that the FAA would refrain from issuing an airworthiness directive. (It was felt that an AD would adversely affect the business interests of McDonnell Douglas and that the company should be free to handle the matter in its own way.) Accordingly, Shaffer stated to the public that all operators were checking cargo doors pursuant to service bulletins. (Service bulletins do not mandate anything.) Inexcusably, no airworthiness directive was issued by the FAA that would have required modifications in the DC-10 to prevent the loss of cargo doors, the collapse of the cabin floor during flight and the subsequent severing of all hydraulic lines, which would cause the pilot to lose control. This, despite the fact that the NTSB had recommended the FAA take such action.

This was a crucial lapse. The FAA is looked to by much of the world to lead in matters of safety. When the FAA took no action, it sent an anti-safety message. Tragedy struck two years later in Paris:

- Paris, 1974: The cargo door on a Turkish Airlines plane blew off while in flight. Again, the high-pressure air in the passenger cabin collapsed the floor between that cabin and the cargo area. Hydraulic lines placed in the floor space were severed. The plane became uncontrollable and crashed, killing all 364 people on board. (The FAA issued the required AD in 1975 and applied the AD to all wide-bodied aircraft.)

- Chicago, 1979: A wing engine tore loose during takeoff, taking with it essential hydraulic lines. The plane crashed killing 275 people. The NTSB partially blamed the manufacturer for a design defect that left the craft vulnerable to catastrophic loss of control.

- Sioux City, 1989: This accident was caused when the rear engine exploded and the metal shards severed all the hydraulic lines that were bunched together in the tail area of the plane. The crippled airliner could only be maneuvered by adjusting the thrust of two remaining engines. The plane made it to the Sioux City Airport and made a crash landing: 111 dead, 187 survivors.

Many survivors and surviving family members of the Sioux City tragedy became enraged because the DC-10 could have been made substantially safer with the installation of a hydraulic check valve. This safety measure would have been relatively inexpensive, costing approximately $10,000 per plane and could have prevented the loss of aerodynamic control. Boeing had installed similar check valves on 747s fleet after a Japan Airlines 747 after the rear bulkhead ruptured, consequently severing hydraulic lines, leaving the pilot without control and causing a crash that killed 520 people.

Yet, McDonnell Douglas did not fully respond to the "lesson learned" and similarly enhance the safety of the DC-10 rear hydraulic lines with a check valve until the crash of UAL 232 at Sioux City. Furthermore, the FAA did not compel the company do so; perhaps suspension, revocation, or similar action, of the DC-10 airworthiness certification would have been a proper response for the agency.

Corrective measures were taken on the DC-10 after these accidents. The FAA assures that the DC-10 is safe; the DC-10 has not been in production since 1984. But the question has to be asked: Why were such seemingly defective designs that should have been readily apparent during certification allowed to pass airworthiness certification standards within the FAA? Could it be that the current certification process, which permits the FAA to rely upon engineers *employed and paid by the manufacturer*, is a system that needs to be reconsidered or reformed?

Many family members of people who died at Sioux City became airline safety advocates after that crash. The survivors became involved in airworthiness certification of the MD-11, the successor to the DC-10. Family members pressured the FAA to deal with the issue of hydraulic failure. That pressure, while not solely responsible for change, did contribute to the agency acting to force McDonnell Douglas to revise the MD-11 design, as evidenced by a letter sent to Tom O'Mara by Leroy A. Keith, of the FAA, dated April 3, 1990, which stated in part:

Through the process of revisiting the design decisions that led to approval of the DC-10, necessary design changes are being incorporated on the new Model MD-11. The initial modification, which will be installed on both the DC-10 and the MD-11, entails the installation of protective devices which act to retain hydraulic fluid in critical branches of one of the hydraulic systems in the event that damage to the system occurs from any source. This feature will ensure that sufficient flight control capability remains to allow change in place on existing DC-10 airplanes by the end of this year. A second phase, comprising a more sophisticated method of retaining hydraulic fluid, is expected to be complete by spring of 1991. The MD-11, is just beginning flight testing and FAA certification will be granted only when the modification is incorporated.

The MD-11 flying and its hydraulic system has been designed with new safety features in place to protect the integrity of the hydraulic control system. It is important to note that the defect in the DC-10 only came to light *after* the plane was in use, a fact relevant to certifying airliners that are equipped with only two engines.

Worries about ETOPS

ETOPS is not the name of a monster in a B-movie, it is an acronym for *extended-range twin-engine operations*; a more descriptive definition is flying long distances—including transoceanic—with a plane that has only two engines. (The industry uses a refined reference: EROPS, *extended-range operations.*)

The primary benefit of ETOPS is efficiency. Two engines consume far less fuel than three or four, and the planes can be flown with a two-person cockpit crew, instead of three. ETOPS craft are also quieter, which promotes compliance with noise abatement standards. So, why is this a safety concern? Two engines provide a precariously reduced level of redundancy. If one engine malfunctions in flight, which is not an unheard of occurrence, the plane will have to get to the nearest airport for an emergency landing on only one engine.

For that reason, the FAA has always taken a cautious approach to certifying ETOPS flight operations. Up until now, the airlines have always been forced to *demonstrate* the safety of a twin-engine model (such as the Boeing 767) for extended distance flights, by testing the reliability of the equipment in *actual flight operations.* This has been accomplished by restricting the distance that an ETOPS craft could be away from the nearest airport as measured by the time it would take to reach the nearest airport flying on one engine. An FAA advisory dated December 30, 1988, restricts newly introduced ETOPS aircraft from operating "over a route that contains a point farther than one hour flying time at the normal one-engine inoperative cruise speed (in calm air) from an adequate airport." That, of course, is not an extended flight operation.

(Calm air is a neutral qualifier for aircraft ground speed; a headwind would lengthen the time required to cover a certain distance; a tailwind would reduce the time required to cover the same distance.)

FAA permission to fly more than 60 minutes from the nearest airport at one-engine speed is based upon certain requirements:

- 75-minute operation: Approval for a 75-minute distance may be given if the requesting airline has demonstrated it's ability to "successfully introduce airplanes into operation" and the "quality of the proposed maintenance and operations program" is approved by the FAA for ETOPS operations.

- 120-minute operation: Each operator requesting approval to conduct extended-range operations with a maximum diversion time of 120 minutes should have 12 consecutive months experience of operations with the specified airframe-engine combination.

- 180-minute operation: Each operator requesting approval to conduct extended range operations with a maximum diversion of 180 minutes should have previously gained 12 consecutive months experience ... in conducting 120-minute extended range operations.

Thus, the usual FAA procedure has been to require more than two years of in-service experience flying the ETOPS craft before permitting an airline to fly a twin-engine transport jet three hours from the nearest airport at the speed flown by one engine in calm air. If ETOPS flights are going to be permitted, this prudent and gradual approach to permitting full extended flights is appropriate and respectful of safety needs.

So, what's the problem? This incremental and cautious approach to certifying twin-engine jets for extended flights is in danger of being changed. The new Boeing 777 wide-bodied jet is destined for ETOPS commercial use. The 777 is intended to fly routes currently flown by such jets as the 747, which has four engines. That means that the 777 will not only fly on transcontinental routes, but will also fly on transoceanic, transpolar, and major desert routes. A plane that loses an engine over the Pacific Ocean might be more than three hours, with headwinds, from the nearest airport.

Pressure is being placed upon the FAA by airlines and Boeing to permit these new aircraft to begin flying extended routes without going through the usual step-by-step certification process for ETOPS certification. This proposal, known as *early-ETOPS*, would immediately allow the 777 to operate 180 minutes—one engine and no headwinds—away from the nearest airport.

Supporters of early-ETOPS maintain that more stringent pre-service testing, tougher regulations in areas such as minimum equipment lists and maintenance standards, would make immediate extended flights safe. Paul D. Russell, chief of product safety for Boeing, in defense of the proposal to permit the 777 to fly ETOPS from the beginning of service, told us that "the 777 is the first plane specifically designed for ETOPS. That was not true of other planes. Also, we now have years of ETOPS experience that have been utilized into the design and manufacture of the new craft. No corners are being cut. Boeing is subjecting the craft to the most extensive certification and testing program ever undertaken. We even plan to fly the plane on commercial routes without passengers to test the plane. The plane will be safe. We are asking for changes in certifications rules that were written between the 1930s and 1950s for certifying propeller-type aircraft."

Pilots are not so optimistic.

When asked whether the concept of a widebody plane being permitted to carry hundreds of passengers over the ocean, hours away from the nearest airport, under an early-ETOPS certification process concerned the Air Line Pilots Association, Captain J. Randolph Babbitt, ALPA president, stated:

> It is a concern. We want the aircraft to spend time in
> service (before being permitted to fly over the Pacific
> Ocean). Little idiosyncrasies in the engine, perhaps,

might not (arise during) six months of operations or a year of intensive testing .... Things come up where the manufacturer has to go back and issue a service directive which might say, "We're not going to operate this type of pump. They all have to be replaced by next January." The newest aircraft, the 777, is going to be permitted to fly over the ocean right out of the box .... And we say "No. Why not fly it around the United States for a year or so. Let's get time on this. It's a new engine, new technology, new software, new components. Let's test it first and then allow them to add time extensions." Build it up over time.

Dave Duff, a spokesperson for the FAA transport airplane directorate in Seattle, which has responsibility for certifying air carrier aircraft, stated that the FAA has not decided to permit early-ETOPS but has merely determined that the concept is "technically feasible." "The manufacturers and airlines would have to meet strict hardware and operational conditions for early-ETOPS to be approved," Duff told us in May 1993. "That decision has not been made. The equipment is still undergoing extensive testing and we have issued proposed requirements that if finalized, would have to be met before early-ETOPS would be allowed." In other words, for the FAA to agree to early-ETOPS, the equipment would have to be so extensively tested that the FAA would be convinced of the reliability of the craft for ETOPS operations.

ALPA's point is that all of the simulated testing in the world is not the same as actual operations in the commercial marketplace. ALPA also believes that the FAA's usual ETOPS certification procedures work well. Perhaps a time-tested approach is applicable: "If it ain't broke, don't fix it."

Donald W. Madole, an attorney who has litigated air crash cases for decades and who has been appointed by the GAO as the chairman of its committee to review the FAA's aircraft certification processes, believes that it might take years for a plane's bugs to be discovered. In fact, he strongly advocates that all aircraft models should have a hands-on physical inspection every six months to determine how the craft is reacting to the conditions in the real world. Such concerns are relevant to the issue of early-ETOPS.

If Madole and the pilots are correct, if the only true test of the long-term safety of a plane's design and manufacture is experience in commercial use, early ETOPS is not a good idea.

Prudence, not expediency, should be the order of the day when deciding issues of safety. Many hundreds of lives will depend upon the reliability of the equipment used in each wide-body ETOPS flight. Put the 777 through its paces over time, in actual use. Make sure that the new engines and related equipment are reliable and highly unlikely to malfunction during flight before allowing the craft to fly transoceanic, hours from the nearest airport. For, as one pilot asked rhetorically, "How would you like to be over the Pacific Ocean, flying on one engine, knowing that you were hours from the nearest place to land?" That might be an unlikely occurrence, but the history of all accidents—nonaviation accidents must be included—is rife with unlikely occurrences that killed many people.

Bomb-resistant planes

"In the next 10 years, I believe the likelihood is pretty good that there will be a bombing of a domestic flight. There are too many dissident groups in the world and too many nuts willing to do the unspeakable in order to get into the history books."

Frank G. McGuire,
editor and publisher of the newsletter
Security Intelligence Report

The issue of sabotage and criminal attacks on aircraft is one that is horrifying to contemplate. But the potential is very real. The statistics are ugly. Witness the bombing of Pan Am 103 over Lockerbie, Scotland, on December 21, 1988 and a similar terrorist attack on an Air India flight in June, 1985. Nearly 1000 aircraft passengers throughout the world have been killed in the past eight years because of terrorist bomb attacks on civilian aircraft.

There are two ways to significantly reduce the possibility of such calamities. Ideally, sufficiently stringent security checks would be in place to prevent any bombs from being smuggled on aircraft. (Airport security issues are discussed in chapter 15.) Because there is no such thing as absolute security, the second potential safety precaution that can be taken if a criminal is able to smuggle a bomb on board a plane is generically called *aircraft hardening.*

Here is the problem: Very small bombs that are difficult to detect have enough power to potentially destroy an aircraft that is in flight. According to the study, *Technology Against Terrorism: Structuring Security*, by the U.S. Congress, Office of Technology Assessment (January 1992), "Explosive devices of the size used in airline terrorist events to date are deadly not because they directly cause catastrophic failure (blow the aircraft to pieces), but because they start a domino effect where the aircraft destroys itself." For example, necessary electronic or hydraulic systems can be destroyed causing the plane to crash. Or radiating cracks in the fuselage can be caused by the explosion, causing the fuselage skin to peel back; hence, the plane disintegrates, which is what happened to the Boeing 747 that was flying as Pan Am Flight 103.

It is difficult to develop detectors that can discover a bomb that is physically small, but contains enough explosive material to cause an airliner to crash after detonation. Research is seeking a way to "harden" the aircraft and the cargo storage equipment (or harden only the cargo bins), so that the smaller bomb cannot create the domino effect of plane loss-of-control or disintegration.

According to Ken Hacker, FAA program manager for aircraft hardening, work is actively being pursued through the FAA on both fronts. "The major manufacturers have formed·a consortium to research ways to make future planes more bomb resistant," he told us. "If planes can be designed to resist bomb blasts like they are with regard to lightning (protection), the increased safety provided may not be so expensive as to make the technology unfeasible."

Unfortunately, the path to building a bomb-resistant plane from research, to design, to manufacture, to use, is decades away. But for the short-term, excellent progress has been made toward the manufacturing of bomb-resistant removable containers that hold luggage. "We have developed an explosive resistant luggage container," Mr. Hacker told us. "We are now in the stage of conducting research to answer the airlines' questions, such as how much will the containers cost, how long will they last, what is their durability, how much will they weigh? The last question is particularly important to the airlines because they view an increase in weight as a decrease in revenue."

Mr. Hacker believes that the remaining work can be accomplished by the end of 1994. He told us, "We are pretty confident that we can do this, and it shouldn't take a lot of money."

Everyone who flies should hope that Mr. Hacker is correct.

The low level and poor quality of airport and airline security measures mandated by the FARs have left domestic flights dangerously vulnerable to criminal attack. Properly applied bomb-resistant materials could save passenger lives in the event of an explosion in a plane while flying—or on the ground. The effort would also act as a deterrent to would-be criminals who would be less likely to attempt a bombing if they knew that their nefarious efforts would lead to naught, even if they succeeded in circumventing security screening. If this plan is workable, it is essential to safety that the FAA compel all airline companies to purchase bomb-resistant containers at the earliest possible date.

Spare parts

"About 39 percent of inventory parts for FAA aircraft were not manufactured by or traceable to FAA-approved manufacturers."

Finding of an investigation conducted by the Department of Transportation Office of Inspector General

As if there wasn't enough to worry about, there is a growing concern about bogus and counterfeit parts being sold to the aviation industry by unscrupulous operators. Indeed, the FAA's inventory of parts for its aircraft fleet has been seriously affected by this problem.

Why is this a concern? The dependability of any piece of equipment relies upon the quality of respective components, whether a jet airliner, a farm tractor, or your automobile. If the part does not meet quality control standards, malfunctions might occur that might cause an accident. Aircraft parts and components are not replaced purely because of failures; replacement might occur when a regular inspection reveals excessive wear that is close to, or beyond, a safe level; replacement might also occur based upon restrictions of time in use—perhaps aircraft cycles or hours of operation.

Spare parts should be compelled to meet rigorous quality control standards for design and manufacture. Unfortunately, neither does the FAA certify spare parts nor inspect suppliers. Some in the industry would like to see the FAA take the lead in regulating part suppliers, but Anthony J. Broderick, the FAA's associate administrator for regulation and certification has rejected the idea as "inappropriate." (Source: *Aviation Week & Space Technology*, March 15, 1993.) The FAA has agreed, however, to cooperate with the industry as the agency seeks ways to accredit part manufacturers and prevent counterfeiting.

A task force has been created to look into this important issue. A desirable strategy would include an intense investigation to determine whether counterfeit parts pose a significant threat to airline safety.

Part V

Airports

"Our industry continues to react to aviation security needs in a dangerously piecemeal and fragmented fashion."

Louis A. Turpen,
director of the San Francisco International Airport,
writing in *Aviation Week & Space Technology*,
June 11, 1990

"The safety problem at the head of my list is the attempt to increase the capacity of airports. Even if you double the runways, you cannot double the airspace."

An airline captain with a major U.S. airline

Most people give little thought to the safety of airports. For most travelers, airports are merely the place they go to at the beginning of their flying experience and the place at which they arrive at the end. Any concerns expressed about the facilities usually concern traffic congestion, parking, or paying through the nose for a taste-less hot dog at an airport concession restaurant.

More consideration should be given by the flying public to the safety of airport operations. One area of increasing concern is se-curity. Civilian aircraft are an inviting target to saboteurs, extor-tionists and the mentally deranged. Accordingly, passengers and members of the public who wish access to a gate are screened for weapons and explosives. According to the Department of Transportation publication, *National Transportation Statistics*

(June 1992), in 1990, 1.145 billion people were subjected to airline passenger screening. From that screening process, 2,853 firearms and 15 explosive/incendiary devices were detected. During this same time period, more than 400 bomb threats were directed against airports and more than 300 bomb threats were directed at aircraft in the United States.

Many people familiar with airport security fear that current security procedures at airports are woefully inadequate, particularly as related to checked luggage and the mail. Some also complain that the screening process for passengers and carry-on luggage is vulnerable to circumvention. The important topic of security and fighting terrorism is discussed in chapter 15.

In addition to security issues, the safety of airport flight operations is another important concern. Accidents caused by on-the-ground runway incursions have taken too many lives. Runway overruns are another safety concern, with pilots criticizing the FAA for permitting runways and/or runway overruns that are too short and for allowing takeoff-abort testing of planes that is unrealistic. The push to increase capacity has resulted in takeoff and landing procedures that are worrisome, plus noise abatement procedures create other potential safety hazards. These topics are covered in chapter 16.

The subject is airports. The issue is their safety, a major challenge for the FAA, the various airport authorities and the flying public for balance of the decade and beyond.

15

Murder most foul

"We know that there is a lot of thievery out of luggage at airports. If something can be taken out of a suitcase, something can also be put in."

Caroline D. Gabel,
professional staff,
House Subcommittee on Aviation

Of all the airline safety issues, the threat of *terrorism* and *sabotage* might be the most emotional. Terrorism has been defined as the systematic use of violence—such as bombing, killing, hostage taking, and hijacking—to promote a political objective. But airlines might be targeted for nonpolitical motives; thus, the term sabotage is usually used in this chapter, defined as any criminal attack against civil aviation regardless of the perpetrator's purpose or motive.

In his article, "Hostage-taking and Terrorism," in the May 1992 issue of *Flight Safety Digest*, published by the Flight Safety Foundation, J.O. Hagelsten, M.D., calls terrorism a "war" stating, "We never know when or where this war will break out, but we must be prepared for it." That makes sense. Criminal attacks can come from any quarter at any time.

So, how prepared are we to conduct this "war"? Are the minimum FAR safety rules governing airport security sufficiently stringent to protect aircraft and the people who fly in them? Are the security measures that are taken at airports performed with the planning, thoroughness, excellence, and professionalism required to prevent would-be saboteurs from succeeding in their intended criminal activity? Disturbingly, especially with regard to domestic flights, the answer is no.

Rules of the security game

"Everyone within the system seems to want to do as little as absolutely necessary when it comes to aviation security."
Victims of Pan Am 103 newsletter, February 29, 1992

In a nutshell, here is how the current airport security system works, according to the 1990 FAA annual *Report to Congress on the Effectiveness of the Civil Aviation Security Program*:

> There are 117 U.S. scheduled and public charter air carriers that are required to adopt FAA-approved security programs. Each of these U.S. air carriers had adopted the Air Carrier Standard Security Program (ACSSP), which was developed by the FAA in consultation with the industry. This program requires each air carrier to implement the same standard of security procedures .... There are 148 foreign scheduled and public charter air carriers that serve airports within the United States. Foreign air carriers are also required to adopt and pursue security programs, and U.S. regulations require foreign air carriers to submit security programs to the FAA for acceptance .... The 265 domestic and foreign scheduled and public charter air carriers serve 402 airports within the United States. Each ... airport ... is required to adopt and use a security program that provides a secure operating environment for these air carriers. Of the 402 airports, 18 airports, designated Category X, have been determined by the FAA to have a need for increased oversight and implementation of special security requirements.

Fred Farrar, a public affairs officer for the FAA, summarized the aviation security requirements mandated by the FAA: "There are two basic parts to the program. The airlines are responsible for greeting passengers and screening them and their carry-on luggage for weapons and explosives. It is the responsibility of the airport to have sufficient law enforcement presence on the property and to deny unauthorized access to sensitive airport operational areas, to the gates and plane loading and boarding areas."

That sounds all-inclusive, unfortunately the truth is less comforting than the appearance. While security involving foreign flights has improved in recent years, gaping holes remain in the minimum security measures required by the FARs and in the implementation of these rules designed to protect commercial aviation against criminal attack. The reasons? Complacency and the financial cost of security.

Screening passengers and carry-on luggage

First instituted in 1973 to foil potential airplane hijackers, everyone seeking access to an airport gate must pass through a metal detector and all packages or luggage that they are carrying are X-rayed so that weapons or dangerous devices can be detected. This system works best when discovering weapons that "everyday" criminals might try to smuggle to a gate, such as metal handguns and knives—but even here deficiencies exist. Unfortunately, the technology utilized at these checkpoints is little changed from the inception of the program and is considered inadequate to catch experts in the methods of sophisticated concealment or weapons made of composite materials such as plastic.

Of more concern is the manner in which the airlines comply with this required security activity. The airlines are not experts at police functions, so they usually contract with a security company to perform these passenger and carry-on luggage screening services. Unfortunately, the people hired to do the actual security screening generally receive little training, are poorly paid, often receiving near minimum wage, find the work boring, and have low morale. This results in a very high rate of job turnover, which has, on occasion, exceeded 100 percent per year. (Source: General Accounting Office; GAO/RCED-87-125FS, April 30, 1987.)

The FAA monitors the effectiveness of these security measures but with the exception of its *air marshal* program—security personnel fly as if they were passengers—does not participate in hands-on security measures. In 1989, the GAO found that the FAA's own test results disclosed disturbing deficiencies in the performance of gate security checkpoint screening. On December 18,

1989, GAO's Kenneth M. Mead testified before the Aviation Sub-committee:

> In general, results of the FAA's testing of passenger
> screening points and the results of our work showed
> that the passenger screening process could not ensure
> that firearms, explosive, and other dangerous weapons
> were not being carried onboard an airplane. On the
> basis of results of FAA tests conducted from September
> 1986 through June 1987, we reported that, overall,
> screening personnel detected approximately 80
> percent of the dangerous test items. In addition,
> detection rates varied widely at the nation's major
> airports, ranging from a high of 99 percent at one
> airport to a low of 48 percent at another. The
> program's effectiveness was also hindered by high
> turnover, low wages, and inadequate training of
> screening personnel. It was clear that in many
> instances air carriers were not placing sufficient
> emphasis on security to ensure that passenger
> screening checkpoints operate at their highest level of
> performance.

It must be reemphasized that those disturbing test results came from the FAA's own monitoring efforts. But there is a real question as to whether the FAA's security oversight tests are a realistic challenge to the integrity of the security system. For example, Congressman Peter DeFazio complained to us that the FAA's ability to monitor airport security checkpoints is compromised by restrictions on the agency that exist in current law: "The FAA is not licensed to have guns, so they can only conduct their security monitoring activities in the most crude manner. They can't disassemble guns and try and sneak them through checkpoints ... the firearms they do possess are large and old-fashioned and encapsulated in plaster during the monitoring checks." In other words, the FAA is prevented from using the types of weapons that a criminal or saboteur might try to sneak past the checkpoints in the real world. A rhetorical question: When was the last time an evil terrorist attempted to smuggle a weapon to an airport gate encapsulated in plaster?

If you think that is bad, read on. It gets worse. "What about screening for check-in luggage?" the FAA's Fred Farrar was asked.

"For European and overseas operations, the airlines must x-ray the luggage and take other precautions to make sure that explosive devices do not get onto planes."

Well and good. "What is the rule for screening of check-in luggage on domestic flights?"

(Pause) "There is no required x-ray screening for explosives contained in checked luggage on domestic flights unless there has been a specific threat made against a specific flight."

That can't be right. Surely the FAA requires the airlines to use technology to screen every piece of checked luggage for explosives. But a review of the FARs confirms Farrar's statement. FARs do mandate the minimum security precautions that airlines must carry out under the law (excerpted):

§108.9 Screening of Passengers and Property

Each certificate holder required to conduct screening under a security program shall use the procedures ... in its approved security program to prevent or deter the carriage aboard airplanes of any explosive, incendiary, or deadly or dangerous weapon on or about each individual's person or accessible property, and the carriage of any explosive or incendiary in checked baggage.

This rule grants the airlines the general right to screen checked luggage for explosive devices under an approved security plan. It does not compel the airlines to utilize screening devices such as x-rays to test for explosives. The airlines are free to use them, but they are not required to under the rule.

The distinction between optional security screening and required security screening is important. As the reader will recall, FARs establish *minimum safety standards* beneath which the airlines cannot conduct business. So long as the airlines meet these minimums, their operations are considered "safe" by the FAA and the agency cannot compel the airlines to exceed FAR requirements.

Under newly enacted FARs, the FAA *can* compel the airlines to conduct x-ray screening or other testing of checked luggage to determine the presence of an explosive or incendiary device for international flights (excerpted):

§108.20 Use of Explosive Detection Systems

When the Administrator shall require, ... each certificate holder required to conduct screening under a security program shall use *an explosives detection system* that has been approved by the Administrator to screen checked baggage *on international flights* in accordance with the certificate holder's security program. (Emphasis added.)

Domestic flights are not mentioned in this rule; thus, under the FARs, the FAA cannot require that an explosive material detection system be used to screen checked luggage for such flights.

These FARs establish an unacceptably low level of minimum safety standards and create the potential for dangerous holes in airport security. (Security reasons forbid a description of the actual measures that are taken by the airlines to screen checked luggage, which might vary from airline to airline.) When asked to justify the relative laxity of the security rules for domestic as opposed to international flights, one official of the FAA explained, "There has never been a terrorist attack against a domestic flight and the risk that one will occur is considered quite small by security agencies."

The official's statement is correct as far as it goes, but the reasoning is way off the mark. (The government judged the prospect of an attack on Pearl Harbor to be quite small before December 7, 1941.) As of this writing, there has never been a terrorist attack against a domestic flight, although there have been cases of sabotage, such as the murders of the crew and passengers on PSA Flight 1711 by the mentally deranged former employee (chapter 6). But does that fact mean that there never will be such an attack? No.

Can the security forces of this country guarantee that they will always be able to detect a security threat before the prospective saboteurs act upon their malicious intent? No reasonable law enforcement or security official would make such a blanket assurance. And what about the criminal who wants to kill an individual passenger and seeks to mask the crime through mass murder? Or the disgruntled former airline employee who wants to hurt his or her former employer? Or a person seeking to cover up a suicide and collect insurance money? Or the nut who seeks publicity for some maligned and twisted purpose? Can the police always detect such a person's dark purposes before an attack? Of course they can't.

That being so, shouldn't the FAA promulgate rules requiring the airlines to use technology to screen all checked luggage for explosive devices now, before such an attempt is made? (If, heaven forbid, there ever is a successful bombing of a domestic flight, you can bet that the rules would be changed and changed fast: Tombstone Imperative.) Shouldn't we anticipate and prepare for the worst, thereby increasing the chance that it can be averted? Haven't we learned the tragic consequences that can follow when security lapses permit a bomb to be smuggled onto a plane? Have we so quickly forgotten the awful lessons of Pan Am 103?

The horror of Pan Am 103

"The nation must act to deter and prevent the use of terrorism against civil aviation as a deadly tool of political policy. The Pan Am experience demands nothing less."

Ann McLaughlin, chairman of the President's Commission on Aviation Security and Terrorism, in a letter to President Bush submitting the commission's report, May 15, 1990

The deaths of the passengers of Pan Am 103 will be remembered as one of the most foul and dastardly acts of aviation sabotage in an era noted for foul and dastardly acts against innocent civilian airliners. (In addition to bombings, several passenger planes were shot down by military action in a 10-year period.) Added to the horror of the Pan Am mass murder is the fact that security measures could well have prevented the tragedy, had they been properly carried out. But that was not to be and 270 people and their families would pay the price with lost lives and grief that time can never fully dispel.

Christmas season, 1988
Frankfurt, Germany
Passengers are boarding Pan Am Flight 103, which is scheduled to fly first to Heathrow Airport in London, and then on to New York City. Unknown to anyone but the criminals who planted the device, a bomb made with plastic explosives has been disguised as a radio that has been smuggled onboard, probably in a suitcase transferred from a connecting flight to the Boeing 747 that is Flight 103.

The plane flies uneventfully to Heathrow and lands without incident. Some passengers disembark. Others board the plane. Most passengers are happy and excited, many are students on their way home to the United States for Christmas.

The plane pushes away from the Heathrow gate at 6:07 p.m. There is a delay on the ground and the jumbo jet does not take off until 6:25 p.m. The plane climbs to 12,000 feet and then to 31,000 feet, leveling off at that altitude at 6:56 p.m. All 259 people onboard—plus 11 people who are going about their business in the little Scottish town of Lockerbie—have only eight minutes left alive.

A small battery sends a small current through a wire. A fuse is ignited. Approximately 14 ounces of a plastic explosive called *Semtex* is detonated. The explosive force of the blast is sufficient to penetrate through the luggage container and pierce the plane's fuselage just below the left wing. A catastrophic chain reaction begins, combining the force of the blast with the high pressure inside the cabin and the low pressure of the environment outside the plane. Cracks in the fuselage are created and begin to spread out. Holes are poked in the roof and the belly of the plane. The hydraulic systems are cut and the craft becomes uncontrollable. But there is nothing left to control as the plane disintegrates and falls to earth in and around Lockerbie.

The force of the impact is so enormous it is difficult to comprehend. The wings and attached fuselage section gouge a crater 140 feet long and 40 feet wide. The impact causes the fuel to explode into a fireball that towers 10,000 feet. A piece of a window frame from a nearby house is blown from its sill and lands three miles away. Winds scatter aircraft debris to the coast of England, some 80 miles distant.

It is the worst security-related disaster in aviation history involving a U.S civilian air carrier.

In the aftermath

The bombing of Pan Am 103 created a fire storm of anger and re-criminations. Grieving family members joined together to demand answers to the question, "How could this happen?" The families became politically active, seeking aviation safety reform and better security precautions to prevent any repeat of the Lockerbie disaster.

Pan American suffered tremendous business losses due to the adverse publicity generated by the bombing. (This business loss might have destroyed any chance that the financially troubled airline had of surviving. Pan American, once one of the world's leading air carriers, is now out of business.) Lawsuits were filed. Some family members settled out of court while others took their cases to court and were awarded millions of dollars in damages against Pan Am for having engaged in "willful misconduct," which contributed to the success of the bombing.

(Under an international treaty known as the Warsaw Convention, damages payable to crash victims and their families are limited to $75,000 when applied to international flights. This damage limit does not apply if the airline is found to have been guilty of "willful misconduct," thereby allowing higher damages in the Pan Am 103 lawsuits. The damage limits of the Warsaw Convention do not apply to domestic flights.)

The jury found that Pan Am failed to follow established security procedures and charged a ticket premium to pay for increased security measures, but then did not use the money for the purpose stated. As of this writing, the case is on appeal.

Under political pressure, President Bush created the *President's Commission on Aviation Security and Terrorism,* which conducted an investigation of the bombing, sought answers as to how the sabotage of Pan Am 103 could have happened, and issued recommendations to prevent such a calamity from recurring.

Some of the most important findings and recommendations of the commission were as follows:

- The U.S. civil aviation security system is "seriously flawed and has failed to provide the proper level of protection for the traveling public."
- "Pan Am's apparent security lapses and FAA's failure to enforce its own regulations followed a pattern that existed for months prior to Flight 103, during the day of the tragedy and—notably—for nine months thereafter."
- "The destruction of Pan Am 103 may well have been preventable. Stricter baggage reconciliation procedures could

have stopped any unaccompanied checked bags from boarding the flight at Frankfort. Requiring that all baggage containers be fully secured would have prevented any tampering .... Stricter application of passenger screening procedures would have increased the likelihood of intercepting any unknowing 'dupe' or saboteur from checking a bomb into the plane at either airport."

- No "amount of government reorganization or technological developments can ever replace the need for well-trained, highly motivated people to make the security system work."

As a result of the commission's work and the political pressure applied on the government to increase security, Congress passed and President Bush signed, the Aviation Security Improvement Act. Among this law's provisions are the following:

- Mandatory criminal background checks are to be conducted for security personnel and people allowed unescorted access to aircraft or secured airport areas.
- The FAA was required to establish minimum training standards for security personnel, as well as minimum educational levels, and language skills.

The FAA, under intense public pressure over the issue of security, also has taken several important security actions in the wake of the Pan Am 103 bombing:

- 12/19/88: The FAA required that U.S. airlines in Western Europe and the Mideast to x-ray or physically search all checked baggage and achieve a positive match of passengers and luggage to keep unaccompanied bags off airplanes.
- 9/5/89: FAA published a final rule giving the agency authority to require airlines to install explosive material detection equipment to screen checked baggage at all domestic and foreign airports handling international flights. (Recall that domestic flights were excluded from this rule.)
- 9/20/89: The FAA-chartered Aviation Security Advisory Committee held its first meeting, focusing on improving aviation's defenses against sabotage attacks.
- 1989 and 1990: *TNA machines* (screening devices that can detect plastic explosives) were being installed at selected airports that serve as ports for international flight. These

machines have proved to be a disappointment, either working too slowly or picking up too many false readings. (See p. 223.)

- 6/14/90: The FAA position of assistant administrator for civil aviation security was created, a position that reports directly to the administrator of the FAA, thereby increasing the profile of security activities within the agency.

- 12/1/90: The FAA begins to implement the requirements of the Aviation Security Improvement Act of 1990, including requiring improved security measures by foreign airlines flying into the United States and the stationing of federal security managers at major U.S. airports, and the posting of security coordinators to foreign countries.

- 1/17/91: Security at U.S. airports was increased to its highest level in the history of civil aviation in response to the outbreak of war in the Persian Gulf. Included in the temporary security measures was the prohibition of nonticketed people past security screening stations and the prohibition of curbside check-in of luggage.

- 6/11/91: The FAA issued a rule requiring airlines to notify aircrew members when there is a specific and credible security threat to their flight. (There is no such requirement of passenger notification.)

These were all welcome steps; however, critics contend that they are not sufficient to protect you and your family against criminal attacks directed against domestic flights. For example, Paul Hudson, whose 16-year-old daughter Melina was killed on Pan Am 103, and who has been deeply involved in airline security issues ever since, told us, "There has been a national rollback of security since the Persian Gulf War. Holes in the system are so glaring that determined terrorists could take out the system in one day."

Moreover, according to several sources, the airline industry's commitment to the new security programs is suspect and some in the industry might be quietly working behind the scenes to attempt to weaken the inadequate rules that do exist. Mr. Hudson told us, "Airlines are tremendous contributors to campaigns and have been trying to get the Aviation Security Act repealed piecemeal, on the grounds that security is bad for the bottom line. For example, at the request of the airlines, a rider was placed on an appropriations bill in the House of Representatives directing that no federal money be spent to enforce requirements that criminal background checks be conducted for security personnel, even though that is a requirement of the law."

Evidence supporting Mr. Hudson's fears can be found in the *Federal Register.* On February 13, 1992, an NPRM proposed a mandatory criminal history records check using the FBI fingerprint-based national criminal history record filing system for all airport and airline employees with unescorted access to sensitive airport areas. That would seem to be a reasonable and prudent step to take considering the risks and was consistent with recommendations made by the President's Commission on Aviation Security and Terrorism.

Apparently the FAA received too many objections about the cost and bother of conducting such searches from airlines and/or airport commentators to go forward with that commonsense proposal. Accordingly, on September 18, 1992, the FAA published a Supplemental Notice of Proposed Rulemaking. The SNPRM, if adopted, will substantially *weaken* the proposal to require an FBI criminal background check contained in the February 13, 1992, NPRM. Specifically, the SNPRM seeks to *reduce* proposed criminal background checks to those instances when an employment history raises questions about the applicant. It also *exempts* current employees with access to sensitive areas from criminal background checks. (These are people who have been hired while there were few security precautions taken to ensure that they were not a threat to safety.)

On a positive note, the SNPRM adds arson to the list of crimes that would prevent an applicant from obtaining privileges for unescorted access, but why was arson left out of the initial proposal, plus why wouldn't a conviction of any felony disqualify the applicant's request for access? Even if the felony was nonviolent, it would seem logical that a person dishonest or unethical enough to have been convicted of a felonious act should not be trusted with sensitive issues of airport security.

The questions must also be asked why security checks for employees at airports shouldn't be at least as tough as those required for a bank teller (who must have an FBI criminal background check). Apparently, the FAA and the airlines do not believe protecting people's lives at an airport or on an airplane deserves the same level of precaution as does the protection of the same people's money in a bank.

Paul Hudson and other surviving family members of Pan Am 103 are not alone in their dismay over the airline industry's apparent resistance to the enactment and enforcement of meaningful security measures. One airport executive whose job requires his deep involvement in security issues told us, "The airlines oppose almost every security measure that comes down the line. Even during the height of the Persian Gulf War, they were grousing about the increased security and were continually pressuring for the restoration of curb-side check-in. They were more concerned with passenger convenience than they were security."

Some officials in the FAA have also expressed similar concern with the attitude of the airlines. One FAA official told us, "The airlines are hostile to spending money on security. And the (further) we get away from Pan Am 103, the more resistant they become."

If these and other critics we spoke with are correct in their complaints, the "anti-security" attitude of the airlines is breathtakingly shortsighted. One of the worst things that could happen to the already miserable financial picture of the airline industry would be a "domestic Pan Am 103." People would lose faith in the safety of flying, much as they did during the Persian Gulf War. Airline revenues would drop like a crowbar thrown off a high building. The FAA would be forced by political pressures generated by the angry and bitter emotions of the moment to create new emergency rules to heighten security at airports. These new mandates would require immediate action that would be expensive and difficult to perform in a rushed fashion. Then, there would be the lawsuits ....

Isn't it better for the FAA to act now by strengthening existing rules and thereby increasing the minimum level of security? Perhaps by taking action today, the specter of a domestic airplane being bombed or hijacked can be prevented tomorrow.

Security improvements that need to be taken

"As terrorist tactics change, it will become increasingly important to be proactive rather than reactive in developing technologies to protect the public."

From *Technology Against Terrorism*,
Congress of the United States
Office of Technology Assessment, January 1992

Many steps need to be taken to improve the security of U.S. airports. These steps should be aimed at making security an integrated system that uses several different strategies that create redundancy and thereby increase the likelihood of success. Some of these are already in place in foreign airports and some are already required for selected international flights. Many recommendations that are described here have been made by the President's Commission on Aviation and Security, the Office of Technology Assessment, or other experts on issues of security.

Foreign carriers must meet domestic standards

U.S. airlines that fly internationally are forced by the FAA to take more stringent security measures than the FAA requires of foreign carriers flying the same route. Bill Jackman of the Air Transport Association believes this puts U.S. airlines at a competitive disadvantage. "U.S. carriers are losing passengers because foreign carriers allow for less hassle," he told us. "Some even permit hotel check-in." Professor Clint Oster, coauthor of *Why Airplanes Crash*, reiterates the point: "Americans have to realize that foreign carriers usually have less security."

This isn't just a matter of economics, but security, and might be a primary reason why foreign carriers have been successfully sabotaged far more often than have U.S. airlines. The following list of explosions on aircraft between 1980 and 1989 (from data compiled by the President's Commission on Aviation and Security) illustrates the point:

Year	Airline	Location	Circumstances	Casualties
1980	United (USA)	Sacramento	Explosion in cargo hold while plane being unloaded	2 injuries
1981	Middle East Airlines (Lebanon)	Beirut	Explosion after plan unloaded	none
1981	Air Malta (Malta)	Cairo	2 bombs explode as luggage being unloaded	2 killed 8 injured

Year	Airline	Location	Circumstances	Casualties
1981	Aerinica (Nicaragua)	Mexico City	Bomb in passenger cabin while plane on ground	5 injured
1982	CAAC (China)	In flight	Explosive device detonated in rest room	none
1982	Pan American World Airways (USA)	In flight near Hawaii	Bomb under seat cushion exploded	1 killed 15 injured
1983	Syrian Airlines (Syria)	Rome	Bomb exploded before takeoff	none
1983	Gulf Air (Bahrain)	In flight	Bomb exploded in baggage compartment	112 killed
1984	Air France (France)	In flight	Bomb in cargo hold	none
1984	Union Des Transport (France)	Chad	Bomb exploded in cargo hold after landing	24 injured
1984	Air France (France)	Tehran	Hijackers blow up cockpit	none
1985	Boliviano (Bolivia)	In flight	Passenger carried bomb to lavatory which exploded	1 dead
1985	Royal Jordanian Airlines (Jordan)	Beirut	Hijackers destroy cockpit	none
1985	Air India	In flight	Bomb exploded in cargo hold	329 killed
1985	American Airlines (USA)	Dallas/Ft. Worth	Explosion in cargo hold after plane lands	none
1985	Egyptaire (Egypt)	Malta	Hand grenades thrown during rescue attempt after hijacking	60 killed 35 injured

Continued on page 222

Year	Airline	Location	Circumstances	Casualties
1986	TWA (USA)	In flight over Greece	Bomb exploded in cabin	4 killed 9 injured
1986	Air Lanka (Sri Lanka)	Sri Lanka	Bomb in cargo hold exploded while plane on ground	16 killed 41 injured
1986	Thai Airways (Thailand)	In flight	Bomb exploded in lavatory	62 injured
1987	Korea Airlines	In flight	Bomb in cabin area	115 killed
1988	BOP Air (S. Africa)	In flight	Bomb in cabin area	17 killed
1988	Pan Am 103	In flight	Bomb in Cargo area	270 killed
1989	UTA	In flight	Midair explosion	171 killed
1989	Avianca (Columbia)	In flight	Bomb under seat	107 killed

That is a lot of carnage by sabotage. The FAA should establish a single minimum security standard for all flights flying under its jurisdiction, while maintaining the freedom to increase security as the need arises based upon individual circumstances.

Improve x-ray and metal detection technology

Most of the current x-ray machines in operation at U.S. airports are outdated and inadequate to the job of preventing bombs from being smuggled onto airplanes. Initially set up to detect guns and knives that would be of use to hijackers, they cannot detect the miniaturized components and computer chips and plastic explosives now used by sophisticated terrorists.

A new generation of enhanced x-ray technology has been developed that can distinguish low-atomic-weight organic materials, such as plastic and other explosives, from other materials. These machines need to be installed at airports and operators should undergo training on how to use the new devices. Magnetic resonance machines (MRI) and/or CAT scan machines might also be extremely useful in detecting weapons and explosives. "MRIs can electronically unpack a bag," one security consultant to airports told us, "and they can do it 10 times faster than the technology in current use. Unfortunately, such machines are very expensive." Perhaps a middle ground can be found whereby the use of this expensive technology would be limited to the inspection of luggage that is highly suspect, based upon profiles and other screening methods.

Continued research on TNA machines

With saboteurs often using plastic explosives, new technology must be created that is able to detect such materials. One technology, *thermal neutron activation* (TNA), can detect plastic explosives and offers hope for improved security. The TNA machine bombards suitcases with slowly moving neutrons that are absorbed by nitrogen nuclei, giving off telltale radiation that is picked up by detectors.

Currently, TNA machines are experiencing several technical difficulties that limit their effectiveness for mass security of checked luggage. The machines are slow, when set to catch small amounts of explosives. They also experience a false alarm rate that is too high for efficient use.

If the problems associated with the TNA cannot be reasonably solved, the Office of Technical Assessment suggests that one application of the technology would be to "use the device only for close examination of individual items selected by other screening methods (x-rays). As an example, if a screening device finds a suspect electronic device in a bag or carry-on item, a TNA device could be used to inspect it for explosives content. Since electronics equipment would have a low nitrogen fraction, and the mass of the equipment would be less than that of large bags, confusing background would be reduced and the false alarm rate would be much lower."

An official at a major U.S. airport who pays a great deal of attention to security issues is enthusiastic about this prospect. "You can have an x-ray machine that automatically passes luggage that is solely packed with clothes on to the plane but (the machine) would divert luggage containing suspect images, such as radios or tape recorders, to a security station for TNA or other high tech or hands-on screening. That would reduce the expense of the human element and allow maximum efficiency."

Profile screening of passengers checking luggage

More than 1 billion pieces of luggage are annually carried on domestic flights. That creates a security nightmare. It is almost impossible to thoroughly check out all that luggage without bringing commercial aviation to a screeching halt.

One possible way to make luggage screening more efficient is for a "profile" to be created of persons likely to be a bomber or likely to be a dupe of a saboteur. (Dupes happen. Several years ago, security personnel for El Al Airlines, the national airline of Israel, caught a pregnant woman who was unknowingly carrying a bomb planted in her luggage by her fiancé.)

The security measures taken at Ben Gurion Airport in Israel are instructive. At Ben Gurion, a highly motivated and well-trained security force performs a personal in-depth interview and profile evaluation of all passengers. The profiling looks at things such as passenger travel documents, their responses to an established set of questions, and the trained observations of the security personnel. (Passengers at Ben Gurion must report two or three hours in advance of their flight.) The aim of the system is to eliminate a large fraction of the passengers who do not appear to represent any possible threat from the time-consuming hand search imposed on those passengers who fit the suspect profile. This system is augmented with a positive luggage and passenger match before the plane leaves the airport.

The depth of the security procedures at Ben Gurion Airport cannot be accomplished in U.S. domestic airports without a fundamental disruption of the system, plus the procedures are not warranted based upon the lower risk levels in this country as compared to the likelihood of sabotage in Israel; however, that does not mean that some sort of profile system, in conjunction with other security measures, would not be desirable and workable in the United States.

According to the President's Commission on Aviation Security and Terrorism, the FAA has already created likely profiles of potential saboteurs. If check-in airline personnel were trained to spot a person meeting the profile, as well as potential dupes of such people, the luggage of such persons could be directed for more intensive screening by TNA or other sophisticated screening devices and perhaps be required to be matched with the passenger boarding the flight. According to the Office of Technology

Assessment, such passenger profile screening would heighten security while making the system more efficient because "the incorporation of an effective profiling system into an overall security system could eliminate a large number of passengers from further screening."

The FAA has been experimenting with an automated profiling system called the *comprehensive passenger screening profile* (CPSP), in which the security person keys the answers to a set of seven questions into a portable computer terminal. The computer then compares the answers against a data base and produces a risk assessment. The operator would then use this assessment to decide on the level of screening the luggage and person would undergo. (The FAA is considering making this system mandatory and has even offered to assume liability for the system's failure. But the airlines are reported to be reluctant because they do not wish to share their passenger profile data with the FAA.)

The FAA should consider mandating the use of profile screening on domestic flights if—and it's a big if—basic civil liberties are not unduly constrained. Increasing airport security through the use of profiles should not be seen as an excuse for an exercise in prejudice. For example, profiles should not be based primarily upon race or ethnic appearance. (It was widely reported that during the Persian Gulf War many people were subjected to vigorous and harassing security checks merely because they "looked" like Arabs.) Also, it must be remembered that profiling is a subjective and uncertain business at best. In overwhelming numbers, those who match a profile are innocent individuals; thus, profiling, if it ever is adopted, must never be used to subject persons to harassment or embarrassing personal searches or interrogation.

There is no question that profiles have the potential to interfere with civil liberties and must be approached with appropriate caution. But we live in a dangerous world. There are people in this country and elsewhere who would target domestic commercial aviation for their own evil purposes. The proper application of profiling can enhance airline security; thus, if profiling is used conservatively and if a positive profile merely directs luggage to greater technological screening, the intrusion into people's privacy can be viewed as light when weighed against the potentially tragic consequences of successful sabotage.

Explosive material detectors at certain U.S. airports

One of the most important security improvements that the FAA needs to require is the placement of explosive material detection devices at airports deemed to be under the greatest threat of attack so that checked luggage on domestic flights can be subjected to the same screening processes as they currently are in international terminals. (Perhaps using profiling to determine which bags are so screened.) If that occurs, curbside check-in of luggage might have to be eliminated because profiling would destroy the convenience of the curbside service. If it is not to be eliminated, then luggage checked at the curb should be screened by an explosive materials detection device. (Current curbside luggage check-in procedures present a potential danger to the flying public. Passengers can check their luggage at curbside with only a very brief and cursory interaction with airline personnel. Moreover, the luggage checked at curbside will be loaded on the plane without assurance that the passenger checked in and boarded the aircraft that carries the checked luggage. Nor is there a requirement compelling the airlines to match luggage checked at the curb with a passenger getting on the plane.) This potential hole in security is too wide and deep for safe operations and must be changed. There would be a potential cost in convenience and perhaps a modest hike in the price of tickets, but the increased security offered by the presence of explosive material screening technology would be worth the price.

Require passenger matching of luggage

Internationally, luggage must be matched to passengers before it is permitted on planes. The reason is obvious. Several bombs have destroyed planes that were contained in unaccompanied checked luggage. (Pan Am 103 and the June 1985 bombing of an Air India flight are two examples.) According to the Office of Technology Assessment, "Ensuring that all checked luggage belongs to passengers who have actually enplaned is an effective first line of defense against this threat."

Luggage/passenger matching is most often accomplished by time-consuming manual procedures. Unfortunately, such manual matching is inappropriate for the fast-paced travel that people in the United States take for granted and would be disruptive and difficult to conduct under the current hub and spoke airport system where people often change planes with little time to spare between their arrival and departure. That being so, it is likely that manual passenger and luggage matching would be opposed by most airlines and passengers.

Bar coding or similar computer technology holds the promise for a more efficient system and should ultimately allow for computer matching of passenger and luggage—even when the passenger has switched planes or airlines (intraline and interline passengers). Indeed, the Office of Technology Assessment has concluded that if bar-code systems were made sufficiently uniform among airline companies, application of bar code technology could solve the interline baggage problem. Further research is clearly warranted.

Notification of threats

One of the big controversies generated by the bombing of Pan Am 103 is whether the government has a duty to alert the general public when a credible terrorist threat against aviation has been determined.

In the Pan Am 103 case, several disturbing events had taken place prior to the bombing that family members and others contend should have led to a public warning of a potential terrorist attack. On October 26, 1988, German authorities had raided a number of residences where members of the violent political group, the Popular Front for the Liberation of Palestine-General Command, had been observed. A Toshiba radio that had been tampered with was discovered in that raid. A few days later, after the suspects had been released by the German courts, another Toshiba radio was discovered among the contents of a car that belonged to one of the Popular Front members. This radio had been rigged as a bomb using plastic explosives and was equipped with a barometric trigger device.

Pan Am and other airlines were alerted by security authorities in Frankfurt about the Toshiba radio-bomb and warned that if anyone attempted to smuggle such a device onboard a plane in luggage, it would be difficult to detect by x-ray. The Telex alert concluded with a stark warning: "It has to be assumed that there will be further efforts to bring similar prepared explosive devices aboard aircraft." (Source: Report of the President's Commission on Aviation Security and Terrorism.) Subsequently, the FAA issued a security bulletin that contained a similar description of the Toshiba radio-bomb, and directed that passenger/luggage matching should be "rigorously applied."

On December 5, a bomb threat was received from an anonymous caller at the American Embassy in Helsinki, claiming that a Pan American plane flying from Frankfurt to the United States would be bombed within two weeks and naming the intended perpetrator. (Fourteen days later, Pan Am 103 which originated in Frankfurt, was destroyed.) Pan Am officials in Frankfurt were notified of the threat.

The warning regarding the Helsinki threat was spread throughout U.S. diplomatic posts, including those of the Department of State and Department of Defense. At no time was the existence of the bomb threat made available to the FAA or the general public. Despite warning its own people of the threat, State Department officials later discounted the threat to the security people at Pan Am.

It was later determined by law enforcement officials in the United States, England, Scotland, and Finland, that the threat received by the Embassy and the bombing of Pan Am 103, were unrelated. No evidence is known to exist, other than the coincidence of time, to prove otherwise.

A controversy in the aftermath of the bombing was whether the passengers of Pan Am 103 should been told of the Toshiba bombs and the general threat made against Pan Am to the Helsinki Embassy. That raises the larger issue of whether bomb threats against airlines or airports should be publicized at all.

This issue presents a challenging dilemma. To publicize threats permits passengers to exercise freedom of choice and decide for themselves whether to fly on an airline or out of an airport that has been threatened. On the other hand, publicizing threats would give tremendous power to wrongdoers, allowing them to disrupt the aviation system merely by making a phone call. Security officials believe that publicizing threats would also alert would-be saboteurs to informers within their ranks, perhaps dissuading disgruntled people from informing on their colleagues and endangering the informer's life, which would reduce the ability of the authorities to keep track of the shadow-activities of terrorists. Moreover, a "cry wolf" syndrome could be generated whereby people would become so used to hearing about threats that they would pay as much attention to them as big city residents do to a car alarm that goes off in the middle of the night.

It is a difficult problem with substantial merit on both sides of the argument. *The New York Times*, in an editorial of April 10, 1989, opposed public disclosure of threats. Taking the pros and cons into consideration, the newspaper's position represents the best policy if, as the editorial stated, the government's security procedures are sufficient to "guarantee traveler's safety." That is an appropriately rigorous standard. As things stand now, the government is a long way from meeting it. If minimum security standards are not dramatically improved in the coming years, the issue of public disclosure of credible threats will have to be revisited.

Review mail regulations

Transporting mail is an important revenue generator for many airlines. Under current law, sealed mail cannot be inspected unless it weighs far more than would be required to create a bomb capable of destroying a large commercial transport jet. This presents a significant security problem. According to an August 1992 FAA unclassified executive summary to Congress, entitled *Security of Main and Cargo in Transportation by Passenger Carrying Aircraft*, "The current restrictions against inspecting and delaying the mail, the lack of commercial processing standards, and a history of letter bombs combine to present vulnerabilities to civil aviation security at least as great as other aspects of aviation operations."

According to the FAA report, approximately six percent of the total mail, by weight, is capable of "containing a device intended to cause catastrophic damage to a passenger aircraft." The number of individual pieces that percentage represents is: 517 million pieces of priority mail, 58 million pieces of express mail, and 632 million pieces of international airmail.

That is a lot of mail to worry about, but the threat is not unmanageable. The President's Commission on Aviation Security and Terrorism recommended that the United States Postal Service "effect a regulatory change redefining the category of mail 'sealed against inspection' to include written materials and those parcels below a specified weight." In other words, large packages would be legally subject to x-raying and other technological security screening. For those people who do not want their large package inspected, the changed law could permit the package to be sealed if reasonable proof of the identification of the sender were provided and the parcel were subjected to a device (currently used in Switzerland and Israel) that subjects packages to depressurization so that a bomb triggered by barometric pressure would explode, with the sender footing the bill for the added security check. Hardened containers, as described in chapter 14, are another answer.

Some of these proposals would take many years to fully implement; however, there is a practical step that can be taken almost immediately. During the Persian Gulf War, in order to protect civilian passengers against the threat of terrorist attack mounted through the mail, the postal service shifted all its mail, except the smallest parcels, to all-freight flights. Planes carrying passengers continued to carry smaller pieces. That is a common-sense policy that would not cost additional funds for fancy machines. It should be immediately reinstated for the protection of the flying public, at least until a long-term reliable security solution can be created.

Paying for security

"Safety is spelled with a dollar ($) sign," says Frank G. McGuire, editor and publisher of the newsletter *Security Intelligence Report.* And there is no doubt that security measures necessary to protect the public are expensive; however, there are some creative ideas being discussed that would alleviate the financial burden on the airlines and airports.

Place security under one federal office *The New York Times* editorial that was previously quoted concluded by stating: "Eventually, the government (might) have to take over airport security—essentially a police function—from airlines and the low-paid contractors now responsible for assuring that the fellow across the aisle isn't carrying a bomb or a Biretta in his briefcase. All of this will change the culture of air travel—but will improve its security ...." The newspaper's position is echoed by a high official of a major United States airport, who told us, "The airlines have not done a good job with security. They react most strongly to costs and customer feelings. What is needed is a security force with a unified chain of command that is responsible for all security issues."

That makes a lot of sense. The FAA was not created to be a law enforcement agency. That might be why it placed most of the burden of security on the airlines and airports.

The existing FAA policy of imposing security responsibilities onto the reluctant airlines is also misguided. Airlines are in the business of providing transportation services to people and shippers of cargo. They are not in the police business. As a result, they contract out many of their policing responsibilities to security firms that usually pay people low wages, offer them little training and have a high rate of employee turnover. At the same time, airports are required to create their own police force and pay for expensive security systems.

Perhaps the time has come to create a professional federal aviation security force that would assume responsibility for most aviation security functions. (We don't force storekeepers to pay for a private police force. Such a centralized security force would make security more efficient and professional. The people working in the security system would be better trained, better paid, more highly motivated and less subject to turnover or corruption. Employment standards would be higher and people with a criminal record would be screened out, a weak area in the current system.

Lease the security equipment A security consultant to a large American airport has a novel suggestion to pay for the needed added security equipment. "Why not have the airlines or airports lease the equipment, rather than buy the security devices? The cost of the lease could be established as a specified price per bag screened. Surely everyone would be willing to pay an extra 50 cents or a dollar if they knew that by doing so everyone's checked luggage would be scanned by high tech security devices." Louis A. Turpen, director of the San Francisco Airport agrees with this general concept: "The way to get past the cost barrier is to break the cost of security down to a unit price per service, which would be recoverable by the airlines.'" Such innovative ideas deserve serious consideration for they would permit a higher level of security without breaking the financial backs of airlines or airports.

Release trust fund money to finance security Almost $7 billion that should be used for aviation safety issues has been coopted by the government to finance the national debt. This unconscionable policy must be reversed and some of the released money invested into improving airport security. The airlines also contend that the government should finance their security expenses because terrorist attacks are not directed against the aviation companies as such, but against aircraft as surrogates for the United States government. The airline corporations might have a point.

There can be no doubt that current security rules are inadequate to fully protecting the public and must be improved. That is easier said than done, but as this chapter demonstrates, many imaginative ideas are available to improve security levels and people committed to carry them out.

Louis A. Turpen, director of San Francisco International Airport, believes that an effective security program should include what he calls a "systems approach." "Mix the tools at each point in the system. Include redundancy. Change the routine on a regular basis so that security measures are not predictable. Play the 'what if,' game. Try and anticipate weaknesses so that they can be filled. Adequately fund your security forces and have a program that can respond to individual circumstances. Bring people into the program who are excited about their work and want to do a good job. Mandate federal law enforcement and security agencies to communicate with the airports about the current threat assessment. Take these steps and the security of aviation would be greatly enhanced." Those important steps are not possible under the current system of divided responsibility and niggardly expenditures on security.

Turpen's prescription is worth investigating. Under the current system, airline security is a reluctant enterprise at best. That is simply not good enough. As the Commission on Aviation Security and Terrorism stated, "Despite the current security requirements at the nation's airports, potential vulnerabilities exist. As a former head of law enforcement for one of the country's largest airports said, 'FAA should move in the direction of closing the gaps now, not wait until we have a significant domestic problem.'" Or, as Paul Hudson so succinctly puts it, "We have to stay at least one step ahead of the terrorists and criminals, or we are lost."

16

Toward safer landings

"In the generic sense, the pressure is on at every operation at airports to move the traffic through."

Captain J. Randolph Babbitt, president of the Air Line Pilots Association

This chapter will cover the more pressing issues of airport safety, other than the subject of security. Several important matters impact the safety of flight operations in and around airports. Perhaps the most important of these is the safety threat posed by runway incursions, which have taken a deadly toll of passengers in recent years. Another is the need to increase the safety of aborted takeoffs, especially the manner in which the FAA tests planes to determine the moment when a takeoff cannot be safely aborted. The problem with general aviation aircraft flying in and around commercial airport airspace will also be addressed along with some of the less than desirable airport operations that the FAA permits or might be considering, in order to increase system capacity.

Airport disaster preparation

"I was very unhappy with the seeming lack of preparation of the people who responded to the accident. When I asked them why they were unprepared, I was told, 'We weren't expecting a crash.' It was really pitiful."

Julia Elhauge,
a survivor of the TWA crash that occurred
July 30, 1992, at Kennedy International Airport

One of the things that most angers Julia Elhauge about her experience in the crash of TWA Flight 843, was not the accident itself but what happened after the passengers escaped from the burning plane. "The people who responded to the emergency were completely disorganized," she states. "We were told to move one place and then, when someone mentioned we were being moved closer to the burning plane, we were told to move somewhere else. Then, someone said, 'Everybody sit. We need a head count. But if you are injured, stand-up.' It was ridiculous. Most of the injuries were leg and knee injuries. No medical people attended to us for a long time, we were herded onto busses and then held 'prisoner' and not allowed to leave for fear we would talk to the press. It was six hours before we were allowed to leave. I believe my injuries were exacerbated by the so-called emergency response."

If the response to the TWA crash was as inept as depicted by Ms. Elhauge, her anger is well placed. One of the most important functions of an airport is to be prepared for the worst. (The quality of the emergency response at Sioux City was credited with saving lives after the crash of UAL Flight 243.)

San Francisco International Airport appears to place a high priority on emergency response preparation. It has a standardized response procedure, preplanned rescue and medical procedures that will be conducted in the event of a crash, and regularly conduct realistic drills so that everyone will be well trained and will understand in advance what to do in the event of an emergency. "Giving everyone a specific job is important," Louis Turpen, the airport director told us. "It's like following a recipe. We even give our custodial crews a specific job to perform in an emergency. Everyone is involved and we all act like a team."

Turpen's emphasis on preparation paid off in 1989 when a 7.1 Richter-scale earthquake hit the area. (Sports fans will remember that the quake hit just as the third game of the World Series was about to begin.) According to R.V. Wilson, director of community affairs for the airport, the quake caused severe damage to the air traffic control tower. The airport was immediately closed and controllers diverted incoming planes while flow control at Washington, D.C., canceled flights to San Francisco that had not departed. Approximately 15,000 passengers and employees were immediately evacuated from the terminal buildings while work began to check the structural integrity of the airport's runways. Clean up activities were begun as soon as power to the airport was restored. Everything moved so smoothly that the airport was reopened the next day.

Why had SFO been able to effectively respond to the earthquake emergency? The airport's disaster preparedness program was the key. (In fact, a full-scale drill had been conducted only months before, presciently assuming a large earthquake at the airport during the afternoon rush hour.) It should be noted that SFO conducts full-scale accident preparedness drills once a year, even going so far as to burn a Boeing 707 in a crash drill to provide a realistic disaster simulation.

"Unfortunately, most airports don't do as good a job as San Francisco in preparing for disasters," said Captain B.V. "Vic" Hewes, a retired international airline captain who is a safety consultant to airports. "The reason is that the FARs do not require a high enough level of airport preparedness. The FAA does issue in advisories that have good safety standards but do not require airports to meet those standards by making them a part of the rules. Heck, the FAR's aren't even as tough as the International Civil Aviation Authority (ICAO) manual."

The ICAO manual, according to Hewes, calls for full-scale disaster drills once every other year and full "tabletop" drills in the off years. "The people involved in emergency response change," Hewes said. "You have to run regular drills so that everyone knows what they are supposed to do and when, like when a new actor joins a running play. You have to have rehearsals." The FARs only require full-scale drills once every three years.

Runway incursions

"One of the more vexing safety problems in the aviation system is the problem of runway collisions and aircraft crossing or getting onto a runway when they are not supposed to. (Runway incursions.)"

From a memo to the members of the House Aviation Subcommittee, from the professional staff, 1991

The FAA defines a runway incursion as "an occurrence at an airport involving an aircraft, vehicle, person, or object on the ground that creates a collision hazard or results in loss of separation with an aircraft taking off, intending to take off, landing, or intending to land." Each incursion creates the potential for catastrophe.

As airports become busier, runway incursions are a growing concern. The February 1, 1991, accident at Los Angeles International Airport is only one example. In that accident, an air traffic controller mistakenly permitted an Air West commuter aircraft to enter an active runway on which USAir Flight 1493 was about to land. The 737 crashed into the smaller plane and a total of 34 people died in collision and its aftermath.

(This accident was probably caused by a failure of air traffic control. The National Transportation Safety Board accident report found that the probable cause of the accident was the failure of the Los Angeles air traffic control facility management to "implement measures that provided redundancy comparable to the FAA's National Operating Position Standards," [meaning, that there were insufficient backup systems in place to catch an error] and the failure of the FAA air traffic service "to provide adequate policy direction and oversight of its air traffic control facility managers." This led to the ground controller having too much work to do, which caused the controller to fail to "maintain an awareness of the traffic situation, culminating in the inappropriate clearances." In other words, the controller, who was an FPL, had too much to do and simply forgot that the commuter plane had been cleared to enter the active runway [by that controller]. Procedures that would have alerted the controller to the error were not in place, leading to the collision.)

The LAX tragedy, while perhaps the most famous incursion accident in recent years, is by no means the only one. In January 1990, an accident eerily reminiscent of the LAX tragedy occurred at Atlanta's Hartsfield International Airport. In that tragedy, an Eastern Airlines 727 landed just behind a general aviation Beechcraft King Air 100. The planes collided and the pilot of the smaller plane was killed. Luckily, none of the passengers or crew of the larger plane were injured. In 1991, an MD-80 and a 737 collided at Newark Airport shortly after both landed. In that accident, the wing of one plane became embedded in the fuselage of the other. Of the 169 people on both planes, only 23 people suffered minor injuries. (One reason for the low injury count was the absence of fire. Had there been fire, the story might have had a more tragic ending.)

A more deadly incursion accident occurred at Detroit Metropolitan Airport on a foggy December 3, 1990:

> It is a cold and foggy day in Detroit. Two Northwest Airlines aircraft are preparing for takeoff. One is Flight 1482, a DC-9, and the other is Flight 299, a Boeing B-727. It is 1:45. The 727 is 24 seconds from takeoff ....
> The DC-9 is lost in the fog.
>
> The captain of the DC-9 is speaking with ground control:
>
> **Captain:** Hey, ground, 1482. We're out here we're stu ... we can't see anything out here. [Lapse of 8 seconds] Ah, ground, 1482.
>
> **Ground control:** Northwest 1482, just to verify, you are proceeding southbound on X-ray now and you are across nine two seven.
>
> **Captain:** Ah, we're not sure, it's so foggy out here we're completely stuck here.
>
> **Ground control:** Okay, ah, are you on a ru- taxiway or on a runway?
>
> **Captain:** We're on a runway we're right by ah, zero four.
>
> **Ground control:** Yeah, Northwest 1482 roger, are you clear of Runway 3 Center?
>
> **Flight officer:** We're on Runway 21 Center.
>
> **Captain:** Yeah, it looks like we're on 21 Center here.
>
> (Expletive.) Pause of 10 seconds from captain's last transmission
>
> **Ground control:** Northwest 1482, y'say you are on 21 Center?
>
> **Captain:** I believe we are, we're not sure.
>
> **Flight officer:** Yes we are.
>
> Pause of 5 seconds from captain's last transmission
>
> **Ground control:** Northwest 1482 roger. If you are on 21 Center exit that runway immediately sir.

A few seconds later, the 727 begins its takeoff roll. It is on Runway 9/27, which intersects with 21 Center. The plane accelerates to about 100 knots when suddenly

out of the fog the DC-9 appears on the right side of
the runway in the path of the right wing of the 727.
The nose of the DC-9 is facing the 727. There is a
sickening sound as the right wing tip of the 727 strikes
just below the first officer's middle window on the
DC-9. The fuselage of the DC-9 is torn down the side
and the wing then tears the DC-9's engine cowl away
from the fuselage at the back of the plane.

The captain of the 727 successfully aborts the
takeoff and stops the plane. No one on board is
injured. The situation on board the DC-9, is not so
fortunate. Three passengers are killed by the impact of
the wing tearing the fuselage. A fire breaks out that
one passenger later describes as looking like a blow
torch coming into the cabin at the right rear where the
engine was torn away from the fuselage. Five other
people, including a flight attendant, are killed by the
fire or by smoke inhalation.

Eight people died on Flight 1482 but it could have been much
worse. Imagine the carnage if the collision had been fuselage to
fuselage instead of wingtip to fuselage.

The NTSB accident report of the event found that the probable cause of the accident was a lack of proper crew coordination
on the DC-9. Contributing causes were deficiencies in air traffic
control services (the ground controller failed to alert the air traffic
controller in charge of the 727 that a possible incursion had taken
place), deficiencies in surface markings, signs, and lighting at the
airport, and the failure of the FAA to correct these deficiencies,
and the failure of Northwest Airlines to provide adequate cockpit
resource management training (*see* chapter 17).

These accidents are the tip of the incursion iceberg. In fact,
hundreds of incursions happen every year. The FAA keeps statistics on airport incursions. The record since 1986, is as follows:

- 1986   325
- 1987   425
- 1988   190
- 1989   210
- 1990   281
- 1991   243
- 1992   217

There is no doubt that these numbers, each representing a potentially serious accident, must be reduced.

Four primary contributors to runway incursions are: improper clearances by ground control to enter active runways (as in the LAX accident); incomplete communications between aircraft and control (as in the Detroit accident); poor ground navigation (as in the Detroit accident); and lack of situational awareness by pilots and controllers (as in both Detroit and LAX accidents). Most often, incursions result from a combination of factors. For example, in Detroit, the pilot of the DC-9 taxied onto an active runway but the ground controller did not issue an alert that a possible incursion was ongoing.

Among the cures being looked at to substantially reduce incursions is the ground radar, known as ASDE, discussed in chapter 11. That technology continues to experience problems and remains behind schedule. A plan to supplement visual warnings on the ASDE system with audio alerts won't be in use until 1995 at the earliest. Other needed reforms, such as standardization of airport signs and markings, will go into effect in 1994. A very good idea to create a standardized lighting system to warn of intersecting runways appears to be nearer to fruition. The airport surface traffic automation (ASTA) system is being prepared which would integrate technology into an all encompassing ground control system. The FAA expects to begin deploying these systems by 1997 (although, if history is a guide, it will be more like 2000). There are also plans to improve the warning lights on small planes to make them more visible. And the FAA has commissioned a tower simulator to train new controllers in tower procedures, which offers hope of increased safety.

There are some other relatively simple, commonsense solutions that could make a big difference in the short term that the FAA should consider. For example, Captain David J. Haase, then the air safety chairman for the Air Line Pilots Association, suggested at the Flight Safety Foundation 44th annual International Air Safety Seminar drawing a red line around the runway. That would be inexpensive and would constitute a "last line of defense that should not be crossed until authorized by ATC." Standardizing the lexicon used between air traffic controllers and pilots is another good idea. There are proposals to install low energy transponders in airport ground vehicles so that they can be tracked and to place electronic maps of each airport in cockpits so that a pilot will always know where the aircraft is located during taxiing.

On a less optimistic note, the GAO has expressed worries that the FAA is not doing a good job managing the development of ASDE technology and other anti-incursion projects. On August 4, 1992, Kenneth Mead of the GAO testified before the Aviation Subcommittee:

> FAA officials expect to set project priorities when the (runway incursion) plan is updated later this year and to provide project costs in quarterly reports to the Congress, rather than in the updated plan. We are concerned about FAA's commitment to follow through with updating the plan and providing cost information to the Congress. Last year FAA stated that it would update the plan by January 1992 but did not do so, and over the past one and a half years, FAA has provided the Congress with only one quarterly report on the plan. Without project status reports, Congress cannot determine if FAA has made progress on the plan or if FAA is allocating sufficient resources to preventing accidents on the nation's runways.

In other words, the GAO is saying that talk is cheap. What the investigating agency wants, and the American people should demand, is consistent excellence in management and a commitment to timely performance in correcting the serious incursion problem that still threatens the safety of airline passengers.

The problem of the aborted takeoff

"For a number of reasons, we (pilots) are forced to fly by the seat of our pants on the decision of whether it is safe to abort a takeoff."

An airline captain who flies for a major U.S. airline

Occasionally, while a plane is on its takeoff roll, it will experience a cockpit alarm or the pilot will somehow sense that it is not safe to proceed. If it is not safe, the plane will be stopped in a procedure known as an *aborted takeoff.*

Aborted takeoffs save lives. But they can also be deadly if the plane is unable to stop before coming to the end of the runway. On September 20, 1989, for example, the pilot of a USAir 737 attempted to abort takeoff at La Guardia Airport in New York and was unable to stop the plane before it ran off the runway and crashed into the East River. The plane's nose landed on a wooden pier holding airport lights in the middle of the river with its tail submerged in the water. Two passengers were killed in the crash and 31 were injured.

This accident was a vivid and tragic reminder that La Guardia Airport has relatively short runways and short airport runway overruns. So do other airports around the nation such as Love Field in Dallas, Texas. (Most of these airports were constructed before the use of widebody craft and for that reason do not have the longer runways required for safe operation of large widebody planes such as the Boeing 747 or DC-10.)

Long runways or short, there are two safety issues of pressing concern required to make aborted takeoffs safer: Extending runways and obtaining accurate information advising pilots when a takeoff abort can be safely performed.

Runway extensions

Current rules require there to be 1000 feet of overrun space at each end of a runway to increase the safety of airport flight operations. The point is to provide an extra margin of safety in the event of an aborted takeoff or a premature landing. Unfortunately, the FAA permitted a grandfather clause to be placed in the rule and thus many older airports do not have to comply with the newer safety standards.

National Airport in Washington, D.C., has already proved that the new standard can save lives. The operators of National Airport decided to build longer overruns to increase the safety of the airport. Since then, and on more than one occasion, planes have aborted takeoffs and stopped on the newly constructed runway extensions. Had the extensions not been built, these planes would have overrun the runway and might have crashed, perhaps falling into the Potomac River. Passengers who walked away from those incidents might have been injured or killed without an overrun.

Studies need to be undertaken to determine the feasibility of building extended runways at La Guardia Airport in New York and at other locations around the country. (The overrun at La

Guardia is only 100 feet long at the end of the runway where the
USAir jet was unable to stop after an aborted takeoff and crashed
into the water, killing two people. A 1000-foot overrun might have
saved those lives.) "The old airports should be forced to meet current runway safety standards," Vic Hewes says. "The new standards have demonstrated that they can save lives."

It must be admitted that extending overruns to 1000 feet might
not be feasible at every airport. But that does not mean that the
runways at these older airports cannot be made safer. Rather than
issue a blanket exception to increasing runway safety by way of a
grandfather clause, the burden should be placed on the airport
operator to prove to the FAA that improvements cannot reasonably be made. (For example, a 500-foot overrun might be able to
be constructed, even if a 1000-foot one could not. Or, a sharp
drop off at the end of a runway overrun could be graded to prevent a plane from breaking up in a crash and would allow for easier emergency response.) Creating an individualized airport safety
improvement program would allow for topographical exceptions
to general safety rules but would also result in an overall increase
in airport safety levels.

Aircraft testing

That brings us to the more pressing concern: improving the manner in which airplanes are now tested to determine the point up
to which a takeoff can be safely aborted. The moment that a takeoff abort becomes unsafe is known in aviation lexicon as V_1.
During the takeoff roll, the member of the flight crew who is not
flying the takeoff, will call out, V_1 when the point of no return has
been passed. After reaching V_1, procedures require the pilot to
take off even if one of the engines fails—on the theory that it is
better to get into the air, make a turn around the airport and make
an emergency landing, than it is to crash—because the plane cannot be stopped before the end of the runway.

Pilots do not question the policy of establishing a V_1 point, but
they do protest the manner in which the V_1 location is determined. One pilot who has years of flying experience with a major
U.S. airline, said, "The tests that tell us when it is safe to abort are
not accurate. First, the pilot knows the test is going to happen. In
a real abort, it takes longer to react. Second, they use brand new
planes, with new engines and unused brakes. That plane will stop
faster during the test than it ever will again. Third, they begin ...

with wheels at the edge of the runway. ALPA ran a test on the issue and discovered that it takes 130 percent of the length of the plane to line up for takeoff under real conditions."

In other words, the test planes will be able to stop more quickly than a plane in actual operation. This means the V_1 point will come later in the takeoff sequence than should be the case. This, in turn, can cause a pilot to abort a takeoff when it is not, in fact, safe to abort.

This working pilot's concerns were reiterated by J. Randolph Babbitt, president of ALPA in August 1992. "The rejected takeoffs have been a big concern for this organization (ALPA) for years. They use new planes, a dry runway and they back the plane up to the edge of the runway. They measure from main (landing) gear to main gear. Of course there may be 80 to 100 feet of plane in front of that main gear. It's really ludicrous."

(Because of the pilots' complaints about the V_1 tests, the FAA promulgated a rule requiring a 2-second pause between the test "event" causing the aborted takeoff and the test pilot trying to stop the plane. The rule was passed in the late 1970s but all planes then in development by manufacturers, such as the 757 and 767 were exempted from the rules, making it essentially a meaningless gesture until new planes such as the Boeing 777 take their certification tests.)

Why would the FAA and the airlines want a V_1 test that is essentially inaccurate? In a word, money. If the plane can be shown to stop sooner down the runway, planes will be certified to fly with heavier payloads—read that to mean, jets filled with more people, cargo, or fuel. "The issue here is weight," Babbitt said in explaining the point. "Let's take La Guardia Airport. La Guardia's runway is about 7000 feet. That's an adequate length for certain aircraft if they are light enough, say 150,000 pounds. But it may be woefully short if you weigh 180,000 pounds. That extra weight is going to require you to achieve more speed on the ground before going airborne." And if tests were accurate? The planes would have to be lighter and something would have to come off: passengers, cargo, or fuel—meaning fewer dollars in the airlines' pockets.

The V_1 tests appear to be another example of antisafety impact of the FAA's dual mandate (fostering safety and promoting aviation). Safety is compromised so that more money can be made by the airlines. But safety should be the first consideration.

There have been too many aborted takeoff accidents to permit this dangerous stacking of the deck in favor of a late V_1 runway location. New tests should be conducted to accurately predict when a takeoff can be aborted safely. The 2-second time lapse should be utilized, the plane should pull into takeoff position as it would during normal operations and the test should be from nose gear to nose gear instead of measured from the main gear. That would be placing safety first. (The problem probably goes even deeper, according to C.O. Miller, safety consultant. "This is an example of the FAA failing to understand the problem and, (similar to) the deicing controversy, to take into account normal human performance limitations.")

Captain Babbitt told us that after much "haranguing" and discussion, the FAA was set to draft an NPRM requiring more realistic V_1 tests. Then, after much anticipation and work, an official silence descended on the plan. The NPRM was never published. After some checking, Babbitt claims ALPA discovered that the proposed rule died in the OMB, which killed the plan on the premise that it would be too costly for the airlines. Let's hope the new Clinton administration puts the safety of passengers before the profit philosophy of the airlines in this important matter and resurrects the plan to make the tests more accurate.

General aviation and commercial airports

"The facts and circumstances of this accident demonstrated the necessity of providing both controllers and pilots with automated systems that can assist them in avoiding midair collisions."

From the 1987 NTSB accident report concerning the midair collision between a DC-9 and a Piper general aviation aircraft

An ongoing controversy is the mixing of commercial air traffic—generally consisting of large transport jets and turboprop commuter planes—with smaller and slower private piston-engine planes flown by most private pilots in general aviation. (There are approximately 220,000 general aviation aircraft, of which 200,000 are piston-engine small planes that carry fewer than 10 passengers.)

Many commercial pilots and their passengers worry about midair collisions between private airplanes and commercial jets in airspace proximate to airports. Indeed, such tragic collisions have occurred twice in the last 15 years at the cost of hundreds of lives. Pilots also worry about the increased workload placed on air traffic controllers when private planes land in front of fast-flying jets. The dramatic difference in speed creates extra work for the controller who will have to make sure that the jet does not run down the private plane.

The danger of midair collisions

In order to avoid midair collisions between commercial craft landing or taking off from an airport and private planes flying near the airport, the FAA created the *terminal control area* (TCA). A TCA is airspace within which all aircraft must be under air traffic control.

To visualize a TCA, picture an inverted round, multitiered wedding cake, with the small part of the cake on the bottom and the largest area, about 20 miles wide, now at the top. The closer to an airport, the TCA is closer to the ground, and even touches the ground in the area directly adjacent to the airport runways. Conversely, the farther away, the higher the beginning and ending altitudes of the TCA. (TCA airspace generally covers altitudes in which transport craft are likely to fly as they approach or leave the airport.)

A private plane that enters a TCA must be fitted with an operating mode C transponder, which will allow the air traffic controller to identify the plane's altitude. Planes not fitted with a mode C are merely blips on a screen and the controller is unable to determine whether the plane is in a TCA or whether it endangers, or is endangered by, other craft.

General aviation pilots that do not comply with TCA rules can be a problem for commercial aviation:

August 31, 1986
Cerritos, California

Aerovanes de Mexico Flight 498, a flight from Tijuana, Mexico, carrying 58 passengers and six crew members, is on approach to Los Angeles International Airport. The plane is being duly flown under IFR and is in communication with the Los Angeles TRACON. The air is clear, visibility 14 miles. All is proceeding uneventfully.

A Piper airplane, carrying three people, has taken

off from Torrance Airport—a general aviation facility
in southwest Los Angeles County—on its way to the
mountain resort town of Big Bear to the southeast.
The pilot of the Piper is flying under VFR and is not in
communication with any air traffic control facility. The
plane is equipped with a transponder but it is tuned to
a setting that is used for planes that are flying VFR and
is therefore unlikely to attract the attention of an air
traffic controller.

The Piper is flown into the Los Angeles
International Airport Terminal Control Area without
clearance from air traffic control. This is a violation of
the FARs. Flight control radar has picked up the Piper
causing a blip, but the blip is not noticed by the air
traffic controller.

The pilot of Flight 498 is warned by air traffic
control that there is "traffic, ten o'clock, one mile,
northbound, altitude unknown." The pilot
acknowledges and seeks a visual sighting. This
sighting is a different plane than the Piper. Los
Angeles Approach Control next advises the airline
pilot to reduce speed and descend to 6000 feet; the
pilot is then told to "hold what you have, we have a
change in plans for you."

There is another GA plane in the vicinity. It is a
Grumman Tiger aircraft flying VFR. The Tiger pilot
contacts ATC as required by all general aviation craft
in a terminal control area. He identifies his plane, his
intended course, states that he is climbing from 3400
feet and asks for clearance to fly at 4500 feet. He is
told by ATC that he is in the middle of a busy TCA
corridor and that jets fly routinely through his area of
sky at 3500 feet. He is also informed that a jet has just
passed him at 5000 feet.

The time it has taken to deal with the Grumman
pilot has taken the air traffic controller's attention
away from Flight 498. The controller suddenly notices
that his ATC computer is no longer tracking the flight.
The Piper has collided with the top of the tail of the
DC-9 at 6550 feet and destroyed the vertical and
horizontal stabilizers. Both planes have fallen into a

residential neighborhood in Cerritos, Orange County. The crash is nonsurvivable. The bodies of the DC-9 flight crew are torn apart by the impact and cannot be autopsied. All of the DC-9 passengers are killed by the tremendous force of the impact. The people on the Piper are decapitated. Fifteen people on the ground are also killed. A total of 82 people have died.

The accident occurred about three miles inside the Los Angeles International Airport TCA. The Piper aircraft did not have a mode C transponder. The NTSB accident report stated: "Without mode C altitude information the air traffic controller could not determine whether the craft was within the TCA because the controller (did) not know the altitude of the craft."

The pilot of the Piper was found by the NTSB to have been a careful and meticulous flyer who had sought advice on avoiding the TCA before leaving for Big Bear and had purchased a map to help him do so. He apparently miscalculated his position, leading him to inadvertently fly the Piper into TCA space without permission from ATC, which led directly to the tragic collision. (Extensive investigation was conducted to determine whether the pilot had suffered a heart attack. It was determined through medical tests and circumstantial evidence that he had not.)

As a result of this accident, the NTSB recommended that the area in which all planes flying with a mode C transponder be expanded to 30 nautical miles from the center of a TCA. The FAA agreed and promulgated the rule, thereby adding a 10-mile safety cushion that will hopefully prevent most inadvertent GA penetrations. This rule should also permit TCAS midair collision avoidance technology to be more effective.

This is well and good but it might not complete the job of preventing inadvertent TCA incursions. According to the Aircraft Owners and Pilots Association, (AOPA), more needs to be done to better prevent another "Cerritos." (AOPA is the principle trade and safety association for general aviation pilots.)

Here is the problem: While mode C transponders help air traffic controllers identify incursions after they happen, the transponders do not help the private pilot realize that his or her plane is in danger of entering TCA airspace. AOPA's idea is help GA pilots better recognize the boundaries of TCAs to avoid inadvertent incursions and thereby increase safety.

One excellent proposal is to take steps to make it easier for a GA pilot to identify TCA airspace. "Current charts identify TCAs through circles drawn on a two-dimensional map. These maps may be difficult to follow while flying," says Drew Steketee, AOPA senior vice president for communications and a GA pilot with many years experience. "Moreover, TCAs are not designed in even circles in many areas because of the local geography or the number of major airports. Some TCAs are so complex that it may be difficult to know whether you have (entered) the airspace. Then, there is the problem of small airports in the area where there will be traffic to avoid. This can create very complex traffic patterns, especially in areas such as Los Angeles." (Indeed, the greater Los Angeles metropolitan area has five major air carrier airports, 18 GA airports, and four military bases. Perhaps that is one reason that LAX has been given a black star as one of the world's most dangerous airports, according to *The Independent on Sunday*, a British paper that cited the International Federation of Airline Pilots as its source.)

The AOPA proposal to clear up the confusion is to create new aviation charts that do two things:

Establish air corridors that VFR pilots can fly through that will permit them to avoid TCAs or help pilots know when they must contact ATC This is the brainchild of Barry Schiff, a TWA captain and private pilot who recently won the $10,000 Wolf Foundation prize for innovation in aviation safety for this idea. Schiff's proposal is to create a map that will inform VFR pilots the altitude and location they can fly to avoid TCA airspace, and identify landmarks on the chart to help them fly the course. The idea has support within the general aviation community. "Current charts only tell private pilots where they *cannot* fly," Steketee states. "That takes their attention away from scanning the sky for other aircraft. Creating a chart that tells pilots where they *can* fly and at what altitude will increase safety by ensuring that the TCA airspace is never crossed, or is recognized, so that ATC can be contacted and the plane can come under air traffic control."

Make TCA charts more usable "It is difficult to know precisely where a TCA begins based on a fictional line on a map when you are flying," Steketee also told us. "Too often, TCAs are designed with concentric circles matching the range rings on a controller's radarscope. But the pilot has no methodology to determine the location of these boundaries in the air. What is needed are *identifying landmarks* on the chart that could be seen from the air and that would tell a pilot when he is straying into controlled space and TCAs designed using straight lines since most flight navigation is based on flying in a straight line from identifiable point to identifiable point." Thus, downtown high-rise buildings, a large amusement park, a power plant, or other notable landmarks would replace imaginary circles, or radio transmission points would serve as the boundaries of TCAs, making it easier for pilots to determine their location and the need to contact air traffic control.

These are good ideas and the FAA should work with GA pilots on ways to identify TCAs. (Indeed, the FAA now consults experienced pilots, known as "user groups," for this purpose.)

Another disturbing aspect of the Cerritos tragedy is that the two planes could have been seen by the respective pilots beginning 1 minute and 13 seconds before the accident—enough time for the collision to be avoided. According to the NTSB accident report, the Piper pilot had the best opportunity to see and avoid the DC-9, but there was a problem:

> The safety board determined that the person
> occupying the right seat in the Piper was not a pilot
> and had never received scan training (the technique
> for seeing other aircraft). Therefore, for this analysis,
> the safety board assumed that only the pilot was or
> would have scanned for other airplanes. Based solely
> on the relative size of the two airplanes, the ... Piper
> pilot had a better chance of seeing the DC-9 than the
> Aeromexico flight crew had of seeing the Piper.
> However, ... the DC-9 was visible through the Piper's
> right windscreen and near the outer limits of a left-
> right scanning pattern. Since the safety board cannot
> assume that any of the passengers would have been
> involved in an active scan for airplanes, the location of
> the DC-9, despite its greater size, would have reduced
> the Piper pilot's ability to see it. Further, given the
> available evidence, the safety board cannot reach any
> conclusion concerning his alertness to the conduct
> and maintenance of an active scan for other airplanes.

In other words, the DC-9 was visible to the Piper pilot at the far right side of the windshield more than a minute before the collision; however, the jet's location in the sky made it easier to see from the right front seat passenger's point of view. The collision occurred because the pilot apparently didn't see the approaching DC-9 and presumably, the passenger wasn't looking.

Now, assume a different scenario: The Piper has a midair collision warning device installed that starts a bell chiming at times of impending collision danger. The respective planes are flying the same routes toward a deadly midair collision about one minute in the future. The Piper's midair collision avoidance device begins sounding the alarm. What would happen? Adrenaline would surge through the pilot's body. His alertness would be heightened and he would lean forward in his seat searching all areas of the sky for the intruding plane. The passengers would ask what the bell ringing was all about. Upon being told it was a midair collision warning, they too would begin searching earnestly for the other plane. The chances that the DC-9 would be seen would be greatly enhanced. Assuming the people in the Piper see the plane in 30–40 seconds, evasive action could be taken. The collision would probably be avoided. (If the jet had TCAS installed, and if the small plane had a mode C transponder operating, the chances of avoiding the collision are further increased.)

This fictional happier ending to the Cerritos tragedy illustrates why midair collision avoidance technology should be researched and ultimately required to be installed in all general aviation aircraft that fly in areas requiring the use of mode C transponders. VFR flight involves the concept of "see and avoid." Under see-and-avoid procedures, the pilot must scan the sky in order to see other craft. Anyone who has flown in a small plane will testify that seeing aircraft, even large aircraft, in a big sky is often easier said than done. Technology can help fill in the gap by detecting and alerting of pending danger.

At present, AOPA opposes rules requiring the installation of technology such as midair collision avoidance systems and ground proximity warning devices in general aviation aircraft. Their objection is based on the cost of safety. "The issue for GA is the cost/benefit relationship of new equipment," Steketee told us. "Many times the equipment proposal will yield very little improvement in safety. Other times, the new equipment will yield little benefit to the GA user who must install it at his own expense."

But the lives of commercial airline passengers who pass through airspace shared between transport planes and general aviation aircraft depend on collision avoidance. The large jets already have TCAS II (although it needs improving) and are supposed to subsequently have TCAS III. TCAS I, designed for commuter aircraft, must be installed by February 9, 1995 (although its development is currently behind schedule.) TCAS I is designed to give 80 seconds warning of a collision during flight and 15–20 seconds warning during takeoff and initial climb, or approach and landing.

Installation of midair collision avoidance technology will depend on it being reasonably affordable. According to an article by Fred George entitled "TCAS I" in *Business & Commercial Aviation* (January 1993), prospective TCAS I system prices are expected to cost anywhere from $22,000 to $65,000 plus installation. That, to say the least, is not affordable for most average GA operators.

However, there is a midair collision avoidance system already on the market specifically designed for GA aircraft, that is affordable. Produced by Ryan International of Columbus, Ohio, the cost of their collision avoidance systems range from $5000 to $11,000. The manufacturer claims that their system is sensitive enough to detect other aircraft as far away as 2000–200 vertical feet, depending on how the device has been adjusted. Horizontal separation is supposed to be detectable as far away as 5 miles. If the Ryan system is what it claims to be, it demonstrates that midair avoidance collision technology can be created for GA aircraft at a more affordable price. Rulemaking by FAA would probably reduce the price even further because other companies would enter the market and the resulting competition would bring the price of the systems down.

The problem of using the same airport

Pilots of general aviation aircraft have the same right to use a large commercial airport as do transport jets; thus, an observer of flight operations at airports such as Kennedy, National, and Los Angeles, will not only see huge jets taking off and landing but small private aircraft as well.

Many commercial pilots would like to see an end to this practice at the larger airports. One pilot told us, "GA planes make landing and takeoff harder and complicate the work of air traffic controllers." Why? "A GA plane may be smaller but it takes up the same amount of airspace. If I am flying approach, I'll have to slow my 737 because I have a small plane in front of me. It just makes things tougher all the way around."

In 1978, a midair collision in San Diego between a PSA Boeing 727 and a Cessna 172 occurred while both planes were under air traffic control. In that tragedy, the 727 essentially ran down the smaller GA aircraft. The collision brought down both planes killing 135 people and was considered by the NTSB as being non-survivable. (After that tragedy, a TCA was created for the San Diego area. But that might not have prevented this accident because both planes were under air traffic control at the time of the collision.)

The time has come for the busiest commercial airports to prohibit smaller planes from using the facilities, at least during peak flying times when the sky and airport are saturated with aircraft. That would ease congestion and reduce the chances for a midair collision between a private plane and a transport craft. (Some airports already charge high landing fees to discourage "consumption.") Another idea being discussed is to segregate smaller and slower craft onto separate runways designated for the use of general aviation aircraft, thereby getting them out of the way of faster transport jets. Surely, the general aircraft community, appropriate government entities, and commercial aviation can reach accommodation on these issues to make flying safer for everyone.

Increased airport capacity

The pressure is on to increase the capacity of airports. During peak flying times many airports are already operating at their maximum capacity (generally about 30–35 planes per hour per runway). Substantial growth can only be achieved at these facilities by building new runways; however, that is a difficult proposition, what with noise problems, political opposition, environmental concerns, and space limitations. As a result, the growth commercial aviation requires for its financial health has reached a bottleneck stifling the industry.

These difficulties have led to a drive to relax some important safety rules, so that a few extra planes can be squeezed in and out of the airports per hour. The airline pilots unions are less than pleased with many of these actual and proposed operational changes. J. Randolf Babbitt, president of ALPA, stated: "We have trouble with some of the calls for increased airport capacity. We'll go along if the moves are accompanied by expenditures for physical airport improvements; however, we find ourselves at odds in those cases where they simply want to shorten space, do tighter parallels (landings and takeoffs), use cross runways with instructions to hold short. We haven't been supportive of the majority. We see them as a compromise, too great a compromise." "Compromises" described by Babbitt include:

Parallel landings

A parallel landing occurs when two planes land at the same time on runways parallel to each other. The FAA permits parallel landings at several airports around the country, including Logan Airport in Boston and at the San Francisco International Airport. (The runways at SFO are only 750 feet apart, forcing landing jets to engage in a form of formation flying as they are landing.)

Currently, parallel landings are only operated in fair weather, when visibility is good. Now, there is talk of allowing such parallel runway use during poor weather, with the proponents depending on technology to keep the parallel planes apart. Such proposed practices must be opposed. Planes fly so fast and are so powerful that even a small deviation could result in tragedy.

Using intersecting runways

Pilots also complain that the FAA permits simultaneous landings on intersecting runways, with the planes being ordered to "hold short" of the intersection until ground control gives directions as to how to proceed. The danger presented by hold-short operations involve the tragedy that might happen if a landing plane finds that it cannot stop in time to hold short before reaching the intersection and a possible collision with another jet. Or, as in the Los Angeles runway incursion tragedy, an error by an air traffic controller could lead to a collision. These hold-short operations are conducted at O'Hare International Airport in Chicago and at National Airport in Washington, D.C., to name two. Now, the FAA wants to expand the program. This is opposed by ALPA at least until specific and adequate rules are created governing the practice.

Reduced separation of aircraft

At one time, the FAA mandated a 4-mile spacing between aircraft during landing and takeoff. In order to increase capacity, spacing has been reduced to 2½ miles. The pilots report that they have even been asked if they mind landing before the aircraft that landed before has cleared the runway. This squeezing of space between aircraft reduces safety because planes are permitted to operate at closer quarters where a mistake can lead to a near miss or even, tragedy.

Noise abatement procedures

Noise abatement is an important program to protect the health of people who live proximate to airport takeoff and landing flying patterns. Accordingly, many localities have established strict noise abatement standards.

Noise abatement is best accomplished by improving the equipment, with quieter engines and new aircraft, but it will be years before the majority of the fleet consists of new and quieter planes.

In the meantime, many airports require noise abatement flight activities that many pilots consider to be less than safe. On September 30, 1991, Captain Richard A. Deeds, chairman of the noise abatement committee for ALPA, stated, "In my opinion, noise abatement is the greatest single (aviation) safety problem in the United States." Deeds states that some noise abatement procedures endanger planes by requiring them to climb at a "negative climb gradient" if the power of one engine is lost. (The plane will fall rather than climb with one engine's power lost.) Other complaints include vertical takeoff angles so sharp that tail strikes on the runway have occurred during "rotation" (the point when the pilot lifts the nose of the airplane off the runway to initiate the climbout); the use of less safe runways based on wind factors to decrease the noise of operations; and using visual, rather than instrument, flying techniques to follow a predefined course. For instance, Deeds reported that noise abatement at the National Airport in Washington, D.C., violate many safety principles because so much attention has to be paid to landmarks: "... the crew (is required) to visually follow the (Potomac) river (but) the nose attitude of the aircraft prohibits seeing the river except for peripheral or side vision. The same departure also requires a deep power cut. All this while operating in visual conditions .... Who is looking out the window for collision avoidance? Visual flight rules require the crew to perform this function and the air traffic control system has no responsibility to provide separation or traffic information."

As long as old airplanes are flying old and noisy engines, noise abatement will be a problem compelling pilots to reduce noise levels at a cost to safe operations.

Build or expand

The best solution to the pressing need to increase the capacity of the aviation system and to alleviate overcrowded airports is the building of new airports and/or expanding those already in operation. But that is a costly, lengthy, and politically difficult proposition under the best of circumstances. In the meantime, alternate answers to reducing safety margins exist if the aviation community is willing to be creative. For example, why not encourage off peak hour operations by having airports charge airlines more per landing during peak periods? They might then charge a lower price for nonpeak flights, (perhaps inducing families with children to fly at these times by offering discounted pricing for infants carried in infant safety seats.) Or, perhaps a combination of travel modes should be considered by building high-speed trains between surrounding communities and major airports, thereby reducing the number of small commuter flights that would fly in and out of hub airports, thus allowing more large transport jet flights, thereby increasing efficiency. The answers are there. We just have to commit our energies to creating them through a more comprehensive national transportation policy, rather than sacrificing safety levels on the altar of increased airport capacity.

Part VI

Man, nature, & safety

"The primary safety problems facing aviation are issues involving human factors. Of course, that's a pretty all-encompassing thought."

John H. Enders, vice chairman of the Flight Safety Foundation

"Everybody talks about the weather but nobody does anything about it."

Editorial in the *Hartford Courant*, August 14, 1897

Part VI focuses on two important areas that have a direct and an indirect impact on aviation safety. Chapter 17 discusses the human element as it affects safety. How does human interaction influence the level of safety? Can management practices improve the safety of flight operations? What part does human fatigue play in safety? Is substance abuse a serious safety issue?

Chapter 18 looks at the weather. Weather related phenomena, specifically severe wind conditions generated by storm activity and icing conditions, can dramatically increase the risk of flight; however, unlike the lament of the newspaper editorial quote, the aviation safety community isn't just complaining—the safety community is doing something, although perhaps not enough. As a result, even though the danger posed by the weather has not been eliminated, weather's threat to airline safety is being steadily reduced.

17

Practice makes perfect

"(There is a) growing concern about civil aviation safety as affected by human performance. These concerns have been highlighted by accident statistics which ... have shown that over the last 10 years, approximately 65 percent of the civil aircraft accidents were directly attributed to flight crew error as a factor to the probable cause."

**From the *National Plan to Enhance Aviation Safety Through Human Factors Improvements*
Air Transport Association of America, April 1989**

Most people are familiar with the term "pilot error," a simplistic term that is often used to describe the cause of an accident in a news report that fails to take the whole web of human causes into account. A better term to utilize is "human failures." High levels of safety, or the lack thereof, can be attributed to the levels of human performance. Whether it is in the initial design of aircraft, the quality of personnel training, management's creation of a "work atmosphere" that is conducive (or destructive) to safe operations or simply the commission of mistakes, it is people, either acting through institutions or directly, that ultimately determine the aviation system's level of safety.

There is no doubt that human failures play a large part in most aviation accidents or incidents. Indeed, the probable cause of many accidents is often human error, whether that error is the pilot's, the air traffic controller's, the engineers' design, the quality of aircraft construction, the failure of maintenance or inspection, in FAA oversight, or a combination of these and other causative elements. Three crashes illustrate the point.

The plane that crashed into the river

According to the NTSB accident report, the USAir Boeing 737 that crashed into the East River during an attempted aborted takeoff on September 20, 1989 (discussed briefly in chapter 16), was primarily caused by a chain of human errors. A recap of the events leading to the crash reveals a series of mistakes that resulted in the death of two people. Among the errors uncovered by the accident investigation were the following (as described in the NTSB report):

- The rudder trim had been moved to full left while the airplane was parked. This affected the ability of the plane to take off, but should not have caused a crash.

- The rudder trim problem should have been detected by the captain on three separate occasions before the takeoff was attempted: during taxi, during the flight control freedom-of-movement check, and during the response to a checklist challenge (when the first officer reads through a printed checklist to make sure everything in the plane is in proper order.)

- The captain did not use the autobrake system during the takeoff roll, as recommended by the aircraft manufacturer and airline management. This failure delayed the onset of braking and extended the plane's stopping distance.

- Both pilots in the flight crew were relatively inexperienced in their respective positions. The first officer conducted the takeoff, his first nonsupervised line takeoff in a Boeing 737.

- Neither pilot was monitoring indicated airspeed and no standard airspeed callouts were performed.

- Computed (takeoff decision) speed was 125 knots and action by the captain to reject the takeoff began at 130 knots.

- Braking during the rejected takeoff was less than the maximum achievable on the wet runway. If maximum braking had been applied, it is likely that the airplane could have been stopped on the runway.

The accident report clearly demonstrates that this accident could have been avoided in a number of different ways between the push back from the gate to the plane's ultimate crash into the East River. Investigation and training to improve human factors is designed to increase the likelihood that mistakes will be avoided and when they do occur, they will be caught and corrected before headline-making tragedies unfold.

The plane that ran out of gas

When a car runs out of gas, the worst thing that usually results is an embarrassing walk to the nearest gas station. But when a plane runs out of fuel, the outcome is often tragic. Such was the case in New York when an Avianca jet that had been "stacked" for more than 1 hour and 17 minutes waiting to land crashed after executing a missed approach at Kennedy Airport. The reason? As ridiculous as it sounds, it ran out of fuel.

The NTSB accident investigation determined that the probable cause of the crash was the flight crew's failure to adequately manage the airplane's fuel load and their failure to communicate to air traffic control that an emergency fuel situation existed. Among the factors cited as a contributing factor was inadequate traffic flow management by the FAA. (Apparently, central flow control allowed too many planes to fly to Kennedy Airport at a time of inclement weather, resulting in long holdings. Traffic management also failed to adequately consider arriving international flights when making flow control management decisions.)

A further contributing cause was the lack of standardized understandable terminology for pilots and controllers during "minimum and fuel emergency states." (The flight crew had requested priority handling and had informed air traffic control that they could only hold for five more minutes because "we run (sic) out of fuel now," but never used the word, "emergency." The flight crew also failed to warn the passengers of the pending crash, which, according to the NTSB report, "may have contributed to the severity of the injuries sustained."

The plane that ran out of fuel is another example of a chain of human errors leading to a tragic result. Had the crew said the magic word "emergency," had Central Flow Control performed to their usual standard of excellence, indeed, had the controller been more curious about the extent of the plane's distress when told, "we run out of fuel now," there might never have been a crash.

The plane that couldn't take off

On August 16, 1987, 148 passengers and six crew members took off on Northwest Airlines Flight 255, from Detroit Metropolitan Wayne County Airport headed for Phoenix. The flight lasted all of 14 seconds. After rotation, the plane never gained significant altitude. The wings of the airplane rolled to the left at 35 degrees and then to the right. The left wing struck a lightpole located about a half a mile from the end of the runway. The plane then crashed through other lightpoles, the roof of a rental car facility and hit the ground. All 154 people on board were killed except for one four year old child, whose mother may have saved her daughter's life by placing her body over her child's as a shield against the crash. Two others died on the ground.

The NTSB determined that the probable cause of the accident was the flight crew's failure to perform the prescribed taxi checklist to ensure that the plane was ready for takeoff; they did not discover that the plane's flaps and slats were not extended as required for takeoff. (Extended flaps and slats allow for proper lift at takeoff.) In addition, for reasons unknown, the electronic takeoff warning system failed to function and alert the flight crew that the plane was improperly configured for takeoff.

The crew's apparent failure to perform the checklist was a violation of the fundamentals of safe flying that cannot be excused. From such seemingly small mistakes can flow large tragedies. Human performance training, much like spring training in baseball, is designed in part to reiterate the fundamentals and prevent the complacency that permits such elementary violations of safety norms.

Improving human performance

"The greater part of maintaining flight safety remains with the awareness and the significance of human performance, both on the flight deck and in the cabin."

**Captain Omar S. Barayan, writing in the
Flight Safety Foundation publication
Cabin Crew Safety, September 1990**

It has long been understood that by taking positive steps to improve human performance, mistakes will be reduced and the overall level of safety within the aviation system will be improved.

Accordingly, the FAA and the industry have been working together to create several human performance improvement programs designed to help reduce errors and improve human
performance when an emergency does arise. These programs
have the potential to make a significant contribution to the safety
of flying and the FAA and industry should be complimented for
creating them; however, as the following discussion reveals, more
needs to be done, especially with regard to toughening training
standards for Part 135 (commuter) flight crews and improving the
vigor of flight attendant emergency response training.

Pilot training

To maintain their FAA certification, pilots must participate in ongoing training programs designed to improve their performance
and increase safety. These training programs are beginning to
branch into the areas of human interaction and the psychology of
safety as well as sharpening flying skills.

Two of the most promising of these newer training approaches are *line oriented flight training* (LOFT) and *cockpit resource management training* (CRM). Both offer great hope for
reducing human error as a cause of accidents and incidents and in
teaching flight crews how to "get out of a jam" if trouble rears its
ugly head.

Line oriented flight training (LOFT)

Sophisticated flight simulators are the primary tool of LOFT, which
permits flight crews to experience in-flight scenarios so that they
can work on their skills in overcoming problems that might be experienced in actual flight. Simulator training is made "real"
through the use of computer interactive technology that permits
trainees to literally see, hear, and feel the simulated flight as if
they were flying a real plane. "LOFT permits us to accomplish
much more than we can through training in a real plane," an enthusiastic pilot told us. "We can experience very dangerous flight
conditions and learn how to get out of them without ever being
in any danger. The lessons learned really stay with you too because you have actually 'experienced' the event." (The simulators
are extremely realistic and the "flights" created by them are
treated by most pilots as seriously as the real thing. It's not fun to
fail either. Paul D. Russell, chief of product safety for Boeing, told

us that he has experienced a "crash" in a flight simulator and left the experience quite shaken.)

Most major airlines are enthusiastic supporters of LOFT. KLM, for example, schedules their pilots three or four times a year for recurrent simulator training, creating different flight scenarios each time. "The scenarios will generally include multiple failures, Captain Martin C. Timmermans, a pilot for KLM told participants in the Flight Safety Foundation's 44th International Aviation Safety Symposium in 1991. "As an example, a flight from Amsterdam to New York could include an engine start failure, and a rejected takeoff. After 'repair' of the 'aircraft' the flight departs again for New York, with a possible diversion later due to a serious system failure."

Adopting the theory that practice makes perfect, simulators permit pilots to practice maneuvers they would never dare try if flying a real aircraft; thus, pilots can practice aborted takeoffs, the loss of power in flight, and can fly through severe weather, all in the safety of a very realistic computer-controlled environment. The "flight" is also videotaped so that the flight crew and trainers can review the entire training session and analyze it in a joint discussion. The FAA views LOFT as being so important that it requires simulator training for Part 121 pilots to teach them the skills of flying out of wind shear, a very dangerous weather phenomena associated with thunderstorm activity that has caused more than one accident (*See* chapter 18).

While the major airlines are making increasing use of the LOFT concept, commuter airlines lag behind. "There is no doubt that simulators provide excellent training," Walter S. Coleman, president of the Regional Airlines Association told us. "In fact, they are better than actual flying because a pilot can practice until he gets something right." Despite this acknowledgment, commuter pilots do not have the same opportunity to experience LOFT as do Part 121 pilots. "The costs are prohibitive for small air carriers," Coleman says "and there are not enough simulators."

John O'Brien, director of the ALPA engineering and safety department, says that the pilot's union wants increased simulator training for commuter pilots but that the regional airlines are resisting. "They're (the regional airlines) trying to get more training in what they call 'training devices' rather than simulators—maybe a simulated cockpit and visual attachments, but no motion. But that isn't good enough. Motion is important. We feel that if you're going to do your training in a simulator and walk on the airplane and actually conduct a revenue flight, you must use a simulator that is very sophisticated."

ALPA also worries about the safety of commuter pilot training using real aircraft. In 1992, O'Brien told us, "In the last year, we've had a couple of fatal accidents for our members as a result of training in an airplane—trying to do things that you really shouldn't do in an airplane and should be done in the simulator. The same thing has also happened in the past with larger aircraft. You can make a mistake in a simulator and walk away, but pilots have died practicing dangerous maneuvers while actually flying on a training mission."

ALPA believes that the FAA should seriously consider mandating increased levels of flight simulator training for all commercial pilots, both in 121 and 135 flight operations. That seems the safest approach, both from the standpoint of protecting pilots and in the increased skill that can be taught through "hands-on" learning. Increased simulator training should improve safety levels and decrease the human error causative factors so prevalent in many air tragedies. It must be admitted that affordability will be a problem. But, with a little imagination that hurdle should be overcome. For example, companies could contribute to the creation of a nonprofit aviation safety training cooperative, that would provide members with simulator training at a reasonable cost. Companies could rent time on a simulator instead of buying one. Businesses offering this service already exist. If increased simulator training were mandated by FAA, more companies could be expected to join the industry, thereby lowering the cost through a healthy injection of competition.

It is especially important that commuter pilots be compelled to participate in simulator training designed to train them how to fly out of unexpected wind shear conditions. Part 135 commuter planes are more likely to fly in bad weather than the large jets that fly over it and the commuters perform more takeoffs and landings. Moreover, commuter pilots are generally younger and less seasoned than pilots of large transport jets that fly for Part 121 carriers, and they often have no experience as a military pilot. (One pilot we interviewed who is a captain for a major domestic airline told us that military flight experience enhances flight safety because military pilots have all been scared "at least once" and might react better in an emergency, however, not all airline pilots agree that military experience necessarily makes a person a better pilot.) Simulated flying would be of special help to pilots who have never "been scared." It would increase their skills in "getting out of a jam," their confidence and, not incidentally, the safety of passengers who are increasingly forced to fly in small commuter planes because of the hub and spoke airport system.

LOFT is an example of how the new computer technologies can make flying safer. But more is needed. Cockpit crews need to learn to communicate effectively and work together as a cohesive unit even if they have never flown before. (This is especially important in the coming era of two-person cockpit crews.) That's where CRM comes in.

Cockpit resource management (CRM)

"CRM training is designed to rid the flight crew of authoritarian attitudes" said Captain William Frisbee, former head pilot for Pan American and an Air Force One pilot. "The idea is to open up communications among flight crew so that they all act as a team."

Why is this important? Poor crew communication and dysfunctional cockpit teams have been found to be a causative factor in many accidents and incidents. "I have known first officers who wouldn't challenge a captain's orders regardless of the circumstances," one experienced pilot for a major airline told us. This pilot told us he had heard of cases where the captain made patently unsafe decisions that were followed unquestionably by the crew. "CRM is designed to end dictatorship in the cockpit," he continued. "I really believe in the concept."

The tendency of some pilots to exaggerate their experience and skill and otherwise fail to communicate accurately and honestly with each other is another threat to safety that CRM is designed to correct. It might not seem that such seemingly harmless "macho" interplay could create a threat to safety, but it can. The December 3, 1990, runway incursion accident in Detroit (described in chapter 16) that killed eight people is a case in point.

Before the fatal taxiing began, perhaps to impress his captain, the first officer exaggerated his military experience and overstated his qualifications. He also overstated his familiarity with the Detroit Airport. This led the captain to unduly rely on the first officer during taxiing in heavy fog, leading to a situation where the blind was essentially leading the blind. This resulted in a runway incursion and the accident previously described. The NTSB accident report of that tragedy stated:

> The safety board believes that a nearly complete and unintentional reversal of command roles took place in the cockpit of the DC-9 shortly after taxiing began. The result was that the captain became overly reliant on the first officer. The captain essentially acquiesced to the first officer's assumption of leadership. This role reversal contributed significantly to the eventual runway incursion.
>
> The sequence of events leading to the role reversal began when the captain asked the first officer if he was familiar with DTW (Detroit Airport) and was told, "yes." The captain then asked him to assist with the taxi clearances and taxiing. The captain's request for help from the first officer was entirely correct, and in keeping with a basic understanding of CRM; however, the first officer's acceptance of the request without reservation or qualification coupled with his failure to clarify the extent of his actual knowledge of the airport, placed considerable responsibility on him.
>
> Although the first officer may have been somewhat more familiar with the layout than the captain, he was not as familiar with the layout as he had led the captain to believe .... The safety board believes that the first officer probably did not want the captain to think he was inexperienced. The first officer apparently realized that the captain was "new" and would need more help than an experienced captain. He later stated that it had been more typical of his experience for airline captains to anticipate taxi clearances and that this occasion was the first time that a captain had asked him to actively assist. This new responsibility was one that the first officer appeared ready and willing to accept. As a result, by the time the crew began to taxi, the first officer began to dominate the decision making in the cockpit.

If the first officer had been totally truthful with the captain, the NTSB accident investigators surmised, it is likely that the pilots would have more readily admitted that they were lost. At that point, they would have contacted ground control for detailed instructions, thereby avoiding the incursion and the subsequent accident. "The captain, however, apparently believed that the first officer knew where he was," the report stated, "and the first officer apparently could not bring himself to admit, or was not aware, that his assertive directions had placed the airline in this predicament." In other words, a little ego went a long way toward creating an unnecessary hazard and eight people died.

CRM uses lectures, audio visual aids, and flight simulator training to enhance effective and honest flight deck communications. According to a presentation made at the 1991 International Seminar of the International Association of Air Safety Investigators, Dr. Alan Diehl (technical advisor for human performance, U.S. Air Force Safety Agency), CRM focuses on five interrelated areas with the intent of preventing common errors and creating an atmosphere of competence and professionalism in the cockpit:

- How to avoid distractions and "error chains"
- Teaching interpersonal skills to improve specificity in communication, leadership, teamwork and a proper division of responsibilities
- Stress management and coping strategies
- Altering hazardous attitudes (authoritarianism or over-politeness)
- Risk management techniques to assist in the rational evaluation of operational hazards

A great deal of time, expense and effort has already gone into CRM and the program is likely to be expanded. So, the question must be asked: Will CRM increase aviation safety? Most pilots and experts in the field answer that question with, "Yes, if ...," if the industry will wholeheartedly embrace the program, if it will back up its acceptance with financial support, if pilots who might be set in their ways are willing to give the program a fair try.

Doubts about the commitment of the industry to CRM aside, the early results are quite encouraging. A study conducted by Robert Helmreich, Ph.D., at NASA's Ames Research Center studied the effectiveness of CRM training. "Is CRM training effective?" Helmreich asked in *Air Line Pilot Magazine*. The answer: "Taken together, the data suggest that the answer is a resounding yes."

Helmreich pointed to several study results to support his conclusion:

- Crew members "overwhelmingly" acknowledge the benefits of CRM
- Behavioral shifts, conducive to safe operations, were observed
- Acceptance for CRM concepts grow over time
- Crews involved in life threatening incidents and accidents have successfully utilized their CRM training with good results

The pilots who saved United Airlines Flight 232 from total destruction are also believers based upon their harrowing experience flying the crippled DC-10 to Sioux City Airport. "I am firmly convinced that CRM played a very important part in our landing at Sioux City with any chance of survival," Captain Alfred C. Hays wrote in *Accident Prevention* (published by the Flight Safety Foundation), in June 1991. His colleague, Captain Dennis E. Fitch, another of the three heroic pilots who helped nurse the crippled DC-10 to its crash landing, is also an enthusiastic booster of the program. Fitch credits CRM training provided by United Airlines for enabling the three pilots to work as a team despite the fact that they had never worked together before.

Captain Fitch has also contended that greater emphasis needs to be placed in CRM within the industry. Speaking in 1991 before the Flight Safety Foundation's 44th safety seminar, he said, "CRM is here to stay, but to be truly effective it must become culture. It cannot be taught and then forgotten. To be effective, it has to be supported by management as a way of life. It has to be practiced through LOFT experiences and shown by example by senior pilots."

CRM is approved by the FAA as part of the *Advanced Qualification Program* (AQP), a method for airlines to provide crew training using advanced training equipment and techniques. AQP, as good a program as it seems to be, is currently a voluntary method of improving crew performance. Many safety experts believe that CRM should be made part of mandatory pilot training through FAA regulations.

One such proponent is Captain Thomas A. Duke, a 30-year Air Force veteran and former director of safety of the Air Force Reserve, who also served with the NTSB. He wrote in the July 1991 issue of *Flight Safety Digest,* that the FAA should require mandatory CRM programs for all air carriers to include methods of improving cockpit coordination and ATC communications. Dr. Helmreich is another proponent of this approach. Because he was so heartened by the results of the NASA study, Dr. Helmreich has also urged that CRM be made a "regulatory requirement" for the industry.

Because preventing human error is such a large part of current aviation safety initiatives, the entire industry must be convinced to participate in CRM training, including commuter carriers, by mandate if necessary. Too many passenger lives have been lost because of mistakes that were caused by poor flight crew communication, complacency, or egotism. Mandatory CRM would go a long way toward improving the personal interaction among all elements within the aviation safety system and should reduce the mistakes that can lead to incidents and accidents and the threat to human life.

Pilot assignments based upon experience

Another safety problem that needs to be addressed is the pairing of an inexperienced *pilot in command* (PIC) with an inexperienced *second in command* (SIC). When both pilots in the cockpit have insufficient experience in the plane being flown or the responsibilities that have been assumed, the level of safety can be reduced.

On November 3, 1988, the NTSB issued a recommendation that urged the FAA to compel airlines to establish minimum experience levels for each PIC and SIC that would prohibit the pairing of pilots inexperienced in their respective positions. (A pilot who is very experienced in flying one model of craft might have far less experience on another, even if qualified by the FAA to fly that particular plane.)

The NTSB issued the recommendation in the wake of an accident at Denver on November 15, 1987, when a DC-9 crashed upon takeoff killing 29 people. The accident report found that the tragedy was partially caused by an inappropriate pairing of an inexperienced PIC and a SIC (who was flying the plane) who had little experience in a DC-9 and who had not flown for 24 days.

(Most airlines allow their pilots to bid for the flight schedules they desire. The bids are generally accepted based upon seniority. Those with low seniority might not have their bid accepted and might be assigned to the reserve pool, where they might have to wait weeks before they receive a flight assignment. This system often prevents newly qualified pilots from using or perfecting their flight skills and increases the likelihood of inexperienced pilots being assigned to the same flight.)

The FAA refused to engage in rulemaking based upon the NTSB's recommendation, choosing instead to issue a nonmandatory advisory circular on the topic. Then, on September 20, 1989, another accident was partly caused by the pairing of inexperienced pilots flying a USAir B-737 at La Guardia Airport, who were unable to execute an aborted takeoff and crashed the plane into the East River killing two people. In that crash, the PIC had extensive experience in the craft—but as a second-in-command pilot. He only had 138 flight hours as a PIC. At the same time, the SIC of the flight had only recently been hired and had just qualified to pilot a 737. Moreover, the SIC was conducting his first unsupervised takeoff in a 737 and his first takeoff after a 39-day period when he had not flown.

At that point, the Tombstone Imperative increased the pressure on the FAA to follow the NTSB's recommendations. In response to the accidents (at Denver and La Guardia) and because many air carriers were not implementing the FAA guidelines on crew experience, the FAA requested an advisory task force to develop recommendations for establishing crew pairing requirements. On September 30, 1990, the task force issued its recommendations requesting the FAA to issue regulations on the subject.

Finally, on March 23, 1993—two and a half years after the task force's recommendations and more than five and a half years after the NTSB initially requested the FAA to act in this area (a recommendation the FAA had called "premature")—the FAA issued an NPRM, that if finalized, will create binding regulations requiring minimum pilot experience on all flights flown under Part 121. (Once again, the commuter airlines flying under Part 135 are excluded from an important proposed safety regulation.)

Now that it has done the right thing, it is earnestly hoped that the FAA will follow through and enact a final rule preventing the pairing of inexperienced pilots. At the same time, similar rulemaking should be undertaken for all commuter flights, where pilot inexperience is already a cause for concern. If these new rules interrupt the bidding procedures of airlines, so be it. Passengers have the right to expect that at least one of the members of the cockpit crew be well seasoned in their position and have significant experience flying the model of aircraft being used on the flight.

Flight attendant training

With so many aviation accidents being survivable, the quality and quantity of emergency response training received by flight attendants is a vital component of passenger safety. But preparing for accidents is not the only purpose for which flight attendants receive safety training. Many other mishaps can occur during a flight, such as an injury or illness of a passenger, cabin decompression, in-flight smoke or fire, and severe turbulence. On these occasions, it is the responsibility of the flight attendants to meet the emergency and/or provide immediate passenger assistance and directions to protect their safety.

That being so, adequate training of flight attendants is a vital component of passenger safety. The FAA recognizes this fact and requires each Part 121 carrier to have an approved flight attendant training program. (This requirement does not extend to Part 135 carriers.) Flight attendants are required to undergo several levels of education, including emergency training that includes evacuations using at least one installed evacuation slide, the extinguishing of a fire using a fire extinguisher, and fire fighting while wearing protective breathing equipment. (FAA rules require that personal breathing equipment (PBE) be available for flight crew use.)

Unfortunately, a special investigation report by the NTSB that was adopted on June 9, 1992, found that there have been several examples of deficient flight attendant performance during emergencies that were laid at the doorstep of inadequate training. On occasion, poor flight attendant performance during an emergency has led to increased passenger injuries.

The NTSB offered several examples:

- In the Detroit runway incursion accident on December 3, 1990, the lead flight attendant had to be assisted by passengers in opening the L-1 door. The attendant did not attempt to manually inflate the evacuation slide and exited before the passengers, giving instructions from the ground.

- On May 5, 1991, an MD-80 was struck by a baggage cart while the airplane was taxiing to a terminal gate. A fire erupted and the flight attendants immediately initiated an emergency evacuation. One flight attendant did not turn on the emergency evacuation lights because that attendant had not been trained to do so. Another began to evacuate through the tail emergency exit, before notifying the pilots (in violation of company procedures) and exited before the engines had been turned off.

- On February 1, 1991, at the LAX accident between the USAir 737 and the commuter flight, two flight attendants got out of their jump seats before the crashing plane had come to a stop, in violation of training. One was thrown to the ground but was able to recover and begin evacuation. Had they been severely injured, they might not have been able to perform their duties.

The NTSB came to some disturbing conclusions after conducting their report. Among them:

- Some flight attendants are not proficient in their knowledge of emergency equipment and procedures. The safety board believes that this deficiency is related to training.

- Differences (among airlines) were noted in the number of hours approved for recurrent training, types of drills, instructor/student ratio during drills and the method of assessing proficiency." In other words, some airlines do a better job of preparing their flight attendants for emergencies than others. (The NTSB blamed this on a lack of FAA standardization requirements and on the agency's lack of "rationale" for approving flight attendant training programs.)

- Many airlines do not perform evacuation drills during recurrent training. (The NTSB report disclosed several cases where the flight attendants did not perform well during emergency evacuations. In one circumstance, a passenger had to take over the flight attendant's job of helping evacuate the plane.)

- Current methods of determining flight attendant proficiency to handle an emergency situation might be inadequate.

- Most flight attendants do not receive CRM training and it is not periodically practiced in group exercises during recurrent training.

Another eye opening revelation contained in the report was the differing level of commitment the airlines have toward recurrent safety training of their flight attendants. The NTSB investigated the practices of 12 unnamed major airlines and published the following results (Note: This analysis doesn't consider the differences in the quality of training that might exist.)

Operator	Emergency Recurrent Training Hours	Security Recurrent Training Hours	Total Recurrent Training Hours	Total Classroom Mock-up Hours	Homestudy Hours
A	8	2	10	8	2
B	10	2	12	10	2
C	12	2	14	10.5	3.5
D	12	4	16	12	4
E	12	2	14	11	3
F	8	2	10	10	0
G	9	2	11	8	3
H	6	2	8	8	0
I	10.5	2	12.5	9.5	3
J	9	2	11	8	3
K	8	2	10	8	2
L	9	2	11	10	1

Recurrent, emergency preparedness training is necessary to prepare flight attendants to be ready to act if a bona fide emergency occurs. This chart reveals that when it comes to this important component of passenger safety, all airlines are not managed equally. This is a matter of some concern. Flight attendants who receive more training, such as the flight attendants working for airline D, can reasonably be expected to be better prepared to assist passengers in time of need than one who received less training, i.e. airline H. (It's unfortunate that the FAA and investigations such as this one conducted by the NTSB allow airlines to remain anonymous. That permits airlines with a lower commitment to safety to be perceived as the safety equal of airlines that commit extra time and resources to flight attendant training. The flying public should be given the facts so that they can decide for themselves which airline they would rather patronize.)

The report on flight attendant training issued recommendations that are probably necessary to improve flight attendant training and thereby increase passenger safety:

• Ensure that flight attendant training programs include instruction in human performance subjects.

- Require hands-on proficiency drills for each type of airplane exit. (There have been several reports of flight attendants being unable to open emergency exits.)
- Ensure that flight attendant training programs provide detailed guidance on the relative probability of hazards associated with emergency situations such as fire, toxic smoke, and explosion.

These are important recommendations and need to be acted upon by the FAA. (The bureaucratic quicksand of Washington, D.C., being what it is, don't look for quick results.)

Another problem with flight attendant training is the exemptions from minimum safety training standards that some airlines request and often receive. (The NTSB has stated that it was "at a loss for understanding the FAA's logic in granting waivers for reduced training hours.")

One recent request is illustrative and deserves a special spotlight. In 1990, United Airlines requested an exemption from the rule requiring all Part 121 carriers to conduct a one-time-only fire fighting training course using a PBE with a real fire. Instead, United Airlines wanted permission to perform the required training using a fire simulation. (The requirement for one-time-only drill training was ordered in response to a tragic in-flight fire that started in a lavatory aboard an Air Canada flight in 1983. The plane landed but before it could be evacuated, 23 people were killed. Many died of smoke inhalation.)

It should be noted that United filed this request months *after* all of the fire fighting training was to have been completed under the rule. One possible explanation for the timing of the request was that United had disobeyed the law. (United also informed the FAA in its petition that it would use other methods to avoid using an actual fire in its training program. Apparently, United believes that if it does not wish to comply with an FAA mandate, the FAA should just go along.)

United made its request for exemption despite the fact that the FAA had made it abundantly clear in the final rule requiring the fire fighting training that the use of a real fire was essential to fulfill the rule's purpose. Specifically, the FAA stated:

> Demonstration and training aids, no matter how realistic, *cannot provide the training benefits and confidence that actual fire fighting experience will have to all crewmembers,* including flight attendants.

Although this is a one-time exercise, it will provide a base of actual experience with combating a fire that a crewmember can build upon later in recurrent training ....

The cost and possible inconvenience of location of suitable training sites should be far outweighed by the *vastly increased competence* and confidence of crew members in fighting in-flight fires. (Emphasis added.)

Having been so unequivocal about the reason real fires were to be used during flight attendant fire fighting training, one would have expected the FAA to tell United Airlines to go ... put out some blazes. Instead, the FAA, ever sensitive to airline desires, revisited the issue and decided to issue a whole new NPRM on the subject.

Fast forward now to August 26, 1992, as the FAA publishes a new NPRM in the *Federal Register* on the issue of crewmember fire fighting, which, if adopted, would:

"... Require crewmembers to combat an actual or *simulated* fire using at least one type of installed hand fire extinguisher appropriate for the type of fire, while wearing the appropriate PBE. This requirement would be designated as the PBE drill, and it would emphasize the correct use of PBE in a fire fighting scenario. The crewmember would perform the drill using PBE while combating an *actual or simulated* fire.

The FAA acknowledges the training benefits of simulation and the various fire fighting scenarios that may be enacted when using a simulated fire in combination with a mock-up of an aircraft cabin, galley, oven, lavatory, or passenger seat .... The FAA also recognizes that many air carriers may choose not to use simulator devices. These carriers would then require their crewmembers to perform the PBE drill using an actual fire, as currently prescribed ...." (Emphasis added.)

In other words, the FAA kowtowed to United Airlines.

What do the flight attendants think about this astonishing flip-flop? To put it mildly, they are not amused. In a letter commenting on the NPRM, the Association of Flight Attendants stated, in part:

AFA opposes this proposed revision and supports the current requirement that crewmembers extinguish an actual fire with PBE on. The FAA was correct in its original rationale that the best way to train crewmembers to put out a real fire with PBE is to actually do so .... One flight attendant who performed such a drill wrote: "The mask does not necessarily turn simultaneously with your head, and everything looks different since you are looking through a flame resistant transparent material. It distorts the appearance of the fire. *It was particularly useful to put the fire out with the mask on* since I knew what the mask would feel like, how the fire would appear through the mask, and how the fire would respond to the extinguisher."

And what is a simulated fire? Flashing electric lights with no heat, no sound. Moreover, the trainee experiences no surge of adrenaline because there is no perceived danger. (Even though a training drill using an actual fire would expose the trainee to minuscule danger, the added realism of a real, hot fire, should increase the concentration of the trainee, increasing the likelihood that the learning would "stick" and be recalled in an actual emergency.) It might make United Airlines happy that they will not have to use a real fire during PBE training, but it is unlikely to thrill flight attendants or passengers that they have expertise in putting out a fancy bank of electric lights.

And people in the FAA wonder why their critics accuse the agency of being in the industry's hip pocket.

Management factors

John H. Enders, vice chairman of the Flight Safety Foundation, believes that airline management inattention to safety issues is the greatest cause of aircraft accidents. "Viewed in the context of multiple causes (of accidents)," Mr. Enders was quoted as saying in the *Flight Safety Foundation News,* of February 1992, "the distribution of contributing causes for the past decade's fatal accidents appears to be approximately 30–40 percent flight crew, 15–20 percent design and manufacturing, 30–35 percent maintenance, and perhaps 60–80 percent management or supervisory inattention at all levels."

Ender's theory is that even when the immediate cause of an accident can be found in the flight operations phase of a flight, the origins of the accident can often be found in enabling factors within an airline's operations or in regulatory oversight that go unnoticed until a critical moment in the flight when the crew is forced to deal with them.

Enders believes that the failure to take these enabling factors into account masks the true cause of many accidents and simplifies the placing of blame. "Care must be taken with this approach," Enders said, "because the progression of events leading to an accident is complex and comprises multiple paths." Under this theory, safety can be significantly enhanced by increasing management's commitment to safe operations and improving intracompany communication.

C.O. Miller, former director of the bureau of aviation safety for the NTSB and now a safety professional, supports the idea that improving airline accident prevention management practices is an important ingredient in increasing aviation safety. "In this author's view, a safety program involves specialized accident prevention efforts in addition to safety being part of everyone's job," Miller wrote in an essay entitled "Investigating the Management Factors in an Airline Accident." Mr. Miller also identified 14 important functions that should be made a part of such safety programs including the development of specific safety plans, the establishment of specific accident prevention requirements, participation in ongoing program reviews, and the implementation of safety education, training and testing. "These are just some of the kinds of things that should be presented in a plan." Miller says. "There may be others depending on the kind of organization."

Many safety advocates agree that establishing an enhanced corporate commitment to excellence in this area is vital if safety levels are to be improved. J.R. Riedmeyer, chairman of the Flight Safety Foundation board of governors, discussed this issue at the 1990 Flight Safety Foundation International Air Safety Conference, stating: "Most companies have organizational entities that oversee safety efforts. Some have strong safety obligations written into the job descriptions of first and second level management. Even with this focused attention, there are many middle management and professional personnel who are unsure about their company commitment to safety. Their perception is that over 50 percent of the mistakes they make are attributable to inadequate training, out-of-date manuals, and poor support."

Captain David A Simmon, Jr., director of flight safety for United Airlines is another supporter of establishing airline safety programs. At the 41st Flight Safety Foundation International Air Safety Seminar (1988), Captain Simmon expressed his belief in the importance of establishing specific centralized safety departments within the airlines. "Care must be taken not to allow subsafety departments to spring up throughout the organization," Simmon stated. "This leads to turfing, inefficiencies and a fragmented approach which prevents important functions from being accomplished."

Captain Simmon also warned against the safety inhibitors that can be found in many companies. "Excessive internal politics is the antithesis of safety because it distracts from the real tasks at hand. Indecision stemming from political concerns can paralyze an organization for months or even years .... The corporate bean counter is another safety inhibitor. Although money changers, accountants, and chief financial officers have been around for centuries, their influence in the airline industry has increased dramatically since the arrival of deregulation. Some bean counters look at safety departments as another expense which must be reduced to the lowest possible cost."

Simmon further expressed his belief that the airlines would have to be sold on the importance of safety programs. "It is unrealistic to expect CEOs, CFOs, or even vice presidents of flight operations to understand the problems, challenges, details, or benefits of safety programs. Our job (as safety professionals) is to present senior management with the facts so they can make informed decisions."

What is the FAA's responsibility to nurture a corporate culture conducive to safety? If John H. Enders, C.O. Miller, David A. Simmon and other safety experts are correct in their belief that it is necessary to create industrywide corporate safety cultures, the implementation of the programs should not depend on the ability of the experts to "sell" management on them. It might be necessary for the FAA to step in and compel their creation through the rulemaking process.

Some safety advocates argue that the FAA should compel airlines to create specific corporate safety departments. C.O. Miller disagrees. "I don't think that it is necessary to compel the creation of a department. It is the program that counts, not being able to prove you have a department on some organizational chart. That and staffing it with qualified people. Having truly qualified people, that is the part of many safety programs that is often overlooked."

That is not to say that Mr. Miller doesn't believe the FAA has an important role in placing safety programs on the front burner of corporate activity. "The FAA should require the creation of safety programs," Miller told us in March 1993, "but the FAA will have to be careful not to go into too much detail. The regulation should specify what needs to be done but should leave the 'how' it is to be accomplished subject to each individual company's business cultures (size, background, and the like). In other words, identify the principles and tasks that are to apply and allow the airlines to use their common sense on how that is to be done, subject to FAA approval."

The FAA also needs to have the power of oversight if the programs are to be successful. Miller says, "One of the problems with corporate safety plans is that decisions are made to implement them and then managers don't follow through with their own mandate. Thus, it will be vital that the company and FAA review each company's program to make sure it remains effective and that they are periodically updated to reflect the differing needs of changing times and turnover of personnel."

Miller's prescription makes sense. If history is any judge, some airlines will never agree to voluntarily expend the money and effort required to successfully administer a specific safety program, unless they are compelled to do so through government regulation. Advisory circulars that are currently issued by the FAA on the topic of corporate safety programs are insufficient because they can be legally ignored. Mr. Miller's approach seems the most likely to cement the commitment to safety at the management level, while allowing for individual airline flexibility and at the same time retaining the FAA's legal ability to enforce safety program guidelines. That might provide the best balance that can be devised. (Mr. Miller told us that "a safety program appropriately monitored by the FAA would be the most important single enhancement in air safety that could be accomplished in short order.")

Passenger safety education

Another area that needs improvement is the education airline passengers receive on how to protect their own safety in the event of an emergency. Safety experts have long been concerned that some passengers have contributed to their own injuries or death and those of fellow travelers because they were not adequately educated on how to appropriately respond in an emergency. This concern is well taken. A review of the accident record reveals that many unnecessary casualties have been caused, at least in part, by passenger panic, their inability to open exits, the blocking of aisles by passengers seeking to retrieve their carry-on luggage during emergency evacuations, and other inappropriate behavior.

The NTSB has long been interested in the topic. In 1985, the safety board conducted a study into airline passenger education (NTSB/SS-85-09) and reported its findings. The report described many incidents involving passengers who either refused to obey safety instructions or did not fully understand them, which lead to injuries:

- On April 3, 1981, a United Airlines DC-10 with 154 passengers and 12 crew members encountered turbulence near Hannibal, Missouri. The captain made an announcement and the seatbelt sign was turned on when cirrus clouds were entered. Moments later severe turbulence was encountered. Passengers who had not heeded the seatbelt sign and announcement were thrown from their seats. A flight attendant and seven passengers sustained serious injuries and several others sustained minor injuries.

- In September 1982, following a rejected takeoff at Malaga, Spain, a DC-10 ran off the end of a runway and struck a building. The tail section of the plane was immediately engulfed in flames and an emergency evacuation ensued. Fifty people died in the aft cabin trying to get out the left overwing exit. None tried to use the right aisle that was clear and led to usable exits. Many of the survivors indicated that their evacuation was not influenced by the safety information they had been presented. Numerous passengers admitted they had not read the emergency briefing card but did remember the oral briefing. The consensus of the passengers questioned was that the written and oral information was of little or no use to them during the emergency. For example, one passenger when asked if the emergency instructions were of any value said that the "information was not retained in a moment of crisis."

- On May 8, 1978, a B-727 with six crew members and 52 passengers struck the water of Escambia Bay, Florida. The airplane settled into relatively shallow water and the cabin was not entirely submerged. Passengers were able to evacuate the plane. Three uninjured passengers drowned after evacuating. Most of the surviving passengers had problems finding, donning, and inflating life vests that were located under their seats. Only 22 percent of the passengers said they had never seen the life vest demonstration. An NTSB survey revealed that only 41 percent of the passengers had read the safety card.

With those events in mind, it is incumbent to the safety of all passengers that everyone traveling by commercial airline know and understand what they are to do in the event of an emergency. The NTSB agrees and in 1985 issued specific recommendations that it contended would increase the level of passenger education and, thereby, the quality of behavior during an emergency. (Note: These recommendations would cost the airlines little or no money.)

Among the recommendations issued as a result of the safety study were the following, along with each recommendation's NTSB status (as of March 3, 1993) based upon the level of FAA response.

Improve the level of oral briefings and demonstrations given to passengers before takeoff and the quality of printed briefing cards The ability of people to understand instructions is dependent on the quality of the information presented. (NTSB Recommendation 85-093; current status, closed —acceptable action.)

Require that emergency safety instructions and demonstrations be repeated to passengers before landing in order to reinforce the pretakeoff briefings Talk about pragmatic—and it would not cost the airlines one thin dime. Most accidents occur during takeoff or landing. People who listen to the preflight safety instructions might remember them during an emergency 10 minutes after hearing them and reading the passenger safety cards, but not recall them at all during an emergency while landing three hours later. Reminding people of what they must do in an emergency when the plane is 15 minutes from landing would induce passengers to think about what they should do if there were an emergency and perhaps save lives. (NTSB Recommendation 85-98; current status, closed—unacceptable action.)

Require that recurrent flight attendant training contain instructions on the use of the public address system and techniques for maintaining effective safety briefings and demonstrations that will motivate passengers to pay attention If the flight attendant doesn't think the briefing is important, the passengers won't. The art of communication is important when conveying important safety information to people. Flight attendants need to be able to improve the motivation of passengers to pay attention to oral briefings and safety demonstrations. (NTSB Recommendation 85-101; current status, closed—unacceptable action.)

Develop a program to test the feasibility and effectiveness of providing safety briefing information in airport terminal gate areas and of providing printed safety information on or inside ticket envelopes The theory here is that repetition creates learning. It works in politics, why not aviation safety? (NTSB Recommendation 85-103; current status, open—acceptable action.)

Encourage all employees and their families, when flying as passengers, to set an example of attentiveness to oral briefings and demonstrations, and of reading safety cards Leadership by example is a very effective tool and could help increase the safety atmosphere of the flight. (NTSB Recommendation 85-105; current status, initial response received.)

Include articles in in-flight magazines that provide additional information and more detailed safety information for passengers Well written articles in airline magazines would provide an extra level of passenger awareness about emergency procedures in the event of an emergency. But the airlines won't permit it. They don't like to remind passengers that there is danger in flying. (Indeed, several airlines, including Delta, Northwest, United, and USAir, were contacted by the publisher seeking to advertise this book in their in-flight magazines. All refused.) But who's kidding whom? Everyone who flies knows that if something goes seriously wrong during a flight, that big time hurt can follow. Providing additional specific information in a place likely to be seen by passengers will enhance safety and increase the likelihood that a passenger will act appropriately in an emergency. (NTSB Recommendation 85-106; current status—initial response received.)

Preflight and in-flight safety demonstrations and presentations are a very cost-effective way of increasing passenger awareness of safety measures and improving the likelihood that passengers who suffer a survivable crash will live. Rather than be unduly alarmed by the increased education, most passengers will appreciate the extra attention paid to their safety. Those NTSB recommendations that have been rejected or allowed to languish, should be implemented by the FAA without further delay. (Chapter 20 describes the things airline passengers need to do every time they get on an airplane to protect their own safety.)

Preventing pilot fatigue

"While taxiing out at the usual position to complete the before-takeoff checklist and set the flaps, confusion arose as a result of a change in the runway. This coupled with the end of the duty day for an all-night flight, resulted in the flaps not being set for takeoff. Upon advancing the throttles, the first indication was the autothrottles not engaging. Upon pushing up the throttles manually, the takeoff warning horn come on. The takeoff was aborted the first 1000–2000 feet."

A report from NASA's
Aviation Safety Reporting System

Pilot fatigue is an enemy of aviation safety. NASA's Aviation Reporting System (chapter 2) is rife with reports of unauthorized landings, aborted takeoffs, pilots dozing during flight, miscommunication leading to operational errors, and other potentially dangerous mistakes, all caused by fatigue and exhaustion.

The current FARs that regulate pilot scheduling by airlines might be a contributing factor to the problem. Under the rules, airlines may force pilots to have "reduced rest periods" of only eight hours, so long as they are given a compensatory rest during the next 24 hours. Moreover, rest periods are measured "from release to report," that is from the time the pilot is released from duty until the time required to report back for duty.

That means actual rest time will be much less than eight hours. During the rest period, the pilot must be transported to the hotel or rest facility, check in, eat, telephone the family, relax in the room and then, hopefully, fall quickly asleep. The next morning, the process is repeated in reverse. Often, this results in pilots who fly having had less than six hours sleep. (This is especially significant if the pilot has changed time zones and the rest period does not coincide with the pilot's normal sleep-time at home.)

The idea behind the rule is to give airlines flexibility in scheduling when an occasional need arises; however, according to ALPA, forcing pilots to fly with reduced rest has become a way of life for some airlines. An ALPA survey of regional air carrier pilots revealed that 86 percent of the answering pilots were provided less than eight hours rest at a rest facility from one to nine or more times per month. Eighty-one percent of those pilots exceeded 16 hours of duty time during a 24-hour period. From one to nine or more times per month. This brutal scheduling leads directly to increased pilot fatigue that can result in a degradation of the pilot's ability to follow safe flying procedures.

The absence of any rules in the FARs defining maximum daily pilot "duty time" is an associated problem identified by ALPA as a causative factor of pilot fatigue. A pilot might be on duty, performing tasks associated with his job, but not actually be flying a plane. (Of the industrialized nations, only the United States and France do not explicitly consider duty time, as opposed to flight time, in their rules governing aviation.) This lapse in the rules primarily affects commuter pilots who often do not have the strength of a strong union-negotiated contract behind them to limit the time they must work, ALPA described how many regional airlines assign heavy on-duty work schedules:

> The airlines have devised a scheduling concept known as the 'stand-up overnight' which is an extremely inefficient use of human resources and ignores physiological rest and sleep requirements. As an example, one airline requires its crews to report at 1759 (5:59 p.m.) hours for a departure at 1844 hours (6:44 p.m.). After three flights and 3:35 hours of flying time, landing is scheduled for 2318 hours (11:18 p.m.). At that time, the crews have approximately 7 hours to wait until their next departure at 0630 (6:30 a.m.) the next morning of just over an hour. After a scheduled duty day of almost 14 hours with 4:40 hours of

scheduled flight time, the crew is released until having to report again that evening for the same trip.

On the third night, the crew reports at 2128 hours (9:28 p.m.) for a scheduled duty of just under 12 hours, with a scheduled flight time of 3:40 hours. On the same night, the crew has a period of approximately 6 hours between the second and third leg of the four flights.

We must emphasize these are scheduled times .... Scheduled times are frequently exceeded, which causes even more fatigue and stress for pilots. Also, this typical stand-up overnight schedule disrupts the pilot's normal sleep patterns and is the ultimate treatment of human beings as machines. The carriers expect that pilots will turn themselves off with no more regard for internal body rhythms than to expect them to be fully functional when needed for flight. (Taken from a petition for rulemaking filed by ALPA on June 21, 1990.)

The carriers respond to this criticism by pointing out that they are scheduling within the FAA-approved legal guidelines. The regional carriers also contend that it is easier for commuter pilots to fly these hours because they usually do not change time zones during their short flights and because a pilot who believes he is too fatigued, has the option of refusing the flight. Moreover, they claim that changing their scheduling practices would be bad for the bottom line and would inconvenience passengers because of fewer or delayed flights and the likelihood that connections at hub airports would be missed.

ALPA responds with the assertion that landings and takeoffs are the most difficult parts of any flight. Regional pilots usually perform more landings and takeoffs in a day than do pilots who fly for Part 121 carriers. Moreover, flying the smaller commuter planes is more stressful than flying large transport jets and requires more attention because since commuter flights fly through weather instead of over it, because there is less flight cruise time on automatic pilot, and because they are working more frequently in crowded terminal airspace. ALPA also claims that it is the rare pilot who will refuse to fly due to fatigue for fear of retribution from their employer.

The pilots' contentions seem well taken. A tired pilot is a pilot who is more likely to make mistakes and misjudgments. Indeed, many reports of operational errors cite fatigue as a contributing factor. (As reported earlier, the authors have been told by NASA that there are more than 800 such reports in its files on Part 121 carriers and that doesn't include reports from Part 135 pilots or those operational errors that are never reported.)

It would appear that under current regulations, pilots can be legally worked too hard and too long in too many circumstances. ALPA is seeking redress of this grievance and has petitioned the FAA to amend the FARs so as to guarantee pilots more rest and sleep. More than three years have passed and no action has been taken.

ALPA's request should be taken seriously by the FAA. More studies need to be conducted, using simulators and pilot questionnaires, on the impact of fatigue. NASA's Aviation Safety Reporting System should be culled for fatigue-related mistakes. Unless solid-evidence is forthcoming that the current rules sufficiently guarantee adequate pilot rest, they should be rewritten to increase the time of minimum rest periods from the current eight hours to at least 10 hours. Maximum daily duty time should also be included in the law as well as a limit on the number of take-offs and landings a pilot can perform in a day. To do less might be to endanger passengers whose safety depends on their pilots receiving a proper amount of rest.

Flight data recorder monitoring

"75 percent of hull loss accidents in the United States commercial jet fleet in the last 10 years has primarily been caused by flightcrew error."

Paul D. Russell,
chief of product safety at Boeing, April 27, 1993

It is difficult to catch flight crew errors as they occur; however, it is possible. Most significant events that take place during a flight are recorded through the *cockpit voice recorder* (CVR) or the *digital flight data recorder* (DFDR). (The former records all of the conversation that takes place in the cockpit; the latter records technical data such as airspeed, altitude, elapsed time between events, and the like.) These two technologies, commonly known as the *black boxes*, often provide invaluable data to accident investigators as to what went wrong in the crucial final minutes before an accident took place. (Part 121 aircraft must carry black boxes; however, Part 135 aircraft need not carry them under the federal rules—another example of the lower safety levels required of commuter air carriers.)

Many in the safety community believe that these technologies can be used in other-than-accident situations. Many believe that pilot performance should be monitored so that deviations from proper flight procedures can be caught and corrected before they cause an accident. This program is called *flight data recorder monitoring* (FDRM).

FDRM is a controversial concept. Pilots are dubious, fearing a loss of privacy and the potential for job harassment and other abuses. The airlines fear that lawyers prosecuting a post-crash litigation, would seek to obtain the collected information in order to prove that the airlines did not take adequate steps to ensure that their pilots followed proper flight procedures. Regulators fear that if they came into possession of such data, they could be forced to reveal it through requests made by media and consumer groups under the Freedom of Information Act.

These are important issues that need to be addressed; however, they are not insurmountable. NASA's Aviation Safety Reporting System is instructive. Recall that NASA is able to obtain detailed reports of dangerous incidents because pilots, controllers and others are assured of anonymity. Were performance monitoring conducted so that it would be anonymous vis-a-vis the outside world, the current roadblocks to creating a safety-enhancing monitoring system could be broken and invaluable information obtained.

Were FDRM practiced universally (a few airlines do monitor), unsafe practices could be quickly discovered and corrected. For example, if monitoring discovered that certain pilots failed to perform their checklists, they could be reminded that reading the checklist is a mandatory procedure. If a rotation (the point where the pilot lifts the plane's nose into the air on takeoff) was performed improperly, extra training could be given to the erring pilot. If the recordings found that the "sterile" condition of cockpits were being violated (under the FARs, during the critical phase of flight, generally below 10,000 feet, pilots can only perform those duties required for the safe operation of the aircraft), the word would go out to cease and desist violating the rule. In short, unsafe practices that could develop into dangerous habits could be eliminated before they cause an accident.

Flight data recording monitoring is an idea that has the potential to significantly improve levels of human performance. At a time when Boeing, (which has one of the world's best aviation-safety data banks) projects one jet transport hull loss every 10 days in the world by the year 2006 (based upon the past 10 years' accident rate for worldwide fleet and expected fleet growth) it is vital that the current accident rate be reduced. One significant way to do that is to reduce flight crew mistakes. Monitoring has the potential to do just that. As such, a regulation requiring flight data recorder monitoring is an idea that should be explored.

Preventing substance abuse

In January 1988, a commuter plane crashed in Colorado killing nine people, including the pilot and copilot. (There were six survivors.) The NTSB found that drug use was a contributing cause of the crash. In that case, the flight captain (who was not flying the craft), had been up the night before using cocaine. As a result of the cocaine and a lack of sleep, he was fatigued for the flight and did not adequately monitor the copilot. The copilot botched a landing during difficult weather and the plane crashed.

To combat drug abuse, the FAA requires random drug testing of 50 percent of all airline employees whose jobs involve safety. (Oddly, pilots receive the drug tests *after* completing their flight circuit, not before.) The tests seem to show that the airline industry does not have a serious drug problem, with less than one percent proving positive.

The airlines would like to reduce the number of people tested randomly each year to 10 percent, which they claim would save them about $90 million annually. ALPA supports the request, although it is opposed by some consumer groups such as ACAP.

Currently, no alcohol testing is required of pilots, unless good cause is shown for the test. If drug testing is going to be conducted, it would seem prudent to add alcohol testing because that drug is legal, easy to obtain, and adversely affects the ability of safety personnel to perform their jobs in a proper manner. (Indeed, three Northwest pilots were found guilty of flying under the influence of alcohol in 1990.) If the level of drug testing is reduced, random alcohol testing should be added to the substance abuse screening program. In that way, the abuse of all substances likely to reduce safety performance, whether legal or illegal, can be deterred.

The FAA also requires that driver's license information be matched with pilot certification records so that drunk driving convictions of pilots can be discovered. The FAA resisted this commonsense approach for years but finally agreed to issue the rule when the NTSB put its recommendation in support of a license/certification matching program on the "Most Wanted List."

Human factors are likely to play an increasing role in improving aviation safety. It will take hard work, commitment, and a willingness to innovate. But if that can be done, if the FAA is willing to put its considerable clout behind the effort in a meaningful, and where appropriate—regulatory manner, mistakes can be significantly reduced, leading to a much safer flying environment.

18

Stormy weather

"Modern aircraft can operate in virtually all kinds of weather, but unpredicted severe weather conditions, such as wind shear or heavy icing, can prove deadly."

From the book *Commercial Aviation Safety*, by Alexander Wells, ED.D.

Birmingham, Alabama
July 10, 1991

L'Express Airlines Flight 508 is approaching Birmingham Airport. The flight crew has been advised that a huge thunderstorm is approaching the area. Approach control contacts the flight at 1803:51 hours (Abridged from the NTSB accident report.):

Approach: Lex five zero eight, just to let you know what's goin' on: I had a Lear (jet) set up on the base from the southeast for the ILS (instrument landing system) to (Runway) five and he got in a little close and saw somethin' on the radar he didn't like so he turned out off the approach and he's holding right now. I do have an Aerostar on the approach and he's on about a two mile final right now. We're tryin' to get a ride report out of him.

Flight 508: Okay, it sounds good. Lex, five oh eight.

Approach: Attention all aircraft, information x-ray is current at Birmingham. The field is IFR, the altimeter two triple niner.

A minute later, the first officer makes an announcement to the passengers: "Ladies and gentlemen we're starting our descent into the Birmingham area at this time. If you would please recheck your seat belts, make sure they are securely fastened and that your carry-on items are stowed underneath the seat in front of you, we'll be landing in Birmingham in approximately 12 minutes. A little bit of weather in the area so, ah, if you would please make sure your seat belts are fastened, ah, ah, we'll try and make this as smooth as possible. Thank you.

Approach: "Lex five zero eight, the Aerostar said that the ride wasn't all that bad but the ah rain had the visibility down to ... to just about zero till they got to three-quarter mile final then he did pick up the airport but he did say that the ride wasn't that bad if you want to try it.

Flight 508: "Understand, five oh eight, we'll give it a try."

Approach: Lex five zero eight, maintain two thousand six hundred 'til established on the localizer. Cleared ILS five approach.

Pilot to First Officer: Okay, I'm established. What can I go down to?

First Officer: Okay, two thousand six hundred until established then we can go down to ah, twenty two hundred.

Pilot: Approach flaps.

First Officer: Approach flaps now.

Approach: Lex five oh eight, I'm just going to hold on to you until you get to the marker and that way if you, ah, have to break out for something—you see something you don't like—you'll be ready to an-

Flight 508: Okay, sounds good, Five oh eight.

Pilot to First Officer: Okay, watch out for wind shear now.

First Officer: Right.

Pilot: If you don't feel comfortable about this, let me know.

First Officer: So far it's all right.

(Sound of rain starts.)

Approach: Lex five zero eight, how's the ride so far?

Flight 508: So far it's good, ah, little bit of rain and ah, pretty light.

Approach: Okay.

Approach: Descend and maintain two thousand six hundred.

One minute later:

Pilot: Climb power.

(Sound of increasing engine speed.)

Pilot: Full power.

(Sound of landing gear warning horn starts.)

(Sound of landing gear warning horn stops.)

(One beep of the landing gear warning horn.)

(Sound similar to engine igniter sound.)

End of recording.

Flight 508 flew directly into a thunderstorm cell, encountering strong vertical wind shafts and turbulence. The flight crew lost control of the plane at about 1,600 feet. The plane crashed into the ground, killing the first officer and 12 passengers. The captain of the flight and one passenger survived. Tragically, the accident was completely avoidable. Four other planes elected to wait out the fast moving storm and all landed without incident shortly after Flight 508 crashed.

Since the beginning of aviation, bad weather has been the bane of aviation safety. In the early days of aviation, flying was restricted to days with light winds and fair weather with excellent visibility. That, of course, is no longer true. Research and experimentation now permit planes to fly safely in all but the most severe weather conditions. Weather predictions, using computer modeling and satellite technology, have become highly accurate. Central flow control is able to restrict the number of aircraft flying in bad weather to a safe level. Commercial aviation is financially viable because problems associated with weather can usually be circumvented or overcome.

Despite these advances, weather remains a significant aviation safety concern. Thunderstorms will thunder, snow will fall, winds will blow and there is nothing that can be done about that except accommodate nature with flight delays and cancellations, or flying over or around significant weather patterns.

Unfortunately, such accommodations do not always keep danger at bay and accidents caused by natural conditions still take their toll. Ice buildup on wings has been the precipitating factor in many accidents. Wind shear, microbursts and other weather phenomena can still cause a plane to crash. Unexpected clear air turbulence can hit a plane, injuring passengers who do not have their seat belts buckled.

This chapter discusses the most significant of these weather-related safety issues and describes what is and what is not being done about them. It will also take a brief look at the technology the FAA hopes to rely on to increase capacity even in the face of poor weather conditions.

Aircraft icing

"We had made very strong recommendations on the icing issue and the FAA just refused to do what we wanted."
Barry Sweedler, director of the NTSB
office of safety recommendations, August 1992

Ice is a deadly enemy of safe flying. Recall from chapter 6 that even a small accumulation of ice clinging to wings and other flight surfaces can severely impair lift and cause a plane to crash on takeoff. Indeed, according to the NTSB, 15 crashes during 23 years were at least partially caused by ice contamination, not including the crash of USAir Flight 405 at La Guardia Airport on March 22, 1992.

The FAA had stubbornly resisted promulgating updated rules governing deicing, believing that decisions about whether to deice should be left to the discretion of the pilot. That approach was not sufficient to protect the public safety. The FAA finally acknowledged that its rules were inadequate after the carnage of Flight 405, when the 27 fatalities in that accident created a Tombstone Imperative, causing the FAA to revisit the deicing rules and promise a new approach.

The result was a new set of final interim rules, which will govern deicing procedures until the final rules are developed. These rules, among other requirements, establish mandatory deicing timetables, require physical wing checks from outside the aircraft for specifically designated "hard-winged" turbo jets with rear-mounted engines (such as the DC-9), and reduce the chance that a plane will attempt to take off with ice contamination.

There is no question that these long delayed new deicing rules enhance the safety of the flying public. But are the new rules sufficiently rigourous? Unfortunately, in the view of many experts, the answer seems to be no. Even a high official of the Air Transport Association, a group not known for wanting tougher rules than the FAA is willing to promulgate, told us in October 1992, "It is generally agreed within the industry that the new deicing rules do not go far enough." Similar comments were heard from pilots and others involved in aviation safety.

This criticism is echoed in a November 1992 GAO report entitled, *New Regulations for Deicing Aircraft Could Be Strengthened.* In that important analysis of the new deicing rules, the GAO detailed four shortcomings.

The regulations continue to permit pilots to check for ice contamination from inside most aircraft It can be difficult to tell whether ice has formed on wings from inside the cockpit or cabin. The FAA recognized this and required all hard-wing jets (aircraft without wing slats) with rear, fuselage-mounted engines, to have physical hands-on inspections made from outside the aircraft to determine whether deicing should be performed. Yet, according to the GAO, only 3 percent of the transport jets flying in the United States are hard-winged turbojets with rear, fuselage-mounted engines. That means that 97 percent of the jet aircraft flying for Part 121 carriers are not covered by this requirement.

The GAO report criticized this solution by stating, "FAA believes that such checks will ensure safety because, under the new regulations, pilots will be better informed and more cautious. In our view, however, the *potential for misjudgment exists.* Obstructed views, distance, and poor lighting can make it difficult, if not impossible, to detect ice from inside an aircraft. Furthermore, FAA's own documents recognize that the only definitive method of detecting ice is to closely inspect the aircraft's exterior." (Emphasis added.)

The FAA has stated they made the decision to limit the number of planes requiring physical inspection because they feared delays that would be caused if the agency required exterior checks of all planes. They further noted that most of the icing accidents involved planes with hard wings and rear-mounted engines.

This explanation seeking to justify inaction is dangerously shortsighted and ignores the phenomenon of "black ice" caused by "cold soaking." (Anyone who has driven in icy conditions knows how difficult it is to see black ice, which is virtually invisible.) Justice Virgil P. Moshansky, the Canadian jurist in charge of investigation into the Dryden crash caused by ice-contaminated wings (*see* chapter 6), explains how black ice can form on aircraft wings: an airplane might "fly in extremely cold, subzero weather, reducing the temperature of the fuel. On landing, the cold can be transferred to the wings in a process known as *cold soaking.* This causes condensation, which quickly freezes. The result is black ice that might be invisible from inside the aircraft, especially if it has been covered with a dusting of snow. This can give the pilot a false sense of security."

Why did the FAA exempt 97 percent of all Part 121 aircraft from an important provision of the rules? Perhaps it is because the new interim rules allow the airlines to continue business with little actual change in operations. Or perhaps the publicity surrounding the new rules allows the FAA to look like they are doing more than they actually are. Indeed, in the spring of 1992 when the FAA announced its intention to issue these rules before the winter of 1992–93, *The New York Times* ran the following headline: "U.S. Would Tighten Rule on Takeoffs in Snow and Ice." The subheadline read, "Aftermath of La Guardia—F.A.A. Plan Would End Reliance on Pilots Checking Wing Ice From Plane's Windows." (*The New York Times*, April 17, 1992.) That subheadline is substantially untrue. The thought that the rule might be designed, at least in part, to create such favorable news headlines might be a cynical idea. Unfortunately, the record of the FAA breeds cynicism.

The new regulations do not apply to commuter airlines

Once again, the FAA permits commuter airlines to fly with reduced safety standards than the already inadequate regulations that apply to larger Part 121 carriers. The FAA's justification for exempting Part 135 carriers is that only one commuter aircraft accident in the last 20 years was caused by ice. (Here we go again with the Tombstone Imperative.) Yet, the GAO reported that at least five aborted takeoffs were conducted by commuter craft pilots since 1988 because of ice buildup on flight surfaces. Moreover, commuter pilots tend to be younger and less experienced and might be more subject to pressure, whether real or imagined, from their employers, to avoid flight delays. Additionally, select commuter airplanes have wings at the top of the fuselage, which means that the wing cannot be inspected by the pilot from inside the plane. Under such conditions, it is not prudent to leave the deicing decision exclusively in the pilot's hands.

ALPA wants the new deicing standards to apply to Part 135 carriers as well as to those flying under Part 121. That would give pilots the guidance they need and the protection to resist pressure from carriers to fly. ALPA should be listened to; when the FAA promulgates the final rules, Part 135 carriers should be included in the regulatory jurisdiction.

The FAA should be more "proactive by verifying that airline personnel have received and understood the initial training material" The GAO pointed out that information distributed about proper deicing in the past has not reached all pilots. The NTSB found that accidents caused by ice usually involved pilots who did not fully understand the dangers of ice. The FAA realizes it needs to get proper information on deicing into the field and has plans to publish a pocket-size book providing pilots with easy access to the data they need while at an airport in freezing conditions. That is a good plan. Oversight of the agency is needed to make sure the job gets done.

Foreign carriers should be included in the rule Americans flying on foreign carriers from the United States might not be as safe as flying on U.S. airlines in icy conditions. That is because the rules do not apply to foreign carriers. That omission is not only a bad idea from a safety angle, but it gives foreign carriers a competitive advantage at a time when the domestic airlines need all the business they can get.

By passing the interim deicing rules, the FAA acknowledged that its passive approach of the past was not the correct way to govern this important safety issue. Yet, despite the improvement that the new rules bring to the subject, such as the creation of holdover deicing timetables, the FAA steadfastly refuses to complete the job and compel outside inspection of all aircraft wings for ice. They are also reluctant to compel Part 135 carriers to comply with the deicing program just as they were reluctant to compel commuter craft to be installed with ground proximity warning systems. This approach is, at best, shortsighted. All aircraft are endangered by the accumulation of ice and all aircraft should be part of an effective deicing program.

(The French have created an innovative solution to the problem that might provide the answer to ice buildup. In Paris during winter conditions, all aircraft must pass through a deicing station, akin to a drive-through car wash, while taxiing to the runway for takeoff. As the plane passes through, its wings are decontaminated. This assures that all planes, big or small, will have been subjected to deicing within a few minutes of departure. That eliminates the need for inspection and timetables. The FAA and U.S. airports should consider the applicability of such a device to domestic use.)

Severe wind conditions

"The two most likely events that could have resulted in a sudden uncontrollable lateral upset are a malfunction of the airplane's lateral or directional control system or an encounter with an unusually severe atmospheric disturbance."

**From the NTSB accident report on
the crash of a Boeing 737 that
crashed in Colorado Springs in 1991**

On March 3, 1991, a United Airlines Boeing 737 was on approach to the airport at Colorado Springs. The flight seemed normal and there was no apparent distress involving the aircraft when suddenly the craft's heading changed, it rolled to one side, gathered speed, and crashed into the ground—all in a period of 6 seconds time. All 25 people on the craft were killed by the crash, which the NTSB labeled unsurvivable.

This accident still has the accident investigation community scratching its collective head. The day was not stormy. No anomalous weather conditions had been detected. Weather is the prime suspect but the crash remains a mystery.

Other accidents and incidents involving severe wind conditions have been much easier to identify.

Wind shear

Wind shears might be the most dangerous weather phenomena affecting aviation. Wind shears (a generic term used to describe quickly changing strong wind currents) are usually associated with thunderstorm activity, although the phenomena can occur in rainy or dry conditions. In the most common wind shear, first there is a *microburst,* a strong downdraft from the base of a cloud. The powerful wind slams into the ground and fans out, looking something like an inverted mushroom. The area affected by the shear will be relatively small but the wind conditions within that airspace can be quite severe. A plane flying in this wrong place at the wrong time could unexpectedly face strong headwinds and tailwinds, both within a few moments of time.

If a plane encounters headwinds on one side of the wind shear while landing, the effect is to increase the craft's lift and indicated airspeed. If the pilot does not know that the craft has encountered a wind shear they might attempt to compensate for the increased speed and lift by cutting power to slow the plane. That might prove disastrous when the plane passes through the center of the downdraft and is suddenly flying in a tailwind, whereupon the lift and indicated airspeed will suddenly change. If the pilot does not immediately increase power, the plane might stall. Before the pilot can break out of the stall, the downdraft and the loss of lift might drive the plane into the ground.

That is exactly what happened to a Delta L-1011 as it tried to land at Dallas on August 2, 1985, during inclement weather conditions. The plane lost speed as it broke through a wind shear and "landed" in a field short of the airport, despite the pilot's throttling all three of the aircraft's engines to full power. The landing gear flattened a car on a freeway at the northern boundary of DFW Airport and then the L-1011 broke into pieces as it crashed into an above-ground storage tank. The crash killed 135 people. Thirty-one people seated in the rear of the plane survived.

Wind shears can also tragically interfere with takeoffs. In May 1984 at Stapleton Airport at Denver, a Continental Airlines Boeing 727 encountered a sudden, unexpected tailwind while taking off. This reduced the craft's speed and the pilot was barely able to get the plane off the ground. The plane had insufficient power to climb and hit the instrument landing system antenna. The pilot managed to avoid disaster by keeping the plane in the air and successfully performed an emergency landing, saving all passengers on board. (A similar takeoff accident was caused by wind shear in New Orleans on July 9, 1982. One hundred fifty-three people on the Pan Am 727 died and nine survived.)

There is good news to report. Most wind shears can be avoided if they are detected, and if they are not avoided, they can be overcome by appropriate recovery action by the pilot. For this reason, the FAA requires Part 121 pilots to receive simulator training in overcoming wind shears. This training should be extended to Part 135 pilots as well.

The FAA is also investigating technology that would alert pilots and air traffic controllers of the wind shear as soon as it appears. In 1988, the FAA issued a directive requiring all commercial aircraft to have onboard wind shear detectors by 1993. Exemptions were soon widely granted delaying the installation until 1995—if the later installed technology *predicts* the presence of wind shear rather than merely reports it as it occurs (when the aircraft might already be endangered). NASA is working with private companies, such as the Lockheed Corporation and Rockwell International, to develop the systems.

The *low level wind shear alert system* installed at about 60 airports around the country provides air traffic control towers with information on wind shear conditions near runways. The technology, which came about as a result of intensive weather research in the early 1980s, is helpful, but still more needs to be done.

The FAA hopes to develop better systems aimed at providing more current weather information. The *automated weather observation system* (AWOS) gathers information from unmanned sensors and broadcasts the information to pilots over VHF radio. The program is installed in many airports, but full deployment has been delayed and is not likely to take place until the late 1990s.

AWOS and similar automated weather reporting systems are typically found at airports that do not have hourly weather observations performed by a qualified weather observer. The large airports typically have a recorded weather report that is updated hourly or when weather conditions warrant. Pilots usually receive any critical weather updates directly from the tower controller when the controller issues the clearance to land.

Doppler radar systems are able to detect microburst winds before they hit the ground, resulting in several minute's advance warning, enabling ATC to direct planes away from danger. The systems are expensive, but research is ongoing as to how they can be distributed to better protect aircraft. Researchers are also optimistic that wind shear detectors on planes can be created to automatically communicate with towers about developing microburst conditions. (The idea is that a plane flying through early wind shear conditions would automatically communicate with the tower about the developing microburst so that a warning could be immediately issued to following aircraft.)

Improved training and new technology offer promise of increased safety in areas of potential wind shear. Yet, discretion remains the better part of valor. (Indeed, several planes approaching Birmingham Airport at the same time as Flight 508, recounted at the beginning of the chapter, avoided danger by flying a holding pattern for a short time until the danger had passed.) Central Flow Control routinely restricts the amount of traffic flying to areas where severe weather is expected. This causes departure delays, but waiting in the departure lounge is the safer option.

Weathering the storms

The aviation industry has substantially overcome other weather-related dangers. Planes are now built to resist damage caused by lightning and airports are designed and constructed to reduce the danger caused by wet or slick runways. (Although there was an accident at Logan Airport in 1982 when a DC-10 ran off the end of the runway after landing, crashing into Boston Harbor and killing two people.) Instrument flight rules permit flight operations in poor visibility and research is ongoing into the *microwave landing system* that will permit increased safety in inclement weather (and increase airport capacity)—if it works. Ways are being looked at to predict clear air turbulence.

Human beings might never be able to do anything about the weather, but they can enhance the safety of flying despite the weather. In the next decade, with improved regulations and technological advances, safety should improve and weather-related incidents and accidents should steadily decrease.

Part VII

Safety first

"It is time for Congress to take back responsibility for our air transportation system. To this end a blue-ribbon commission should be impaneled to make recommendations on reorganizing federal oversight of the aviation industry."

Theodore P. Harris speaking before the
Board of Commissioners of the
Port Authority of New York and New Jersey, October 29, 1992

These are troubled times for commercial aviation. The airline industry is losing billions of dollars a year, the FAA is overwhelmed with work and underwhelmed with resources, the aircraft fleet is aging, the sky is growing increasingly crowded, terrorism may be a growing threat, and the aviation system, when taken as a whole, appears to be suffering a slow motion slide toward less safe conditions.

Here is something else to consider: If safety levels do not improve but merely remain static, most experts agree that there will be an increase in the number of accidents per year and an increased casualty toll. Earl F. Weener, Ph.D., chief engineer of airworthiness, reliability and maintainability, and safety, for Boeing told the participants in the Flight Safety Foundation's 43rd International Air Safety Seminar (1990), "Even if the accident rate trend continues its gradual decline over the next 15 years, we could encounter, on average, five more accidents per year by

2005." That is not an isolated fear, but is so well accepted in the safety community that it can be called the conventional wisdom.

Will the accident rate decline, absent concerted effort by regulators and airlines to increase current safety standards? That is highly doubtful. Further advancements in safety will be hard to come by. "The past 30 years of safety improvements have been largely due to new technology and improved designs," J.R. Riedmeyer, chairman of the Flight Safety Foundation, told the 43rd annual International Air Safety Seminar. "We see nothing to equal the benefit impact of jet engines and microprocessors." With technology having a reduced impact on improving safety, crash survivability improvements and increased emphasis on operations and training will have to take up the slack.

But that costs money and the price of safety is no longer automatically factored in to the price of a ticket as it was under CAB oversight. Once such expense items were no longer guaranteed, spending on improving safety became vulnerable to corporate belt tightening. And now that the term "airline profits" seems to have become an oxymoron, what is the likelihood that the airlines will voluntarily invest in more rigorous safety measures? And what will happen if the aviation accident rate begins to rise?

The status quo is unacceptable. Complacency and self-satisfaction must be overcome. The slow decline that appears to be developing in the level of safety must be reversed. This will not be an easy or a quick-fix process. It will take a long-term commitment from all levels of the aviation industry from regulators to airlines to unions to passengers. There will be setbacks but the job can be done.

The final two chapters in this book discuss some of the important issues that need to be addressed in improving the aviation safety system to meet the challenges of the decade and beyond. Chapter 19 considers topics of systemic and regulatory reform. Chapter 20 discusses the need to create a powerful consumer voice that could represent passenger safety issues in the halls of power—along with a proposal as to how that can be accomplished. Chapter 20 also suggests actions that a passenger can take now to protect their safety and increase the likelihood of survival if they are in a plane crash.

19

Toward a safer tomorrow

"By allowing the 'free hand' of the market to rule, we have been hurting the good carriers and rewarding shoddy operators."
Congressman Peter DeFazio, November 20, 1992

"We are not spending enough on safety."
Louis A. Turpen, director of
San Francisco International Airport

It must be clear to any reasonable observer that the government's approach to aviation in the 1980s has been destructive to the industry and has threatened the level of safety. Deregulation, unrestrained by antitrust and safety enforcement, created havoc in the industry. The FAA has failed time and again to adequately regulate safety, the ATC modernization effort has been plagued with delays, and the air traffic control system has been troubled. Commuter airlines are a growing segment of the aviation industry, yet safety regulation has not caught up with this new reality. Clearly, the time has come to consider change.

It's time to reregulate

"Before deregulation, we had the newest fleet in the world. Now, we are 48th out of 51 (August 1992). The airlines cannot afford new planes. We can't move forward to increase capacity and

improve safety because of the money. Deregulation has reduced the margin of safety."

Captain Duane E. Woerth,
ALPA first vice president

It has been more than 10 years since the country began its experiment with airline deregulation. Promoters of the experiment in free markets promised lower fares, increased competition, better service and a new and safer era of air travel. Instead, deregulation as administered by the Reagan/Bush team, created almost the opposite. Let's review the facts:

Industry finances are a shambles

Between 1989 and 1992, the airline industry lost approximately $8 billion. Several airlines have gone out of business or have merged with other companies, including Eastern, Pan American, Piedmont, and Midway. Others, such as Continental Airlines and TWA, have sought the shelter of bankruptcy courts. Continental subsequently emerged from bankruptcy protection. Northwest Airlines and USAir have fallen so deeply in debt they have been forced to seek an infusion of cash and are now partly owned by foreign airlines. Even relatively strong airlines such as United Airlines and American Airlines, have canceled the purchase of new aircraft and announced layoffs. As a result of all of the delayed and canceled orders, Boeing, the country's largest civilian airline manufacturer, has announced mass layoffs of its workers. Moreover, the industry pleads poverty anytime needed safety regulations are suggested.

The use of commuter airlines has increased

Recall that deregulation has increased the public's reliance on small commuter airlines. These carriers have a worse safety record, are subject to more lax safety regulations, and fly planes that, for the most part, do not have as much safety equipment as larger jets. Moreover, pilots for commuters often do not have military aviation experience, have less training, and fewer flight hours than their colleagues who fly large transport jets. Many commuter pilots view their work as akin to playing baseball in the minor leagues, where they pay their dues until they are ready to be called up to the major leagues and fly for Part 121 carriers.

The lower level of experience and training of pilots required by the FAA under Part 135 rules sometimes leads to pointless tragedy.

One such accident took the life of Senator H. John Heinz III. Senator Heinz and others were flying in an air taxi when the pilot started the landing approach and attempted to lower the landing gear. While the pilot could see that the gear had lowered, a light in the cockpit did not indicate that it was locked in place. The pilot apparently did not know that the landing gear on that particular make and model of aircraft is automatically locked into place by a spring mechanism when it is lowered; thus, if the wheels could be seen, they were ipso facto, locked in place.

The pilot received permission to fly past the airport tower where it was confirmed that the gear was lowered. But that wasn't good enough. The pilot wanted more assurance. A helicopter pilot agreed to fly close to the plane to confirm what was now quite clear—that the landing gear was lowered. During a close pass, the plane and helicopter collided. Both craft crashed. Everyone on the plane and the helicopter were killed—a senseless tragedy caused by a pilot who had not received sufficient training to understand the workings of the airplane.

Money problems have raised questions regarding airline safety

"You can't have airline safety without airline profits," says Christopher J. Witkowski, former director of ACAP, now director of air safety and health for the Association of Flight Attendants. Many of the threats to aviation safety described in this book have been caused, at least in part, by the poor financial condition of most of the major airlines and/or the refusal of the FAA to compel airlines to invest in safety.

Take the aging aircraft problem as an example: Safety is adversely impacted by geriatric aircraft in several ways, even if the improved aging aircraft maintenance procedures prevent another tragedy similar to Aloha Airlines.

- Aircraft built before 1985 do not have cabins that have been made more fire resistant, nor are they outfitted with the sturdier 16-G seats unless there has been a complete overhaul of the aircraft interior.

- Older aircraft require more intensive maintenance.

- Older aircraft are noisier and less efficient. This might lead localities to force pilots to maneuver in a less safe manner on takeoff and landing.

- Older aircraft often have older engines and other important mechanical systems that might be more likely to malfunction.

Then there is the question of the safety reliability of financially troubled airlines. When Eastern Airlines began to sink under its self-created red ink, to save money, the airline began to conduct business in a criminal manner. Specifically, it falsified maintenance records, claiming to have performed repair work when, in fact, it had not done the work. As a result, the airline pleaded guilty in federal court to six counts of falsifying records and was charged a fine of $3.5 million. (In the plea bargain, 53 counts were dismissed in return for the plea.)

Is Eastern Airlines the only airline to falsify maintenance documents? As of the date of this writing, it is the only one criminally indicted for the practice. But sources have informed us, and the press has reported, that USAir, another financially troubled major carrier, is being investigated (as of May 1993) by the FAA because its mechanics have reported mass pencil whipping. (The airline and the mechanics have been involved in a heated labor dispute. USAir contends that any problems in its maintenance operations are isolated and an aberration. As this book goes to press, the FAA has not come to any conclusions on the matter.)

If the allegations as reported by some USAir mechanics are true, commercial aviation could be rocked to its foundation. It would indicate that the Eastern Airlines debacle might not have been an industry anomaly. It would also illustrate the need for vast improvements in FAA oversight and the necessity that the Department of Justice strongly pursue criminal cases against airline employee wrongdoers so that individuals would have a powerful incentive not to cut corners in an act of misguided company loyalty or in response to management pressure.

Airports are overcrowded

The hub and spoke airport system has caused overcrowding because there are fewer direct flights between smaller cities than before deregulation and because of the proliferation of small commercial planes that carry few passengers but take up as much airspace as the largest commercial jet. This overcrowding has put a strain on ATC, caused regulators to ease up on safety rules in order to increase capacity, and has created additional security problems because of the frequent need to transfer luggage between planes.

Let us admit that full economic deregulation of the airlines is a failed policy that should be discarded, or at the very least, redesigned. It might not be feasible or even desirable to return to the days of full government control of prices and routes; however there is a middle ground that can be found between total government control and government abandonment of the field.

Professors Paul Stephen Dempsey and Andrew R. Goetz have written a challenging book on the topic, entitled *Airline Deregulation and Laissez-faire Mythology* (1992, Quorom Books, Westport, Connecticut). In it, they describe several steps they believe would revitalize commercial aviation and promote safety. Among their suggestions are:

Take steps to increase entry of new carriers into the industry Deregulation was supposed to increase competition but it didn't work out that way. Instead of expanding over time, the industry has become more concentrated because of monopolistic practices by larger airlines, leveraged option buyouts, mergers, and structural problems in the industry that drove the new carriers out of business or onto the sales block.

One method advocated by Dempsey and Goetz to revitalize the industry and promote healthy competition is to limit the number of airport hubs any individual carrier might dominate. This antitrust action would force airlines to open up airport slots that they control to smaller airlines. This, in turn, would allow for more competition and the ability of niche airlines to carve out markets. (For example, before they were swallowed by a larger carrier, People's Express operated nonstop flights between Los Angeles and Chicago. That forced the other airlines to keep fares down and service up on that route.)

Eventually, as niche airlines prospered, the inefficient hub and spoke system could become obsolete, to be replaced by direct-route airlines. (Southwest Airlines is the model.) That would lessen airport overcrowding, reduce the need for small commuter flights, and improve service while serving various regions of the country in a less expensive and more time efficient manner.

Institute price guidelines According to Professor Dempsey, "Free market economists predicted that pricing under deregulation reflect carrier costs. Instead, rates reflect the level of competition." This has created several contradictory problems for the industry:

- Underpricing: In markets where the competition remains fierce (Los Angeles to New York, New York to Washington, Los Angeles to San Francisco, and the like) prices are often so low that the airline loses money even if the plane is full.

- Overpricing: At the same time, when an airline enjoys a virtual monopoly, it might charge outrageous prices. This often results in the surrealistic practice of an airline charging passengers a higher fare to take a short trip than it does a passenger taking a longer flight in the next seat flying on the same plane; thus, a passenger flying to New York from Los Angeles via a Midwestern hub, might pay less than the passenger who disembarks at the Midwestern hub. In addition, people living in communities where there is little or no competition often suffer skyway robbery with fares that are tremendously overpriced. (Dempsey and Goetz suggest a law, similar to one applied to railroads by Congress in 1887, prohibiting the airlines from charging higher fares for shorter flights than they do for longer flights going in the same direction.)

Limited price regulation should be reinstated. State regulation of the insurance industry could provide a loose blueprint. Insurance was first regulated because unscrupulous companies would underprice the product to obtain business and then be unable to pay claims when they were made; thus, insurance regulators prohibit pricing that is too low to ensure company profitability and the ability to pay claims. At the same time, in theory at least—but too often, not in practice—insurance regulation is intended to prevent price gouging. Conceptually, if not always in reality, insurance regulation prevents over- and under-charging, leaving companies with a wide latitude of pricing and services that can be offered.

Something similar could be instituted for the aviation industry, although unlike insurance, every price change should not require a regulatory approval. The airlines should be given a broad latitude over their prices and their services; however, monopolistic practices such as predatory pricing designed to drive competition out of business would be prevented while at the same time, outrageous fare rip-offs would be stopped. (Predatory pricing can offer bargains over the short term but once market control is obtained, the airline can charge whatever the market will bear. The creation of a virtual monopoly can also have a psychological impact on regulators who might not wish to come down too hard on the dominant carrier and thereby deprive a region of the country with easily accessible air transportation.) At the same time, anti-trust enforcement should vigorously intervene to prevent collusion by competing airlines in setting unreasonable prices.

Under such a system of "semiregulation," it would be vital that a consumer-driven consumer watchdog organization be created to represent the public interest on issues of ticket pricing. It would be created along the *citizen utility board* (CUB) concept, organizations that act as watchdogs over utility companies in Wisconsin, New York, Oregon, and California. (*See* Coalition of Airline Passengers (CAP) in chapter 20.)

Semiregulation should allow the airlines to pursue specific markets. For example, to lure families, airlines might wish to offer huge discounts for children during flight times when few business people fly in order to fill otherwise semiempty flights. Those discounts would be allowed because they would be intended to improve efficiency and not drive competitors out of business.

Partial reregulation makes a lot of sense. As Dempsey and Goetz suggest, the government would set the parameters within which airlines could legally operate but would not control their business behavior within those parameters. Partial regulation also incorporates a healthy competitive philosophy while preventing the manipulations and abuses that destroyed the economic foundation of the industry during the 1980s. It would also assure passengers that money would be available to pay for safety.

With the laissez-faire radicals now out of power, and with the prospect that antitrust laws and financial fitness standards would be enforced, there is a chance that the wreck that is deregulation will be towed to the shop for repairs. Ultimately, that would prove beneficial to passengers and the industry alike.

President Clinton announced plans to appoint a 15-member commission to investigate ways the government can help stimulate the airline business. Among the proposals to be considered were loan guarantees to the airlines, low interest loans to the airlines, increased foreign investment, and a change in the computer reservations systems that currently favor the major airlines.

If the government is going to "bail out" or otherwise assist the industry, taxpayers are entitled to a quid pro quo. Any corporate welfare should be reciprocated with airline "safefare." The government should insist that some of the benefit received by the airlines be used to enhance airline safety, such as refurbishing cabins to make them fire resistant and taking other steps to improve crashworthiness. Absent that, taxpayer assistance to bail out airlines—businesses that have created most of their own financial problems—should be vigorously opposed.

Reform the FAA

"There is something that has gone amiss in the bureaucracy."

Federico Peña,
secretary of transportation, quoted in
***The Washington Post,* March 8, 1993**

The overall performance of the FAA throughout the eighties and into the nineties was, to put it politely, inadequate, despite a projected budget for fiscal year 1994 of $9.2 billion. (The agency's FY 1994 budget request breaks down, according to documents supplied by the FAA, as follows: $4.576 billion for "operations"—a less than one percent increase of $38 million over the FY 1993 level. These funds pay for air traffic control, inspections, and the regulation and enforcement functions of the agency; $2.524 billion for facilities and equipment, an increase of seven percent over FY 1993, to pay for modernization of ATC and other technological systems; $250 million for research, engineering and development, a nine percent increase over FY 1993 (RE&D pays for research and development of new technologies in the areas of security, air traffic control, and technology, designed to increase capacity); $1.89 billion is requested for airport improvement grants to enhance capacity, emphasize safety needs, and reduce noise. Seventy-five percent of the agency's budget is financed by user fees contained in the Airport and Airway Trust Fund, which typically has a multibillion dollar surplus.)

This book is rife with disappointing examples of the agency's refusal to promulgate needed regulations in a timely manner, of halfway measures, of incompetent management, of shortsighted decision making and kowtowing to airline desires. The few times when the agency's work has demonstrated excellence, as with the aging aircraft issue and central flow control, merely highlight the agency's usual less-than-desirable level of performance. To say the least, it is not a record that causes one to stand up and cheer.

In fairness, it must be said that many of the FAA's problems are not entirely of its own doing. Looking back over a dozen years, it is easy to see why the people who work at the FAA would feel overwhelmed. Deregulation dramatically increased its responsibilities to certify a growing number of new airlines just when the Reagan administration cut the agency's budget. The PATCO strike and subsequent firings hamstrung the FAA's ability to expand the air traffic control system. The antiregulatory political climate of the 1980s and the politicization of the DOT and OMB, made real safety reform difficult at best. In many ways, it was the worst of times to be a safety agency.

But now there is a new political climate in Washington and a chance that the old laissez faire ways can give way to a more enlightened approach to the important work of promoting aviation safety. But that will not occur if the FAA is allowed to continue with business as usual.

The time is ripe to reform the FAA. Here are some ideas that deserve consideration:

Eliminate the dual mandate

As we have seen, the FAA's purposes for existing are often at cross purposes. On one hand the agency is charged by law to promote the economic health of the aviation industry. On the other, it is required to foster safety. When the two purposes come into conflict, money wins out over safety almost every time.

It is time to amend the law so that the FAA's sole function is as a safety agency. Congressman Peter A. DeFazio (D-OR), who serves on the House Aviation Subcommittee agrees. "Let the Department of Commerce or some other department promote the industry," he told us. "Safety should be priority of the FAA. Safety and nothing else."

At the very least that would send a powerful message to the people who work in the agency, who are often accused of acting as if their job is as a facilitator of the airline industry. It would also allow the FAA to focus exclusively on safety and make the FAA less vulnerable to protestations by the airlines that resist reasonable safety regulations.

Make the FAA an independent agency

A growing belief by many in the aviation safety community is that the FAA should be removed from the Department of Transportation and changed to an independent agency with the purpose of removing the agency from the political machinations of Washington, D.C.

No doubt that the Transportation Department and, by extension the FAA (which is controlled by the DOT), have been compromised by politics in the past. One career staff person in the Department of Transportation told us, "In the last 10 years, we've been blinded by economic theory and that has impacted the ability of the DOT to do its work." This regulator's frustration stemmed from the department's unwillingness to enforce airline financial fitness standards due to the laissez faire politics in control during the 1980s, but that has not been the only area where politics interfered. Pressure was placed on the FAA by free trade radicals in the Reagan and Bush White Houses to induce the FAA to certify more foreign airline repair facilities to service U.S. airlines—this despite the fact that civilian airline maintenance is one of the few U.S. industries that continues to dominate the world's markets. "Reagan and Bush pushed the FAA to give authority to overseas applicants," one knowledgeable source told us. "Three hundred were approved and more than 1500 are pending. One huge complex is being built 15 miles inside Mexico. This is bad for the American economy and has safety ramifications." (Some of these ramifications: logistical problems in FAA oversight, perhaps a less well trained work force, a greater opportunity for saboteurs to infiltrate the maintenance facilities, and the like.) These criticisms were repeated by other industry and government insiders who expressed their belief that the FAA expanded foreign maintenance certifications because of political pressures and industry demands.

It is important to insulate the FAA from such pressure. One union official told us, "An independent FAA is the best answer for the troubles that plague the agency. It would prevent political micromanaging by the DOT and would liberate the agency from many of the bureaucratic rules that hamper its effective management." The Air Transport Association, a group usually in conflict with the safety positions taken by the union official quoted above, is in agreement. "The DOT is a highly politicized department," William

Jackman of the ATA told us. "The FAA needs to have independence if it is to do a proper job."

Some worry that an independent FAA would soon be dominated by the airlines and manufacturers. Indeed, the Air Transport Association is a strong supporter of an independent FAA. But that does not make independence a bad idea. Industry dominance of the agency already exists. "FAA personnel see themselves as facilitators of the industry," one consultant to the FAA and other government agencies told us. "That's just the mind set of the agency." (To which we add: If the agency doesn't see itself that way it sure acts as if it does.)

Among the benefits cited by supporters of an independent FAA (regardless of the form), are increased freedom from politics, removing the agency from the bureaucratic equipment procurement process (the ATC modernization fiasco), increased freedom to make management decisions involving personnel, and increased control over its own budget. The general proposal has widespread support throughout the aviation community and should be given serious consideration by Congress and the administration.

Appoint the FAA administrator for a tenured term

Pending more substantive long-term reform, many propose that the FAA administrator be made a tenured position with a term of four to six years.

That makes a lot of sense. Certain failings of the agency during recent years have been partially caused by the high level of turnover of administrators, six in the 12 years of Reagan/Bush, not counting interim administrators. "Every time the agency changes administrators, priorities change," says William Jackman of the Air Transport Association. "That doesn't bode well for continuity of performance." Joseph Del Balzo, acting FAA administrator, admits that instability at the helm can cause disruption. "Every time a new administrator comes on board," he told us in August 1992, "it can take months to acquaint them with all of the ongoing activities of the agency."

They are right, of course. It is difficult for any organization to perform well if there is no continuity of leadership. One of the benefits of a tenured position is that it would be assumed that the person receiving the appointment would serve for the entire term, thereby bringing stability to the agency. Moreover, it should increase the professionalism of the FAA. In the recent past, many administrators of the FAA have been appointed for political purposes or as a political reward rather than a demonstrated commitment to promoting aviation safety. The post of FAA administrator should not be viewed as patronage or as a step on the road to career advancement. By making the position tenured, the president is more likely to appoint a "professional," and the Congress would be likely to take a longer and tougher look at appointees, so as to weed out political hacks and dilettantes.

Give increased weight to NTSB recommendations

Under the current system, the FAA can ignore NTSB safety recommendations with impunity. That needs to be changed. A system needs to be devised whereby NTSB recommendations are given greater official consideration.

One idea that would seem to hold promise would be this: When the NTSB has formally issued a recommendation, the FAA would be compelled by law to publish an NPRM on the subject (if applicable, all NTSB recommendations do not require NPRMs), say within 90 days and promulgate the rule within one year, unless it could positively demonstrate that the recommendation is ill advised. In other words, instead of placing the burden on the NTSB to convince the FAA to enact the proposal, the burden would be on the FAA to prove that it should not follow the proposal. That would reduce many of the frustrating delays that exist under the current system and prevent the FAA from killing good proposals through inaction.

Spin off ATC from the FAA

There is growing support in the aviation community to separate the ATC function from the regulatory purposes of the FAA. Cornish Hitchcock, former director of ACAP says, "It might be a good idea to sever the ATC system from the FAA's regulatory function. The former is an operational function, akin to the Postal Service. By severing the operational from the regulatory, management can focus better. That would improve the ATC modernization effort and allow for greater accountability." Such a move would also remove ATC from the budgetary approval process and user fees could assure them a continual and reliable source of funding. It is certainly worth a careful look.

These are a few of the ideas that could improve the FAA's level of performance. One point is clear: If the safety record is to improve, if safety regulations are going to raise minimum operating standards, it will require a tougher FAA. Reform of the agency might be the only way to break the current safety gridlock.

Repeal the cost/benefit rule

"The cost/benefit rule, as currently applied, is a disgrace in that it grossly oversimplifies a decision process that should be followed in the public interest."

**C.O. Miller,
air safety professional, May 1993**

The cost/benefit rule as it has been applied to regulation since the presidency of Ronald Reagan, has served as a roadblock to safety and an excuse for inaction. There is also the suspicion that the cost benefit rule reigns supreme—unless the FAA and industry do not want it to. (Interestingly, when the aging aircraft crisis arose, there was little cost/benefit controversy—even though the costs of the program will be significant—while only one person had died because of an aged aircraft.) The time has come to rescind Executive Order 12291. The time has come to try a different more rational approach to airline safety.

That is not to say that cost should never be considered when the FAA decides whether to promulgate a rule. Cost should be *a* factor—but it should not be the *only* factor or even the primary factor, at least not as costs are defined under the present system. (For example, the "cost" to the airlines if business is lost due to a public perception that failing to enact a rule has reduced safety, is not considered a cost.)

What formula or process could replace the current cost/benefit rule? Here are two alternatives:

A reasonable passenger standard

Safety always extracts a cost, whether in money, time, convenience or all of these. (That's in the short term. In the long term, increased safety saves money, time, and heartbreak.) A "reasonable passenger standard" of determining the cost of safety would consider this question: "If given a choice between a flight in which the proposed safety rule were in place and a flight where the proposed rule were not in force, would a reasonable passenger be willing to pay the additional price (whether time, money, or convenience) for the flight with the heightened safety?" For example, if safety rule "X" cost $2 per ticket and required the passenger to arrive at the airport 10 minutes earlier, would the passenger agree to pay the price? If the answer were affirmative, the rule would be passed, if negative, the rule would be declined.

The reasonable passenger standard would utilize a broader application of the term "cost" than the existing cost/benefit rule. Money would no longer be the sole criterion and there would be more give and take to fashion a rule that would be "reasonable." Moreover, for the first time, passengers would have to be brought into the rulemaking process because their opinions would be required to determine the reasonable passenger's point-of-view.

The "total picture" approach

While the reasonable passenger proposal is better than the cost/benefit analysis currently in place, we prefer a different approach than comparing "costs and benefits." Why not look at the total picture? How many injuries are expected to be prevented? How many lives saved? Will the public resist the change or applaud it? Over how long a period of time will the benefits of the rule be experienced versus the increase in costs? What is the impact on society as a whole? Are there any spin-off benefits, such as improved technology? Will employment be increased or decreased? Are there other ancillary benefits to society? Can the cost of the proposed rule be reduced and still provide the increase in safety? What are the costs when amortized? Such in-depth analysis would bring a greater depth and breadth to the safety process—something like adding color to a system that is currently operated in black and white.

Either of these more enlightened approaches would permit costs to be taken into account during consideration of a proposed safety rule, but do away with the odious system of placing an arbitrary dollar value on a human life and then cold heartedly measuring whether the money spent to increase safety is more or less than the so-called value of the lives that would be lost if the rule were not promulgated. In other words, the complete long-term picture would be considered, not just dollars and cents.

Strengthen Part 135 regulation

"It's time that commuter airlines be required to meet the same safety standards as Part 121 carriers."

David Traynham,
professional staff,
Aviation Subcommittee, August 1992

"The FAA has not kept up with the evolution of aviation," Ira Rimson, a well-respected aviation accident investigator told us. "Its regulatory attitude is still mired in the days when commuter airlines were a very small part of the commercial airline industry. The regulations, the mind-set of the inspectors assigned to commuters, the whole approach, is outdated."

The tremendous growth of commuter airlines since deregulation has created a multifaceted safety problem. Commuter carriers were originally subject to less onerous safety regulations because the industry was generally made up of air taxi businesses that had little money and carried relatively few passengers.

With deregulation, that has all changed. According to statistics provided by the Regional Airline Association, total passengers enplaned grew from 15.4 million in 1981 to 42 million in 1991. The number of planes in service increased from 1463 (in 1981) to 1992 (in 1991). The commuter industry is generally quite profitable.

That being so, there is a growing belief by safety experts such as Mr. Rimson, C.O. Miller, John H. Enders, union officials, government officials, and others, that the time has come for the FAA to bring the minimum safety standards that govern regional carriers governed by Part 135 into line with large carriers that operate under Part 121. "It's time to create a single standard of safety," J. Randolph Babbitt stated. "This is especially important for the commuter ridership that picks a commuter airline because it has the same colors and name as a large airline and the pilots wear the same uniforms."

Captain Babbitt is referring to the marketing practice of regional airlines and major airlines holding themselves out as if they were a single business entity. "They (passengers) like the standards set by the large airline," Babbitt told us, "and may say, 'Gee, I'm buying the big airline. They've got a good safety record. They must have good standards,' when in fact they may well be flying under less stringent safety standards and on an airline in which the major carrier has no ownership interest. We don't think that's right."

The business practice of large airlines and commuter airlines appearing to the general public as if they are part of the same company, is known as *code sharing*. Here's how code sharing works. A passenger retains a travel agent to purchase tickets to New York, telling the agent he prefers to fly American Airlines. To get to New York, the passenger will first have to be transported to a hub airport. So, the travel agent will book the passenger on American Eagle to the hub airport and then to New York on American Airlines. The passenger would believe that American Airlines flew him from the beginning of the flight to his destination in New York when that was not the case. (The authors telephoned American Airlines flight reservations at 1-800-433-7300 and asked the reservation operator which airline flew commuter flights for American Airlines. The answer was, "American Eagle." The operator was then asked whether American Airlines owned American Eagle. The answer given was "Yes." As the chart describes, American Eagle flights are flown by four different companies.)

According to documents from the Department of Transportation, dated September 17, 1992, the following commuter airlines were sharing codes with the major airline but were really separate companies:

Major Airline	Commuter Airline	Actual Owner
American Airlines	American Eagle	Four airlines fly under the tradename American Eagle: Executive Airlines, Flagship Airlines, Simmons Airlines, and Wings West Airlines
Continental Airlines	Continental Express	Two airlines fly under the tradename, Continental Express: Britt Airways and Rocky Mountain Airways
Delta Airlines	The Delta Connection	Sky West Airlines
Northwest Airlines	Northwest Airlink	Three airlines fly under the tradename, Northwest Airlink: Big Sky

Major Airline	Commuter Airline	Actual Owner
		Transportation Company, Simmons Airlines, and Northeast Express Regional Airlines Inc.
TWA	Transworld Express	Two airlines fly under the name Transworld Express: Transworld Express, Inc. and Air Midwest, Inc.
United Airlines	United Express	Three airlines fly under the tradename, United Express; Air Wisconsin, Inc. Mesa Airlines, and Westair Commuter Airlines
USAir	USAir Express USAir Shuttle	Three airlines fly under the tradename, USAir Express: CCAir, Inc., Jet Express, Inc., Stateswest Airlines, Shuttle, Inc. flies under the tradename USAir Shuttle

According to the Regional Airline Association, there were 41 code sharing agreements (computer codes used by travel agents when booking flights) between regional and major carriers in 1992. Of those, 14 airlines were owned outright by major carriers, four were partially owned and 23 were "pure marketing alliances devoid of any ownership by the major airlines." In 1991, 93 percent of industry's passengers were transported on airlines with code sharing agreements.

This is not to say that the airlines listed above are not safe or that they are doing anything illegal; however, there is a subterfuge being practiced with the intention that passengers take comfort in believing that they are flying on a major airline. Moreover, the level of safety required of the large carrier by the FAA vis-a-vis its commuter "affiliate," are often quite different. The public expects to fly safely whether they are in a Boeing 747 or a 19-seat commuter plane. The FAA should hold all commercial airlines to the same level of safety, regardless of the size of the plane. Also, in the interest of honesty, the agency should also require public disclosure of the actual name of the commuter airline flying under a tradename meant to associate it with a major carrier in the minds of the flying public.

Enhance whistle-blowing protection

"I was fired from Eastern Airlines because I implied that they were not following safe maintenance practices. The kinds of problems I tried to bring to the FAA's attention later led to the criminal indictment of Eastern Airlines."

John King,
whistle-blower and
former mechanic for Eastern Airlines

"Aviation safety runs on the honor system," a high official of the FAA has said. Very often that is true. The FAA does not have the manpower or resources to adequately police the industry. The FAA does not make optimum use of the people available to ensure that the industry is following all of the safety guidelines.

That being so, "whistle-blowers," people who observe unsafe or illegal practices and report them, are an extremely important part of the aviation safety system. Aviation whistle-blowers usually work for airlines or manufacturers, where they are in a position to observe practices that an FAA inspector, who is not on site, might never see. Whistle-blowers need to be protected and encouraged because their no-cost eyes and ears can significantly protect the safety of the flying public.

The FAA recognizes the importance of whistle-blowing and has established an 800-number hotline for people such as mechanics and pilots to call and report safety violations they have observed. If requested, the caller can remain anonymous. The hotline is important; however, it needs to be improved. "If a complaint is made on the hotline," a high union official told us, "the matter will be referred to the airline's POI (the inspector in charge of the airline's oversight) for follow-up. What is the POI's incentive? To prove that the report is unfounded. Otherwise, it looks as if he has not been doing a very good job of inspecting. I have even heard of POIs pressuring people they suspect of calling the hotline to recant."

Our source has a valid point. It is contrary to human nature to expect inspectors to enthusiastically follow up leads that would prove they might have been remiss in their duties. This union official would like to see the FAA turn whistle-blower tips over to an independent inspector who would have no compunction about "discovering" unsafe practices or other safety deficiencies that the POI has missed. That does seem like a prudent step, one that could improve the quality of FAA follow-up on hotline reports.

The law also needs to better protect the job security for whistleblowers. In 1987, John King tried to tip off the FAA that Eastern Airlines was systematically falsifying its maintenance records. He called the hotline. According to King, the FAA contacted Eastern and told them about the report and permitted Eastern Airlines to investigate itself about the then anonymous allegations. Surprise, surprise: Eastern determined that the report was unfounded.

Unable to get action through proper channels, King went public and was fired by Eastern. The reasons for the termination were set forth in a letter to King dated July 27, 1987:

> On July 22, 1987, you appeared on local TV and were quoted on local radio in Boston. The message you conveyed to the public through the media was that Eastern Airlines management is consciously compromising aircraft safety. Additionally, a tape-recording of a conversation you secretly and illegally taped with a member of Boston management was released to local media as well as Cable News Network.
>
> Based on your public statement the company has conducted an investigation of our allegations. This investigation has revealed the following:
>
> 1. Upon repeated questioning from Eastern Management you could not provide the company with any information involving aircraft that have been flown illegally....
>
> 2. You brought your allegations and secretly recorded tape to the attention of the FAA who upon investigation did not find Eastern in violation of FAA regulations.
>
> 3. You failed to bring allegations concerning safety infractions to other members of management in the chain of command above your supervisor.
>
> 4. After the FAA did not find a violation of regulations, and without bringing the allegations to the attention of

management you chose to approach the media with your allegations.

5. You secretly tape-recorded a conversation with your supervisor during which you were repeatedly asked if you were tape-recording the conversation. You evaded the question several times and ultimately denied taping the conversation.

This constituted a false statement to your supervisor.

The false statements you made to the media and the release of the tape-recording can only be viewed as an attempt on your part to undermine and cause harm to the company's business reputation by falsely and without foundation casting doubt on the safety of flying Eastern with the travelling public....

We can only assume you made these false statements based upon your ill feelings toward the company due to your termination for sleeping on the job last year and your concern of allegedly being forced to work overtime.

Your conduct as described above is a serious violation of company rules and regulations. As a result, your employment with Eastern is hereby terminated effective immediately.

One of the persons receiving an official copy of the termination letter (according to the "cc:" on the letter) was one Thomas Lewis, then an executive of Eastern Airlines who had responsibility over the airline's maintenance program. According to King, this same Thomas Lewis was later an arbitrator at the arbitration in which Mr. King unsuccessfully sought to have his job reinstated. Mr. Lewis would later be indicted by the U.S. government, along with Eastern Airlines and other individually named defendants, for falsifying maintenance records. That indictment contended that the fraud began in 1985, two years before King was dismissed for telling the world that Eastern was engaged in the kind of maintenance fraud that King had described. Eastern Airlines would plead guilty to six counts of the indictment and would be fined

$3.5 million. (The criminal cases against Thomas Lewis and other individuals are pending (May 1993). The government has neither dismissed the case nor brought it to trial. Under the law, Mr. Lewis and the other named individuals must be considered innocent until proven guilty.)

Whether Mr. King had a grudge against Eastern that led him to whistle-blow is not important. What is important is that he tried to alert the FAA to pencil whipping and got fired for his efforts. On August 30, 1989, the FAA would write a letter to Eastern Airlines charging the company with falsifying records "beginning February 1988 to, on, or about February 1989," and flying aircraft that were not in an "airworthy condition," and offering to "accept $839,000 in settlement of this matter." Thereafter would come the indictments and the Eastern Airlines guilty plea.

It is important that people be encouraged to blow the whistle on unsafe aviation practices and that their jobs be protected when they do. This is especially important considering that the FAA is usually unable to make surprise inspections on airlines because of the voluminous records that must be assembled before an inspection can begin.

The Congress has recognized the importance of whistle-blowing by passing the Whistle-blower Protection Act of 1989. This law is intended to protect government workers from retaliation for reporting unsafe or improper activities by government agencies.

Similar protection needs to be extended into the private sector. Airline whistle-blowers need to be assured of anonymity and that they can report perceived safety violations without fear of reprisal, harassment, or job loss. Whistle-blowers often face protracted legal battles that they must often wage at personal expense. Some means must be found to provide legal help for those facing retaliation, lawsuits and/or loss of jobs. Whistle-blowers should be given immunity from job actions, except if it can be shown that the employee lied or should have known the charges were false, even if their complaint cannot be completely proven. (The FAA often is unable to substantiate bona fide claims.) True, there is the danger of disgruntled employees making false claims, but for the sake of safety, some accommodation must be made to permit employees to whistle blow—even when they make a good faith mistake—without fear of retribution.

Force the carriers
to compete on safety

*"All of the major airlines meet minimum FAA safety
requirements, although some may do more. There has been an
unspoken agreement among the carriers. We don't go after each
other on safety."*

**William Jackman,
Air Transport Association, October 1992**

"If the public believes every carrier to be equally safe, where's the
financial incentive for a carrier to do better than minimum standards? What's the reward for being the best?" That query was pos-
tulated by Robert W. Baker, senior vice president of operations for
American Airlines (as quoted in the September 1987 issue of *Air
Line Pilot Magazine*). It is an important question. Why don't the
airlines compete on safety?

It is unfortunate but true, the airlines with the cooperation of
the FAA, have created the impression that when it comes to safety,
they are all the same. But that isn't true. Some spend more on
safety than others. Some have better training programs than others. Some do a better job of maintenance than others. Insiders
might know which airline is which, but it is virtually impossible
for the general public to find out which airlines are "some" and
which are "others."

Christopher J. Witkowski, former director of ACAP and now
director of air safety and health for the Association of Flight
Attendants, has testified before the Aviation Subcommittee, stating
in part: "In this age, when consumers can get ready information
about a variety of products, air travelers have no means of weigh-
ing the safety of individual airlines and aircraft. As a result, there
is no accurate way for prospective airline customers to reward
carriers that strive for safety excellence or to avoid carriers that
perform poorly .... By making air carrier and airplane safety information available to consumers, a market incentive will be created
that forces carriers to improve safety performance and fly aircraft
with a better safety record. Carriers will benefit as they phase out
substandard safety performance factors and aircraft with a poor
safety record."

The FAA doesn't see it that way. Its only interest is in ensuring
that the airlines remain within the minimum guidelines estab-

lished in the FARs. Those airlines that exceed the guidelines do not get "extra credit," and often, those that do not meet the minimum standards are quietly reprimanded, often with little or no public notice.

All carriers are not equal when it comes to safety. The blank wall of obfuscation that prevents consumers from differentiating among the airlines on issues of safety must be demolished. The airlines should be induced to compete on issues of safety perhaps with public disclosure of safety indicator statistics as the key. That is the best way to create an aviation system where the minimum safety standards set by the FARs are exceeded by the airlines as a matter of good business practice. Wouldn't that be better than the current system where the financial incentive is to cut costs so long as practices do not dip below acceptable FAA standards?

The issues discussed above are just some of the areas that need to be addressed in a committed and systemic fashion if aviation safety levels are going to improve dramatically, as they must, over the next decade. Of course, they are not the only ones. Many others have been discussed throughout the book and there might be new issues that arise as developments unfold.

But there is yet more that should be done to promote safe flying. You, the passenger, need to become involved in safety to protect your own welfare and to improve the aviation system. That is the subject of chapter 20.

20

Protect yourself

Jet Passenger Hurt In Jet Turbulence Dies
Headline in *The Washington Post*, October 21, 1990

Tragic headlines are often made doubly disturbing because many casualties of flight are avoidable if passengers are willing to take the time and effort to protect themselves. This chapter describes the tactics you can take to protect yourself whenever you fly. The text will also describe the ways you can become an aviation safety activist and help make flying safer for everyone.

Self-help

"God helps those who help themselves."

Folk wisdom

Imagine you are about to take the dream vacation of a lifetime. You are really excited. You have been looking forward to this trip for the two years it took to save the money to pay for it. Now your head is filled with thoughts of the new sights you will see, the interesting people you will meet, the "good time that will be had by all." The only thing between you and fun is the five-hour plane ride from your home to unexplored new horizons.

In order to enjoy that vacation you will first have to arrive safely at your destination. The overwhelming odds favor just such a happy conclusion to your flight. But, you never know what will happen. The time has come to prepare yourself for safe flying.

What to do at home

Protecting your flying safety begins at home:

Choose the clothes you will be wearing when you fly In the unlikely event of an accident, fire will probably be your worst enemy, if you survive the impact of the crash, which is likely. That means you should wear clothes that will not increase your risk of being burned. Clothes made of natural fibers, especially wool or wool blends are good for traveling. Leather jackets can provide protection too. Your clothes should cover as much of your body as possible. Some experts suggest avoiding synthetic blends that can melt on your skin in intense heat. Be sure to wear shoes that will serve well in an emergency—no high heels. If losing your eyeglasses would incapacitate you, wear a leather safety strap to be sure they remain in place.

Bring your own smoke hood Until airlines are compelled to provide smoke hoods for passengers, if you want that protection, you will have to bring your own. (Many aviation professionals carry their own PBE (smoke hood) when flying. Others do not.) Several companies sell the device. You should choose one that works by filtering out smoke, carbon monoxide, cyanide, and other gasses. (It should not carry its own source of oxygen.) If you choose to carry a smoke hood, you should also purchase a "practice hood." Smoke hoods that utilize filter systems come in a sealed pouch. If you break the seal, the hood will lose its efficacy. By purchasing a practice hood, you can rehearse donning the hood so that you won't have trouble getting it on during the intensity of an emergency.

Be sure to keep your smoke hood immediately at hand when flying. If you put it in carry-on luggage that is stowed away from your seat, you might not be able to get to it. Plus, you will not want to block an aisle during an emergency while you look for your hood. (A bonus to carrying your own smoke hood is the protection it affords in high-rise hotels. Witness the people who died of smoke inhalation at the MGM Grand Hotel in Las Vegas.)

Smoke hoods, including the price of the practice hood, can generally be purchased for approximately $200.

Take an infant safety seat Recall that it is virtually impossible to hold on to an infant during a crash sequence or during strong in-flight turbulence. Infants who are held in laps can be seriously injured or even killed. It is as much your responsibility to protect your infant from injury while flying as it is while you are driving. The best way to do that is to make sure your baby is restrained in an infant safety seat.

Under new FAA regulations, airlines must permit you to bring an approved infant seat on the aircraft. You might have to pay for your child's seat or the airline might offer it free if the plane is not full. (Your best chance for flying on a plane that is not full is during nonpeak hours.) If you must pay for your baby's seat, ask if the airline offers a discount. If it does not, check around with other airlines that might better respect your desire to protect the safety of your infant by offering significant price breaks. Contact your carrier or travel agent for further details.

According to the FAA, recommended child seats are those manufactured after February 26, 1985, and have labels stating that the restraint is certified for use in motor vehicles and aircraft. Also recommended are seats manufactured between January 1, 1981, and February 25, 1985, with the label: "This child restraint system conforms to all applicable federal motor vehicle safety standards."

If you have questions about the use of your child restraint seat, contact your airline's customer service department.

What to do at the airport

Being alert and taking safety precautions at an airport can prevent tragedy:

Never leave your baggage unattended Unattended baggage is an invitation to theft. But there is another danger. Someone could plant contraband or an explosive device in your unattended bag.

Never carry any article, package or baggage of an unrelated or unknown person This especially applies if you don't know the person well. You never know what might be inside.

Report anything unusual to airport police or the airline crew If you see unattended baggage, report it. If you see someone who appears to be acting suspicious or furtive, report it.

Airports are vulnerable to criminal attack. The need to be vigilant is a price of the times in which we live.

Cooperate with security screening Airport security is designed to protect the safety of everybody. If you are asked to reenter a metal detector or to open your bag, do it without protest. Be ready to prove that the computer or radio you are carrying is bona fide. (This is usually accomplished by turning it on.) Don't argue or give security personnel a hard time.

What to do when you are on the plane

When you are on the plane, you should prepare yourself for self-protective action in case of an emergency:

Locate the nearest emergency exits Once you have found your seat, look around for the nearest emergency exits. Count the rows between you and the exit and memorize the number so that if you are blinded by smoke you will still be able to locate the exit. Make a mental note of at least two exits in case there is an emergency and one is blocked by fire or debris.

Mentally plan your escape Take a moment and plan what you will do if there is an emergency evacuation. Which way will you turn? How many rows must you travel? Is there an alternate route if an aisle is blocked? Don't expect to rely on a flight attendant's instructions, because the flight attendants might be injured or otherwise unavailable during an emergency.

Review the safety briefing card No matter how often you have flown, *carefully* read the safety briefing card. It will tell you how the emergency exits operate. Make a mental note of it. It will tell you how to don life vests. Make a mental note of it. It will tell you how to operate oxygen masks in the event of a loss of pressure. Make a mental note of it. In other words, study the card very thoroughly.

Listen carefully to the oral safety briefing Pay attention to the safety briefing, even if you have heard them many times before. The announcements are important. They demonstrate important safety equipment. Recalling the briefing can save your life during an emergency.

Ask questions If there is anything in the safety briefing or on the safety briefing card that you don't understand, ask questions. In an emergency, what you did not understand could definitely hurt you.

Report anything that appears amiss Passengers tend to be reluctant to report problems they perceive because they are afraid of looking foolish or nervous. That is a mistake. Sometimes passengers can prevent accidents by pointing out problems to flight attendants or flight crew.

At least two accidents described in this book could have been avoided if passengers on those flights had taken this advice. According to the NTSB accident report concerning the Aloha Airlines accident caused by metal fatigue, "After the accident, a passenger stated that as she was boarding the airplane through the jet bridge at Hilo, she observed a longitudinal fuselage crack. The crash was in the upper row of rivets along the S-10L lap joint, about halfway between the cabin door and the edge of the jet bridge hood. She made no mention of the observation to the airline or ground personnel or flight crew." If she had spoken up, it is possible that plane never would have left Hilo and the top would not have ripped off the plane.

Similarly, *The New York Times* reported on March 27, 1992, that some of the survivors of the USAir Flight 405 that crashed on takeoff on March 22, 1992, because of ice buildup, actually saw ice on the right wing before the takeoff. "We take off like this, we're all dead," one of the passengers was reported by the *Times* as saying. "We're on the plane to hell." These passengers apparently relied on the flight crew to see what they had observed. The crew did not see the ice. The plane crashed.

A letter to the editor in the *Times* dated April 10, 1992, discussed the correspondent's experience when aboard a jet at La Guardia in winter conditions similar to that faced by Flight 405.

> "The plane was fully loaded and we sat locked inside for two hours while the plane was deiced, taxied out, came back for a second deicing and got in the takeoff line again. After we had waited for about a half hour, the wind shifted, and we had to go to the other end of the runway, with ice all the while building up on the wing, next to my window ....
>
> "When the pilot announced that we were next in line for takeoff, I rang and requested that a stewardess

ask the cockpit if they were aware that what seemed an inch of ice had built up on the wings. The flight engineer came back into the cabin and observed the wings. The pilot announced that we had to return for deicing again ...."

This passenger might have saved hundreds of lives by asserting his concerns (and risk looking foolish) rather than assume that the professionals knew what they were doing. His example is well worth emulating.

Be sure your carry-on luggage is securely stowed Loose luggage can be transformed into a lethal missile during an accident or severe turbulence. Luggage in an aisle or between seat rows can hinder or prevent evacuation.

Know your responsibilities if you are seated next to an exit If you are seated in a seat row containing an exit, you are required by law to be able to accomplish the following:

- Locate the door and quickly follow instructions.
- Be able to physically open the door.
- Determine when to open the door or determine if opening the door is too dangerous.
- Devote full attention to an emergency.

The emergency exit opening procedures are printed on the door. Be sure to review them and understand them before the plane takes off. Also, if there is an escape slide at your exit, be sure to read the instructions on its operation.

Remain alert during takeoff Many people "fortify" themselves for flight by taking a tranquilizer or a stiff drink before flight. This isn't wise. Most accidents occur during takeoff and landing and it is important that you remain alert and ready to take appropriate action if an accident occurs.

What to do during your flight

During flight you should remain vigilant of your own safety:

Remain seated with your seat belt fastened Even if the seat belt sign is turned off, remain seated unless you have to get up to go to the lavatory or for some other reason. Unexpected clear air turbulence, while rare, can hit at any time. If you are restrained in your seat there is little danger; however, if you are out of your seat and the plane unexpectedly encounters severe turbulence, you could be injured or even killed.

If there is a rapid decompression, put on the oxygen mask In a decompression the mask will fall in front of you from the bulkhead or ceiling. (You should know where based on your preflight emergency preparation.) Follow the instruction on your safety briefing card or from the flight attendant.

Fire If there is an in-flight fire, remember:

- Do not use the oxygen mask. The air in the mask is partially recirculated from the aircraft's air supply. Using the mask while there is a fire could expose you to toxic fumes.
- Use a wet paper towel or article of clothes over your nose and mouth.
- Move away from the source of the fire if it is possible to safely do so.

Don't use personal electronic devices during takeoff or landing It is against the FAA rules to use devices designed to transmit signals or receive very high frequency transmissions during flight (portable radios, cellular telephones, CB radios, and the like). It is not a good idea to use other electronic devices, such as laptop computers and tape players, during the critical phases of landing and takeoff. It is suspected, but has not been proved, that such devices can cause airliner navigation and communication systems to malfunction, endangering the flight. Some airlines prohibit the use of such devices during takeoff and landing.

Prepare for landing When the plane is close to landing, repeat the safety precautions you took before the flight: review the safety card, plan your action in an emergency, locate the nearest exits, and the like.

If there is an emergency

If you are in an emergency, remember:

- Stay calm. Panic kills.
- Follow flight attendant instructions.
- Assume the "crash position" as described on the briefing card.
- Leave your carry-on luggage behind. (That should be obvious,

but more than one crash has had evacuations inhibited by people blocking the aisle trying to retrieve their luggage.)

- If there is fire or smoke, don your smoke hood if you have one, stay low, count the number of seats to the exit, follow the floor proximity lighting and exit the aircraft as quickly as you can. Don't crawl on your hands and knees; you could be trampled.

- If there has been a water landing, be sure to take flotation devices, such as your seat cushion or life vests (if any).

- Before opening a door or emergency exit, look through the window to be sure it is safe. Check for fire, smoke or other hazard.

- If you evacuate on a slide, jump into the center of the slide with your arms across your chest and your feet together. The airlines advise that you do not take your shoes off, so do not wear high heels when you fly.

- Once outside, move away from the aircraft and help fellow passengers who need assistance.

As you can see, there is a lot you can do to protect yourself. But there is more you can do. As a citizen, you can have an impact on the safety of the aviation system.

Become a safety activist

"There is a need to formalize consumer input into the regulatory process."

Congressman Peter De Fazio, November 1992

Sure, I care about aviation safety, you might be thinking, but I'm just one person. What can I do about it?

The answer is simple; get involved. Tom O'Mara had never thought much about aviation safety until his daughter was killed at Sioux City in the crash of United Airlines Flight 232. He subsequently became a tireless safety advocate. "I was told by someone I respect, 'It's often the victims that fix the system because the rest of the traveling public very quickly forgets the tragedies in aviation.' And my wife, a therapist, says that passengers simply practice denial. Once you have survived a crash or had a close family member killed in a crash, denial is no longer an option."

Tom began an individual crusade to improve safety, starting with pressuring the FAA to improve the DC-10. His efforts expanded and he became the president of the Aviation Consumer Action Project (ACAP).

That is not to say you have to go out and head your own safety organization. Few people have the time or money for that. But you can support organizations that already exist and support measures to make it easier for airline passengers to create a powerful safety group.

Join ACAP

The Aviation Consumer Action Project is a nonprofit organization founded in 1971 by one of the authors to promote airline safety and the rights of the traveling public before federal agencies of the executive branch and Congress. It is the only nonprofit consumer organization working full-time on aviation matters. ACAP is supported entirely by contributions from the public and is a tax-exempt organization under 501(c)(3) of the Internal Revenue Code. Contributions are tax deductible.

Since its founding, ACAP has scored some big victories for airline passengers, including:

Preventing the FAA from changing the definition of near midair collisions After the firing of PATCO controllers, the FAA attempted to reduce the definition of a "near miss" from 500 feet vertically and/or one mile horizontally to 500 feet horizontally or vertically, or if the pilot believed a near collision had occurred. Using the Freedom of Information Act, ACAP discovered that this new definition created an underreporting of near misses and many incidents that had not been made part of the government statistics. ACAP began an intense public advocacy campaign to reverse this public relations gambit by the FAA, including testifying before congressional committees, and working with the Department of Transportation and the FAA. Thanks in large part to ACAP's efforts, the policy of redefining near misses was abandoned.

Urging safety measures on the FAA Over the years, ACAP has been on the cutting edge of safety improvements in aviation. For example, on August 8, 1973, ACAP petitioned the FAA to set standards on smoke and toxic gas emissions during a fire, and continued to advocate improvements for more than a decade.

The FAA would not get around to mandating improvements until 1985, and then, only on planes built after the date the rule became effective. The political pressure brought by ACAP over those years was one factor leading to the improvements. In 1979, ACAP sought a court order requiring the FAA to increase the safety of passenger seats on airlines. In 1974, ACAP attempted to prevent radioactive hazardous materials from being transported on passenger aircraft. That contest continues.

Replying to proposed rules and petitions ACAP is the only full-time organization representing the safety of passengers by replying to NPRMs and petitions for rulemaking in front of the FAA and other governmental bodies. This is an important function. ACAP is able to act as a "consumer cop" on the beat, working to prevent rules that would degrade safety and urging regulators to adopt those proposals that will make flying safer. As the reader will recall from chapter 4, rulemaking is a labyrinth where those interests with the money to pay for lobbyists or "trade organizations" have the ability to press their positions on important safety issues. ACAP represents passengers and safety in these contests. Their presence is an important safeguard for airline passengers. (For example, the FAA is currently considering a drastic reduction in full-scale evacuation testing using real people when aircraft are up for certification. (It must be shown that the plane can be evacuated in 90 seconds using half the exits.) Tom O'Mara of ACAP said, "It is unconscionable that the FAA would listen to an attempt to eliminate evacuation testing. ACAP intends to vigorously represent the interests of passengers in this issue by contesting this proposal unless door exits are ordered placed in airliners every 30 rows.")

Engaging in other pro-passenger activities ACAP has improved the environment of flight for passengers by successfully working to require "no smoking seats" for all passengers requesting them and supporting legislation that banned smoking on aircraft flying domestic routes. ACAP was also part of the fight compelling the airlines to notify passengers of their overbooking practices, provide increased compensation for bumped passengers, and seek volunteers before involuntarily bumping passengers off flights. ACAP has also been active in seeking improvements for aviation security efforts, and has served as the consumer representative on FAA's Research, Engineering, and Development Advisory

Committee and on several subcommittees of the Aviation Security Advisory Committee as well as the Aviation Rulemaking Advisory Committee and frequently offering testimony on behalf of consumers before various congressional committees.

ACAP needs your membership if it is to be able to vigorously represent the interests of passenger safety and consumer rights. Membership begins at $35 per year and included in the price is a periodic newsletter and some of the best advocacy your money can buy.

We urge you to join ACAP: To do so, the toll-free number is (800) 836-0236, or you can mail your tax-deductible $35 membership check to:

ACAP
P.O. Box 19029
Washington, DC 20033

Support the creation of the Coalition of Airline Passengers (CAP)

Clout in Washington, D.C., depends on power. Power comes from either money, numbers, or both. As things now stand, the airlines and the industry have the money. As a special interest, they donate liberally to political campaigns and pay the costs of full-time advocacy trade groups such as the Air Transport Association.

One way to bring balance to this equation is for the creation of a passenger advocacy group that would have a large number of voters, who could provide a counterbalance to industry political power and represent the interests of the airline consumer.

One problem in forming and maintaining such a group is getting the message about its existence out to the general public. Consumer organizations rarely have the money to pay for mass mailings or advertising, and if they did have the money, it is probably best spent promoting the group's agenda rather than draining time and dollars on soliciting more money to keep the group in operation. But there is a possible answer: The Coalition of Airline Passengers (CAP).

CAP would be a passenger financed and managed advocacy group that would operate in a similar way as do Citizen Utility Boards (CUB). CUBs are organized state-based advocacy groups whose purpose is to give residential utility rate payers a voice in the regulatory proceedings. The purpose of a CUB is simple: Make sure you and your neighbors get a fair shake from utility companies, state regulators, and lawmakers. This voluntary "joining together" of individual utility customers who use their money in the form of dues and their talent in the form of services and the political power of their numbers, is a very effective tool in the consumer self-defense strategy against the exercised power of the utility industry.

CUBs were initially formed by state law in Wisconsin, Illinois, and in the City of San Diego, California, compelling utility companies to place inserts in their utility bills announcing the existence of the CUB and containing a coupon for consumer membership. The industry hated the idea of consumer empowerment and took the CUB to the U.S. Supreme Court, which, in a bizarre split decision, struck down the insert laws as a violation of the utility monopoly's right to remain silent; however, the CUB movement didn't collapse, as the utility companies had hoped. (The big shots don't like level playing fields.) The CUB movement continues, with Illinois now placing CUB inserts into state government mailings with New York about to do the same.

CAP would work in a similar manner. It would be an advocacy group that would have the purpose of achieving the goals of accident-free, affordable, and efficient air travel by representing passenger interests before the FAA, the NTSB, the aircraft manufacturers, the airlines, the courts, and Congress. In short, it would be a passenger association that would match the power of the vested interests that already are organized to advocate for the industry's agenda.

Joining the group would be voluntary, but individuals and corporations whose employees fly frequently, would have a strong incentive to participate. The group would be a private sector organization and would cost taxpayers nothing. Notice of the existence of the group and membership coupons would be printed on all airline ticket jackets. Once a minimum prescribed number of people joined, the management would be elected and the work would begin.

Airlines and manufacturers employ squads of lawyers, economists and accountants to develop and present their corporate views to the government. To supplement their in-house efforts, airlines spend millions more for law firms, trade associations, and lobbyists. The only effective way to counter this power is through a joining together of a large number of committed consumers into an advocacy group, that would have the power and clout to promote aviation safety in an effective and organized manner.

Many family members and survivors of airplane tragedies are already joining to create a passenger safety organization. Perhaps their work can provide the foundation for the CAP.

Individual advocacy

Whether or not you join a passenger advocacy group, you can and should involve yourself as a citizen in promoting aviation safety. If any issue or issues in this book have alarmed you or motivated you to help create a safer flying environment, you are urged to express your beliefs by phone calls and letters to your elected representatives.

You should write the chairs of the congressional and senatorial subcommittees with jurisdiction over transportation (Congressman James Oberstar and Senator Wendell Ford), who chair the House and Senate committees primarily involved with safety regulation. The address is:

U.S. House of Representatives (or U.S. Senate)
Washington, DC 20515.

If you want the level of safety regulation to be improved, let the FAA know about your feelings. Write to:

Administrator
Federal Aviation Administration
800 Independence Ave., NW
Washington, DC 20591

We're sure the FAA will appreciate hearing from you.

Epilogue

Aviation is a subject that, like the tides, is always in flux, always in a state of change. For example, as this book is literally going to press, new and profound concerns have been raised about the air quality within the passenger cabin of new airplanes. Pressurization systems on older aircraft circulated fresh air into the passenger cabin every 3 minutes. But systems on newer airplanes permit that time to be modified and in order to save money, domestic airlines are recirculating the air every 7 minutes or longer. (The air in the cabin is 50 percent fresh and 50 percent recirculated.) This practice has not only been claimed to be responsible for passenger and flight attendant headaches, nausea, and other discomforts, but might also transmit communicable diseases, including tuberculosis.

U.S. government health officials have initiated health studies on the issue. Pending the results of the studies, the FAA should immediately require airlines to circulate fresh air throughout the cabin every 3 minutes. After all, if the health risk is real, delaying any action will unnecessarily endanger the health of the cabin crew and passengers—perhaps endanger their lives.

Beyond new safety concerns that might arise, other aviation issues—like *The Man Who Came to Dinner*—never seem to go away. For example, recall the discussion in chapter 15 that details the Warsaw Convention's unfair restrictions on crash victim compensation to $75,000 on international flights, unless willful misconduct can be shown. Even this inequitably narrow door that permits crash victims to obtain full compensation in cases of willful misconduct is in continuing danger of being slammed shut. Proposed amendments to the Warsaw Convention—the amendments are known as the Montreal Protocols—would limit all compensation, regardless of circumstances or airline misconduct, to approximately $130,000 on international flights.

Lee S. Kreindler, the venerable aviation attorney who represents many of the surviving families of Pan Am 103, puts it this way:

> The Montreal proposal is, simply stated, foolish. It eliminates the willful misconduct exception currently

in place in the Warsaw Convention. (If the Montreal Protocols had been effective when Pan Am 103 was bombed, Pan Am's liability to the families would have been restricted to just over $100,000 apiece, despite the jury's finding that Pan Am's willful misconduct involving security procedures led to the catastrophe.) The proposal is destructive as well because it undermines the basic tenet that the wrongdoers should be responsible for the damages that they cause; the proposal imposes a huge cost on passengers—passengers and their families would have to bear most of the tremendous costs resulting from serious aviation accidents—and it would perpetuate an unwarranted limit of liability that undermines an important financial incentive toward safe business practices, a limit that is unavailable to almost anyone else in our society.

The U.S. Senate has so far refused to ratify the Montreal Protocols, but advocates keep trying, refusing to let it die and repeatedly bringing the matter back to the Senate floor. If and when the matter is brought up again, it must be defeated—for good.

This book has attempted to describe the most important safety issues facing commercial aviation today in the belief that shining the light of knowledge on these issues is the best way to pierce the fog of obfuscation that too often surrounds aviation safety in the FAA and official Washington. We earnestly hope that the problems and challenges that have been described here will serve as a motivator to involve yourself in issues of airline safety. The stakes are high and your participation is crucial.

We anticipate that there will be voices decrying this book as presenting a pie-in-the-sky wish list for reform that would, if implemented, bankrupt the industry. Many of the suggestions for reform in this book are expensive and some will take time to be fully implemented. But do not lose sight of the fact that the airlines and the FAA have been foot-dragging on needed safety reform for years and in some cases for decades. That cycle must be broken.

Remember this too: "Expensive" is a relative term. The commercial aviation business is a $75 billion industry that is accustomed to spending tens of millions, hundreds of millions, and even billions of dollars in business transactions. Indeed, according to Boeing, a single 747-400 transport jet costs an airline $140–$165 million, delivered; a 737-500, Boeing's most inexpensive jet, costs $29–$43 million; thus, if an industrywide safety reform is projected to cost $150 million, that is merely the cost of one 747 or approximately eight 737s.

Also keep in mind that the debt incurred by the industry to finance its business machinations and other poor management practices during the era of deregulation have been major contributors to the current financial state of the airline industry. That should evoke less sympathy when they predictably "cry poor" about safety.

In conclusion, we reiterate our call for you to get involved in your own safety as airline passengers. If the "powers that be" know that you are watching and that you care, they are going to do a better job of safeguarding your safety. That's the reality of government. Safety can be as simple as that.

Appendix

NTSB accidents

In the 25 years after the safety board was established on April 1, 1967, 3711 passengers and crew were fatally injured in 161 scheduled commercial aviation accidents involving airplanes certificated with eight or more passenger seats. Of these, 3059 fatalities occurred in 67 Part 121 accidents. Not included are accidents involving all-cargo aircraft, rotorcraft, or ground incidents of an unusual occurrence. (Nonsurvivable accidents have an asterisk*.)

Date	Location	Airline	Aircraft	Fatalities
06-23-67	Blossburg PA	Mohawk	BAC 1-11	34*
07-19-67	Hendersonville NC	Piedmont	B-727	79*
11-06-67	Erlanger KY	United	B-707	1
11-20-67	Constance KY	United	Convair 880	69
01-08-68	San Diego CA	Imperial Commuter	Beech E18S	3
05-03-68	Dawson TX	Braniff	L-188	85*
06-28-68	Vichy MO	Purdue	DC-3	1
08-10-68	Charleston WV	Piedmont	FH-227	35
10-08-68	Las Vegas NV	Catalina Vegas	DeHavilland DH-104	4
10-25-68	Hanover NH	Northeast	FH-227	32
11-23-68	Santa Ana CA	Cable Commuter	DeHavilland DHC-6	9
12-02-68	Pedro Bay AK	Wien	F-27	39*
12-24-68	Bradford PA	Allegheny	Convair 580	20
12-27-68	Chicago IL	North Central	Convair 580	27
01-06-69	Bradford PA	Allegheny	Convair 440	11
01-18-69	Los Angeles CA	United	B-727	38*
02-05-69	Port Angeles WA	Puget Sound	Beech C-45H	10
02-18-69	Lone Pine CA	Hawthorne Nevada	DC-3	35*
03-05-69	San Juan PR	Puerto Rico	DeHavilland DH1142	19*
09-09-69	Fairland IN	Allegheny	DC-9	82*
07-06-69	Monroe GA	Air South	Beech B99	14

Date	Location	Operator	Aircraft	Fatalities
07-25-69	Kekaha HI	Trans Isle Air	DeHavilland DH-104	1
10-03-69	Denver CO	Metro Commuter	Beech 65-B80	5
10-11-69	Loiza Aldea PR	Air Indies	Beech C-45H	1
11-19-69	Glens Falls NY	Mohawk	FH-2278	14
01-22-70	Aspen CO	Rocky Mountain	Aerocommander 680V	8
01-28-70	Cleveland OH	TAG Airlines	DeHavilland DH-104	9
02-10-70	Waterford CT	Pilgrim Aviation	DeHavilland DHC-6	5
03-22-70	Binghamton NY	Commuter Airlines	Beech C-45H	3
11-14-70	Huntington WV	Southern	DC-9	75*
11-27-70	Anchorage AK	Capital	DC-8	47
12-28-70	St. Thomas VI	Tran Caribbean	B-727	2
05-06-71	Coolidge AZ	Apache Airlines	DeHavilland DH104	12
06-06-71	Duarte CA	Hughes Airwest	DC-9	49*
06-07-71	New Haven CT	Allegheny	Convair 580	28
08-19-71	Augusta ME	Downeast Airlines	Piper PA-31	3
09-04-71	Juneau AK	Alaska	B-727	111*
10-21-71	Peoria IL	Chicago Southern	Beech E18S	16
10-24-71	Bath PA	Monmouth Airlines	Beech B99	4
02-16-72	Jackson MI	Hankins Airways	Beech D18S	2
02-20-72	Fairfield IN	Sun Valley	Beech 65-B80	5
02-22-72	Molokai HI	Alii Air Hawaii	Beech D18S	8
03-03-72	Albany NY	Mohawk	FH-227B	16
05-19-72	Albuquerque NM	Ross Aviation	Beech 65-B80	9
06-24-72	Ponce PR	Puerto Rico	DeHavilland DH114	5

* Nonsurvivable

Date	Location	Airline	Aircraft	Fatalities
06-29-72	Appleton WI	North Central	Convair 580	5
06-29-72	Appleton WI	Air Wisconsin	DeHavilland DHC-6	8
12-08-72	Chicago IL	United	B-737	43
12-20-72	Chicago IL	North Central	DC-9	10
12-29-72	Miami FL	Eastern	L-1011	99
04-19-73	Davenport IO	Air Iowa	Beech E18S	6
07-23-73	St. Louis MO	Ozark	FH-227B	38
07-24-73	Honolulu HI	Alii Air Hawaii	Beech C-45G	5
07-31-73	Boston MA	Delta	DC-9	88
08-28-73	Los Angeles CA	TWA	B-707	1
09-27-73	Mena AR	Texas Int'l	Convair 600	11
11-03-73	Albuquerque NM	National	DC-10	1
01-06-74	Johnstown PA	Air East	Beech 99A	12
01-30-74	Pago Pago AS	Pan American	B-707	96
02-02-74	Honolulu HI	Pan American	B-747	1
04-11-74	Hilo HI	Island Air	Beech H18S	11
04-30-74	Galveston TX	Metro Airlines	Beech 99	6
09-11-74	Charlotte NC	Eastern	DC-9	71
12-01-74	Berryville VA	TWA	B-727	92*
12-26-74	Riverton Heights WA	Harbor Airlines	Britten Norman BN-2A	4
01-09-75	Whittier CA	Golden West	DeHavilland DHC-6	12

Date	Location	Airline	Aircraft	Number
06-24-75	Jamaica NY	Eastern	B-727	112
08-30-75	Gambell AK	Wien	F-27B	10
11-30-75	Elko NV	Scenic Airlines	Cessna 402	2
04-05-76	Ketchikan AK	Alaska	B-727	1
04-27-76	St. Thomas VI	American	B-727	37
06-11-76	Summit Lake AK	Alaska Aeronautics	Cessna 402	2
12-12-76	Wildwood NJ	Atlantic City	DeHavilland DHC-6	3
04-04-77	New Hope GA	Southern	DC-9	62
08-13-77	Yates City IL	Brower Airways	Cessna 402A	3
09-06-77	Iliamna AK	Alaska Aeronautics	DeHavilland DHC-6	13
12-19-77	Vieques PR	Vieques Air Lines	Britten Norman BN-2A	5
02-10-78	Richland WA	Columbia Pacific	Beech 99	19
03-01-78	Los Angeles CA	Continental	DC-10	2
04-27-78	Upola AS	South Pacific	Cessna 402	10
05-08-78	Pensacola FL	National	B-727	3
09-25-78	San Diego CA	PSA	B-727	135*
12-04-78	Steamboat Spgs CO	Rocky Mountain	DeHavilland DHC-6	2
12-28-78	Portland OR	United	DC-8	10
02-12-79	Clarksburg WV	Allegheny	Nord 262	2
03-01-79	Gulfport MS	Universal Airways	Beech BE-70	8
05-29-79	Chicago IL	American	DC-10	271*
05-30-79	Rockland ME	Downeast Airlines	DeHavilland DHC-6	17
06-17-79	Hyannis MA	Downeast Airlines	DeHavilland DHC-6	1
07-24-79	St. Croix VI	Prinair	DeHavilland DH-114	8

* Nonsurvivable

Date	Location	Airline	Aircraft	Fatalities
12-03-79	Nome AK	Evergreen	DeHavilland DHC-6	4
03-21-80	Houston TX	Eagle Commuter	Piper PA-31	7
06-12-80	Valley NE	Air Wisconsin	Swearingen 226TC	13
07-21-80	Tusayan AZ	Scenic Airlines	Cessna 404	8
07-25-80	Philadelphia PA	Air Pennsylvania	Piper PA-31	3
01-20-81	Spokane WA	Cascade Airways	Beech 99A	7
04-17-81	Loveland CO	Air US	Handley Page HP-137	13
12-31-81	Durango CO	Sun West Airlines	Piper PA-31	4
01-23-82	Boston MA	World	DC-10	2
01-13-82	Washington DC	Air Florida	B-737	78
02-21-82	Providence RI	Pilgrim Airlines	DeHavilland DHC-6	1
07-09-82	New Orleans LA	Pan American	B-727	153
01-09-83	Brainerd MN	Republic	Convair 580	1
10-11-83	Pinckneyville IL	Air Illinois	HS-748	10
01-19-83	San Francisco CA	Wings West	Beech C-99	1
08-17-83	Peach Springs AZ	Las Vegas Airlines	Piper PA-31-350	10
10-28-83	Middletown PA	Pennsylvania	Shorts SD3-30	1
08-02-84	Vieques PR	Vieques Air Link	Britten Norman BN-2A	9
08-24-84	San Luis Obispo CA	Wings West	Beech C-99	15
09-07-84	Naples FL	Provincetown Boston	Cessna 402C	1
12-06-84	Jacksonville FL	Provincetown Boston	EMB-110P1	13

Date	Location	Airline	Aircraft	
01-21-85	Reno NV	Galaxy	L-188C	70
02-04-85	Soldotna AK	North Pacific	Beech 65-A80	9
02-06-85	Altus OK	Altus Airlines	Cessna 402B	2
08-02-85	Dallas TX	Delta	L-1011	135
08-25-85	Auburn ME	Bar Harbor	Beech 99	8
09-06-85	Milwaukee WI	Midwest Express	DC-9	31*
09-23-85	Grottoes VA	Henson Airlines	Beech B99	14
11-01-85	Bethel AK	Hermens Air	Cessna 208	2
03-13-86	Alpena MI	Simmons Airlines	FMB-110P1	3
10-28-86	St Croix VI	Virgin Is. Seaplane	Grumman G-73	1
01-15-87	Kearns UT	Sky West Airlines	Swearingen SA-226TC	8
03-04-87	Romulus MI	Fisher Brothers	CASA-212-CC	9
04-01-87	Anchorage AK	Wilbur's	Cessna 402	2
05-08-87	Mayaguez PR	Executive Air	CASA-212-CC	2
08-16-87	Romulus MI	Northwest	MD-80	156*
11-15-87	Denver CO	Continental	DC-9	28
11-23-87	Homer AK	Ryan Air Service	Beech 1900C	18
12-07-87	San Luis Obispo CA	PSA	BAe-146	43*
12-22-87	Chadron NE	G.P. Express	Cessna 402C	2
12-23-87	Kenai AK	South Central Air	Piper PA-31-350	6
12-23-87	Maunaloa HI	Panorama Air Tours	Piper PA-31-350	8
01-19-88	Bayfield CO	Trans Colorado	Fairchild SA-227AC	9
02-19-88	Cary NC	AVAIR	Fairchild SA-227AC	12
04-28-88	Maui HI	Aloha	B-737	1

* Nonsurvivable

Date	Location	Airline	Aircraft	Fatalities
08-31-88	Dallas TX	Delta	B-727	14
02-24-89	Honolulu HI	United	B-747	9
07-19-89	Sioux City IA	United	DC-10	111
09-20-89	Flushing NY	USAir	B-737	2
10-28-89	Molokai HA	Aloha Island Air	DeHavilland DHC-6	20
12-26-89	Pasco WA	NPA/United Express	BAe-3101	6
09-03-90	Kaltag AK	Frontier Flying	PA31-325	3
12-03-90	Detroit MI	Northwest	DC-9	8
02-01-91	Los Angeles CA	USAir	B-737	34
		Skywest	Fairchild SA-227	12
03-03-91	Colo. Springs CO	United	B-737	25*
04-05-91	Brunswick GA	Atlantic Southwest	EMB-120 RT	23
07-10-91	Birmingham AL	L'Express	Beech C99	13
08-20-91	Ketchikan AK	TCMSCO Helicopters	Britten Norman BN-2A	4
09-11-91	Eagle Lake TX	Continental Express	EMB-120	14
12-10-91	Temple Bar AZ	Las Vegas Airlines	Piper PA31-350	5
01-03-92	Gabriels NY	Commutair	Beech 1900C	2
01-23-92	Clewiston FL	Air Sunshine	Cessna 402C	2
03-22-92	Clewiston FL	USAir	F-28	27
06-07-92	Mayaguez PR	Executive Air	CASA 212	5
06-08-92	Ft. McClellan AL	G.P. Express	Beech C99	3
10-31-92	Grand Junction	Alpine Aviation	Piper PA-42	3

* Nonsurvivable

Abbreviations

Many aspects of aviation are controversial, but one truth is not controversial: The industry is rife with abbreviations and acronyms. Here is a key to those used most frequently in this book.

ACAP Aviation Consumer Action Project

ALPA Air Line Pilots Association

ATC air traffic control

ATA Air Transport Association

CRM crew resource management or cockpit resource management

DOT Department of Transportation

FAA Federal Aviation Administration

FAR Federal Aviation Regulation

GA general aviation

GAO General Accounting Office

GPWS ground proximity warning system

IFR instrument flight rules

NATCA National Association of Air Traffic Controllers

NASA National Aeronautics and Space Administration

NTSB National Transportation Safety Board

NMAC near midair collision

NPRM notice of proposed rulemaking

TCAS traffic alert and collision avoidance system

TCA terminal control area

VFR visual flight rules

Glossary

aborted takeoff When a pilot decides it is unsafe to take off during the acceleration of the takeoff roll and the pilot takes action to stop the aircraft.

Aviation Consumer Action Project (ACAP) A nonprofit consumer advocacy group that represents the interests of passengers in matters pertaining to airline safety and consumer rights.

accident An event that causes serious injury or death to a person or persons that are on an aircraft; also, an event that causes serious damage to an aircraft.

advisories FAA documents that provide guidance on aviation issues. Advisories are not mandates and do not have the force of law.

aging aircraft Aircraft that have exceeded a given number of cycles (*see* cycle). Aging aircraft might develop safety defects primarily caused by metal fatigue and/or corrosion.

Air Line Pilots Association (ALPA) The largest labor union representing commercial pilots. An advocate for increased safety regulations.

Aircraft Owners and Pilots Association (AOPA) The largest organization representing the interests of general aviation.

airport surface detection equipment (ASDE) Ground radar technology designed to prevent dangerous runway incursions by taxiing aircraft.

air route traffic control center (ARTCC) Also referred to as *center*. An ARTCC is in charge of a specific area of airspace above geographical boundaries; that area is divided into smaller parcels of airspace (*see* sector). An ARTCC will oversee most of an airliner's route of flight. (*See* terminal control area and tower control).

air taxi An air carrier certified by the FAA to provide on-demand public transportation. Air taxis are governed by FAR Part 135.

air traffic control (ATC) A service usually operated by the FAA to keep planes at safe distances from each other and to promote safe, orderly traffic flow. A nonfederal control tower might be operated by controllers that are not employed by the FAA. ARTCC controllers are federal employees.

Air Transport Association (ATA) The trade and lobbying group of the major airlines.

airworthiness certificate FAA documentation that an aircraft has been designed and manufactured according to prescribed safety standards. The certificate is required for all airliners and practically all general aviation airplanes. (Extremely lightweight aircraft might not carry an airworthiness certificate; these aircraft are prohibited from operating at or near large airports.)

Airworthiness Assurance Task Force FAA-sponsored safety committee that studies issues involving aging aircraft.

Association of Professional Flight Attendants The union that represents flight attendants employed by American Airlines.

Aviation Safety Reporting System (ASRS) An incident-reporting data base that is administered by NASA.

Aviation Subcommittee The United States House of Representatives Committee on Public Works and Transportation, Subcommittee on Aviation. The primary legislative committee in the House of Representatives with jurisdiction and oversight regarding aviation issues.

cabotage The proposed practice to allow foreign flag air carriers to fly domestic air routes.

Capital Investment Plan (CIP) The FAA's ATC modernization program.

center *See* air route traffic control center.

Central Flow Control A facility at the FAA's offices in Washington, D.C., that oversees primarily the movement of airliners operating within the continental United States.

certification A license from the FAA. Pilots and mechanics must pass FAA-mandated tests to obtain a certificate. Airline companies must meet FAA-mandated criteria for certification.

checklist A prescribed sequence of procedures followed by a cockpit crew in preparation for different phases of operation: engine start, taxi, pretakeoff, takeoff, landing, and the like. Additional checklists are utilized when the pilots must respond to a specific problem, such as a comparatively minor mechanical malfunction, or noteworthy emergency, such as an engine fire.

Civil Aeronautics Board (CAB) A defunct U.S. government agency that was in charge of economic regulation of commercial aviation. CAB was phased out by deregulation.

Civil Aviation Authority (CAA) The principal aviation authority in Great Britain, similar to the FAA in the United States.

cockpit resource management (CRM) A form of safety training that seeks to increase communication and teach the skills that will allow the flight crew to act as a team.

code sharing The business arrangement whereby a major airline permits a commuter airline to appear as if it were a part of the major airline's flight operations. ("Code" refers to the computer code of the major carrier in computer reservation systems.)

cost/benefit rule An executive order that prohibits the FAA (and other regulatory agencies) from promulgating a rule unless the benefits of the proposal, as measured in dollars, exceeds the dollar cost of complying with the regulation.

commuter aircraft Smaller commercial aircraft that carry 60 or fewer passengers.

commuter airlines Airlines that operate commuter aircraft according to FAR Part 135.

controller A person who operates ATC equipment and controls aircraft that are flying according to instrument flight rules regardless of the weather conditions: cloudy or clear. (*See* instrument flight rules.)

cycle A cycle is a way of measuring the age of an aircraft. A single cycle is takeoff, pressurization, depressurization, and landing.

deicing The process of placing special fluid on wings and other aircraft surfaces, typically prior to takeoff, to remove ice and permit safe operations during inclement winter weather conditions.

Department of Transportation (DOT) The department in the executive branch of government that has authority over the FAA and has the direct responsibility of ensuring that airlines are financially able to operate.

deregulation The current economic policy that permits commercial aviation to operate free of most government economic controls.

dual mandate A term used to describe the sometimes conflicting legal mandate of the FAA to promote aviation and foster safety.

extended-range twin-engine operations (ETOPS) The practice of flying aircraft with two engines over long distances and far away from the nearest airport. Special FAA certification is required for ETOPS.

Federal Aviation Administration (FAA) The federal agency primarily responsible for promoting aviation and fostering aviation safety. The FAA is responsible for promulgating the FARs.

Federal Aviation Regulations (FAR) The regulations governing aviation operations in the United States.

final rule A rule that has undergone the bureaucratic process and has been published in the *Federal Register* as an enforceable regulation. (*See* Notice of Proposed Rulemaking.)

Flight Safety Foundation A nonprofit organization, funded primarily by aviation commercial interests, that researches and promotes safe aviation practices.

full performance level (FPL) Describes an air traffic controller that is fully qualified to handle all elements of a specific ATC duty station. FPLs are the most experienced controllers.

fuselage The central body portion of an airplane, housing passengers, cargo, and crew.

General Accounting Office (GAO) The nonpartisan branch of government that investigates and analyzes the workings of government and issues recommendations for improvement.

general aviation (GA) The term used to describe all aviation that is not commercial or military, primarily made up of private pilots and business aircraft.

ground proximity warning system (GPWS) An electronic device in the cockpit of an airplane that provides visual notice, aural warning signals, plus voice recommendations (how to maneuver the airplane) when a plane is in danger of crashing into terrain.

holding Also known as stacking. When an aircraft flies a preestablished pattern, often an oval route, similar to a horse racing track, at a prescribed altitude, until receiving an ATC clearance for a landing or another maneuver.

hub and spoke system A system of airline operations where major carriers operate primarily out of centralized large "hub" airports. Passengers that depart from smaller communities (spoke airports) are often flown to the hub airports on commuter aircraft. The hub and spoke system evolved after deregulation.

human factors A technology that, when applied, improves human performance. Human factors training such as CRM seeks to reduce human errors and improve aviation safety.

incident An infraction of aviation safety standards that does not result in an accident.

incursion An unauthorized entry onto an active runway or any occurrence at an airport involving aircraft, vehicles, objects, or people that creates a collision hazard with an aircraft.

inspectors Personnel employed by the FAA who inspect airline operations to ensure the carriers are obeying safety regulations. Inspectors also inspect new airlines to determine their eligibility for FAA certification.

instrument flight rules (IFR) Rules governing flight using instruments for guidance rather than visual sightings. All air carriers fly IFR.

International Civil Aviation Organization (ICAO) An agency of the United Nations whose members agree to comply with the agency's minimum safety standards as set by agreement.

lap infant A child under the age of two held by an adult during flight instead of being restrained in an infant safety seat. Lap infants can be unnecessarily injured during severe turbulence or the forces generated by a crash.

minimum equipment list (MEL) The equipment, systems, and other components that must be operating properly for a flight to be authorized.

mode C transponder A device that provides information to a radar screen to help the controller identify aircraft altitude. (*See* transponder.)

National Air Traffic Controllers Association (NATCA) The labor union of air traffic controllers that was founded after PATCO was decertified.

National Aeronautics and Space Administration (NASA) In addition to being the space agency for the United States, NASA researches new aeronautical technologies and otherwise promotes the safety of flight by overseeing the Aviation Safety Reporting System.

National Transportation Safety Board (NTSB) An agency established to investigate aviation and other transportation-related accidents and to issue recommendations to improve safety.

near midair collision (NMAC) A safety violation where planes almost collide in flight. The FAA keeps statistics on NMACs and identifies them by the severity of the safety risk created.

Notice of Proposed Rulemaking (NPRM) An NPRM is published in the *Federal Register* publicizing the intentions and contents of a proposed regulation. Interested parties are then permitted to comment, after which time a final rule is issued, or the proposed rule is amended, or is withdrawn. (The *Federal Register*—published every day, except on the weekend and federal holidays—is commonly found in any public library.)

operational error An air traffic control event where separation standards between aircraft were violated because of an air traffic controller's mistake.

Part 121 The section of the FARs that controls regularly scheduled large commercial air carriers. Part 121 has the strongest safety standards.

Part 135 The section of the FARs that control commuter airlines and air taxis. Part 135 has less stringent safety standards than Part 121.

passenger protective breathing equipment (PPBE) A smoke hood or mask that provides breathable air for a short period of time so that an airline passenger may have an opportunity to exit an aircraft through toxic smoke and fumes that might result during an emergency evacuation from a burning aircraft.

pencil whipping The practice of falsifying maintenance records to claim that maintenance work on aircraft has been performed when no maintenance was accomplished.

pilot deviation Pilot action that results in a violation of ATC standards.

Professional Airway Systems Specialists (PASS) The labor union that represents FAA inspectors and the specialists that maintain and service ATC equipment.

Professional Air Traffic Controllers Organization (PATCO) Now defunct, PATCO was the air traffic controller labor union prior to decertification when PATCO members went out on strike and were fired by President Ronald Reagan.

profile A security method that identifies personal traits expected to be exhibited by a person that might pose a threat to aviation security. Once identified, the luggage and person fitting the profile might be subject to increased security measures.

recurrent training Training designed to reinforce existing safety skills and impart new information for aviation professionals such as pilots, flight attendants, air traffic controllers, and ground personnel.

Regional Airline Association The trade and lobbying organization representing commuter air carriers.

rotation The point where the nose of an aircraft lifts off the ground at a speed sufficient to commence flight.

safety indicators Proposed statistical data that would measure the level of safety in the aviation system. Ideally, safety indicators would allow regulators and the public to identify areas of degraded safety before accidents occur so that corrective action could be taken.

sector A defined area of airspace under the control of a single controller.

Semtex A plastic form of explosive material believed used in the sabotage of Pan Am 103.

separation The spacing of aircraft horizontally and vertically. The FAA establishes minimum separation standards that must be followed during flight.

stall The loss of lift when the angle of an airfoil (typically a very steep angle) or the velocity of the airfoil (too slow) fail to create sufficient lifting forces to maintain controlled flight. Wind shear might cause a stall due to disturbed airflow over the wings. (Aircraft stall and automotive stall are different. An aircraft stall is an aerodynamic situation; an automotive stall is a mechanical situation.)

survivable accident An aviation accident where the crash forces are insufficient to kill all of the people on board the plane. Contrary to popular belief, most accidents are survivable.

taxi Movement on the ground by an aircraft while under its own power.

taxiways Paved areas at airports leading to and from gates and runways.

traffic alert and collision avoidance systems (TCAS) An electronic device in the cockpit that is capable of providing a warning to the pilot, who can initiate appropriate evasive action to avoid a midair collision. The reliability of TCAS alerts has prompted a controversy between pilots and air traffic controllers.

terminal control area (TCA) Controlled airspace around major airports. All planes flying within TCA airspace must have a mode C transponder and must be under air traffic control.

terminal radar approach control (TRACON) A terminal air traffic control facility in charge of aircraft leaving and approaching one airport or perhaps more than one airport. TRACON controllers will "hand off" airplanes flying through their airspace to a tower controller, if the plane is landing, or hand off the airplanes to a center controller, if the planes are departing. (*See* air route traffic control center and tower control.)

tower control Air and ground traffic controllers who work in the airport tower and are in charge of aircraft that are taking off, landing, and taxiing.

transponder An electronic device on an airplane that transmits specific information to a radar site; the information is translated by a computer into an electronic display that appears on a controller's radarscope. The controller is able to watch the aircraft identification, track, ground speed, and altitude. (*See* mode C transponder.)

turbulence Atmospheric conditions that cause a plane to deviate from smooth flight, often experienced as a shuddering and shaking. Turbulence is commonly associated with the frontal boundary between high pressure and low pressure weather systems.

V_1 The point at which it is presumably no longer safe to abort a takeoff based upon the speed and weight of the aircraft and the remaining runway length during the takeoff roll.

visual flight rules (VFR) The rules that govern many general aviation aircraft operations. Pilots flying VFR use visual sightings to avoid unsafe conditions.

wind shear A change in wind speed and/or wind direction in a short distance resulting in a tearing or shearing effect. It can exist in a horizontal or vertical direction, and occasionally in both directions. The shear is often created by a microburst where a strong downshaft of wind hits the ground and fans out like an inverted mushroom; typically, the downshaft is produced within or in the vicinity of a thunderstorm, but not always. Wind shear conditions might cause airfoils to lose lift and produce an aerodynamic stall.

References

The following written materials were helpful during research and preparation of this book.

Barley, Stephen 1990. *The Final Call*, Pantheon Books. New York.

Cox, Matthew, and Foster, Tom. 1992. *Their Darkest Day*, Grove Weindenfeld, New York.

Dempsey, Paul S., and Goetz Andrew R., 1992. *Airline Deregulation and Laissez-Faire Mythology*, Quorum Books. Boston.

Eddy, Paul, and Potter, Elaine, and Page, Bruce. 1976. *Destination Disaster*, The New York Times Books. New York.

Nance, John J. 1986. *Blind Trust*, William Morrow and Co., Inc. New York.

Oster, Clinton V., and Strong, John S., and Zorn, Kurt C. 1992. *Why Airplanes Crash*, Oxford University Press. New York.

Savage, Peter. 1988. *The Safe Travel Book*, Lexington Books. Lexington, Massachusetts.

Taylor, Laurie. 1988. *Air Travel: How Safe Is It?*, BSP Professional Books. London.

Wells, Alexander. 1991. *Commercial Aviation Safety*, TAB Books, a division of McGraw-Hill, Inc. Blue Ridge Summit, Pennsylvania.

Wood, Richard H. 1991. *Aviation Safety Programs*, IAP, Inc. Casper, Wyoming.

Additionally, stories in newspapers and periodicals were helpful, including: *Air Line Pilot, Aviation Week & Space Technology, The Los Angeles Times, Newsweek, The New York Times, The San Francisco Chronicle, The Wall Street Journal, The Washington Post*, reports from seminars, and materials published by the Flight Safety Foundation.

Other written materials were prepared by government sources, including reports of the General Accounting Office, National Transportation Safety Board, U.S. Department of Transportation, Federal Aviation Administration, Congress of the U.S. Office of Technology Assessment, President's Commission on Aviation Security and Terrorism, and the official record of testimony given by various parties before committees of the U.S. House of Representatives and the U.S. Senate.

Index